The
Message
Is the
Medium

THE
MESSAGE
IS THE
MEDIUM

Online All the Time for Everyone

TOM KOCH

   **Westport, Connecticut**
                                                London

Library of Congress Cataloging-in-Publication Data

Koch, Tom.
    The message is the medium : online all the time for everyone / Tom
Koch.
        p.   cm.
    Includes bibliographical references and index.
    ISBN 0–275–95549–4 (alk. paper)
    1. Online information services.   I.   Title.
QA76.55.K63   1996
302.23—dc20   95–53001

British Library Cataloguing in Publication Data is available.

Library of Congress Catalog Card Number: 95–53001
ISBN: 0–275–95549–4

First published in 1996.

Praeger Publishers, 88 Post Road West, Westport, CT 06881
An imprint of Greenwood Publishing Group, Inc.

Printed in the United States of America

(∞)™

The paper used in this book complies with the
Permanent Paper Standard issued by the National
Information Standards Organization (Z39.48–1984).

10 9 8 7 6 5 4 3 2 1

Copyright Acknowledgment

The author and publisher gratefully acknowledge permission to
reprint SouthStar Network. "All Surgery Risky, Doctor Says." *Kitchner
Waterloo Record.* January 10, 1994, D10.

For Tara and Kevin in September

Contents

1

"The Medium Is the Message" and Other Myths of the Evolving, Electronic Age

The message is the medium by which we seek the answers to the problems of our lives. Marshall McLuhan, the erudite but generally unintelligible Toronto professor who insisted that "the medium is the message" got it backwards.[1] Online, offline, broadcast news, or Morse code: The medium merely carries the data we all require. It is through the messy complex of reported facts, opinions, perceptions, reports—the disparate elements of fact and surmise that we retrieve from every conceivable source—that each of us attempts to make sense of our individual lives and shared times. From the perspective of the user, the medium is not the message any more than the crushed velvet little box holding a diamond ring is the real present bestowed, on traditionally bent knee, in the time-honored form of a request for marriage.

Imagine that you have a dread disease and a new drug offering hope of a cure has just become available. Do you care what medium carries that message of health and hope to your home? It may be an article in the latest issue of the *Journal of the American Medical Association;* a telephone call from the doctor, whose colleague read a report on the drug; or it could be a fact overheard in a patient's self-help support group. It may be a datum reported on the Internet, or a fact gleaned from an online electronic search. What is important to the patient is not the carrier, but the signal it conveys. Whether it comes by jungle drum or on the 11:00 nightly television news, it is the promise of hope that the fact of a new drug or new treatment that is crucial to us, not the means by which the news traveled to our hospital rooms.

In an age of rapid technologic advances, we are forever blasé about the forms of our public exchanges. In this century fax, photography, radio, telegraphy, and television all have signaled significant advances in technology. All are now assumed, taken for granted. Whatever the technology, it takes only a decade or so to bend its power to the harness of our culture and our will. Then we forget its newness and concentrate on the facts and data it transmits. What does Auntie Mildred say? Well, give her a call! Mauna Kea is erupting again? Quick, turn on CNN! Is there a new treatment for multiple sclerosis? Let's check the medical journals, or ask the erudite members of some online discussion group. None of us, except the occasional academic, care about the medium that delivers our messages. It is the data that they present to us all which we so desperately seek.

Unfortunately, the newest technologies have been the subject of more hyperbole and hype than a circus sideshow. Electronic communication and "virtual reality" are the future, today. John Perry Barlow, a founder of the Electronic Frontier Foundation, says of the evolving realm of online electronic tools that "we are in the middle of the most transforming technological event since the capture of fire."[2] Neil Postman, on the other hand, says in his accusatory way that with these new technologies, "We have transformed information into garbage."[3] Both men are wrong. Computers are not as significant as the introduction of fire. They won't heat our food, keep us warm, or fend off predators at night. Nor has the technology of electronic transmission transformed precious information into common garbage. After all, as other critics remind us, newspapers, newsmagazines, and TV talk shows have been doing that for years. The reality of online technologies lies somewhere beyond the rant and hyperbole of those whose business it is to praise or condemn. Amazingly, those who make grand eloquent claims or forceful condemnations have paid little attention to the way normal people are utilizing these electronic resources in their lives. Thus critics and crusaders alike argue in a vacuum. The only important question, for the user, is whether the online resource is comprehensible, reliable, and efficient. If it does a better job than other technologies, most of us will use it; if not, then all the hype and hyperbole in the world will not assure its success.

If the medium is not the message, then data are not information. There can be no "information highway," because information remains, whatever the medium, a precious commodity. Data are the bare facts, the unsupported opinions, the informed suggestions, the books, journal items or news clips that help us in our search for answers. Data lead to information and build to an informed position supported by more than hope or prejudice. Information is what we need, and data are how we get it. In traditional and electronic venues alike, information is the end point of our travels and not the path of the seeker's journey. Thus, while this book *is* about the logic and structure of online systems, about how to understand the medium that people use in their search for facts, it is *not* about the mythical and misnamed "information highway." Online is simply yet another venue in our continuous search for relevant data that may be transformed into information to answer the questions we may present. At best, online resources create a "databahn," a multilane digital road paved by unsupported facts and partial truths that must be accumulated before "information" can be achieved.

Whatever that databahn may be, it is not the Internet. There are any number of electronic avenues that lead down data paths toward the goal of supported information. They include, in a partial list: the Internet in its many parts, America Online, CompuServe, Dow Jones Information Service (DJIS), Genie, Knight Ridder Information Service (KRI), LEXIS-NEXIS, Prodigy, local online bulletin boards, specialized data services like the legal resource Westlaw, and a host of other venues. To speak of the Internet as "the information highway" is like calling New England the United States at large. It is as if Canada's eastern region, the maritime provinces, declared themselves to be the whole of the Confederation. Internet, in fact, is a confederation of resources that includes the World Wide Web, UseNet, Gopher Sites, FTP, and Telnet. Each has its uses, and all have their place on the databahn. It is vast—by September, 1995, there were 6.6 million host systems across the Internet, each a computer with its own Internet numerical address that could be accessed by more than 25 million online users. But large as it is, that congregation of online entry points is still only a *part* of the evolving online world, not the digital world itself.

It is the logic of that evolving whole that is the subject of this book. Whatever service an individual uses, whatever online sources are regularly accessed, the same logic and organizational structure will be evident. While each online resource is unique, all share a common network and a similar organization. All are part of the standardizing but not yet standardized medium whose reality is maturing, year by year, as more and more people explore its potential. Mail flows easily between most online centers, and users of, say, Prodigy can easily access Internet addresses. But because each service is a little different, and most require a financial commitment, choices have had to be made. In this book, examples are drawn from my own experience and thus emphasize the services I know best. These include the general online service CompuServe, where I am an assistant sysop (systems administrator), and the Internet, especially its evolving World Wide Web,

KRI's detailed and specialized library services, and DJIS for business news. Each has its advantages. But what one uses is far less important than partisans of any single service insist. The crucial issue is to understand how to choose the source that best fits an individual's needs, and then how to find the data that can answer the problems we all face in our lives.

The medium is important because it brings the message forward. Whatever carrier most consistently assures swift access to the best available data will win the loyalty of users. This is not, however, because the medium is attractive, but because it carries material we need, and need to trust. Across the world of knowledge, information, and data, in the world of online communication and traditional resources alike, the question is always: Where can I get the most reliable data most efficiently and least expensively? If it is the Internet, fine. If it is in a local newspaper, that's OK. From an online, electronic self-help group? Great. In this book, as in life, the measure of the medium is the data it carries, the ability of the resource to assist a user in finding the answers to questions he or she is compelled to ask. The best venue is always the one where quality data can be most easily retrieved.

Individual media, the lanes of the databahn, can be either easy to use or difficult to understand; slow in service or speedy in delivery; intuitively organized or chaotic in their construction. Typically, we seek the simple, the quick, and the well organized because those qualities facilitate data retrieval. In today's environment of proliferating online systems offering a variety of services, it is necessary first to choose the online service that best meets an individual's needs. Which service carries the data required, and if more than one are providers, then whose service is cheapest? Is one online venue easier to learn than another?

Can the whole be arranged like a road map, allowing users to see the advantages of different routes, and can it be so portrayed that nontechnical, average folks with questions can make intelligent choices between online venues? Fortunately, the answer is yes. A goal of this book is to explain the organization of online resources so an average reader can make informed choices in choosing data venues. There is a logic to the whole, and it is that order which this book seeks to describe.

This is not, however, another text for those who wish to "surf the net." Surfers are hobbyists who are more concerned with glitter than substance, with a medium's general appearance than the data it may make available to us all. Surfers spend happy hours skimming the surface and admiring the technology itself. This book, on the other hand, is for those want to "dive for data," those who have gone online because electronic resources seem to offer the best chance of providing the facts contained in an individual report, news clip, journal article, or personal insight. Data divers search digital resources for the answers to specific problems. For them the medium is merely a way to find the facts that will help them resolve an issue, treat a patient, improve a stock portfolio, or plan a trip. What is important for the data diver is the message returned, wherever it is found: online or in a print library, in a self-help session, or in a conference group.

Because this is a book about online resources, its focus is on these electronic tools, both how they are used and the degree to which average folks have found them to be the best way to retrieve a pertinent fact, opinion, or perspective simply and quickly. But because it is about data, comparisons and analogies are frequently made between information technologies we know—the telephone, the mail, and the print library—and their online incarnations. In discussing problems that may arise online, the cautionary tales of past searchers offer important cautions. Thus, in describing these electronic data systems, there are frequent references to the experiences of users who have or have not found online answers to the problems they sought to answer.

Today's online technologies are commonly perceived and typically touted as an unprecedented, quantum leap to the future. The old is out. Newspapers are dead. Libraries passé. The future starts now. Pfui. Nothing could be further from the truth.

The medium is not the message; data are not the same as information. And there is nothing revolutionary about electronic data sources. Let us demythologize the new, separating the dreams of the converted from the condemnation of those who believe evolving technologies are necessarily radical, threatening, and dangerous. Electronic data and communication technologies are part of the slow march of the technologic evolution. Thus these new resources do not represent a revolutionary break with tradition, but rather a continuation of its strengths. For the user, this is good news. It means that skills already mastered through the use of older technologies—including the mails and the library—largely are applicable to learning these newer tools.

Even revolution builds upon its immediate past, incorporating the best of what was in an attempt to forge a better future for us all. The evolving "information society," as it is now almost universally named, is no different. All history—revolutionary and evolutionary—cannibalizes the past, keeping what was best as it incorporates new ideas and technologies. The marriage of personal computers with vast data storage facilities linked by telecommunication lines through a message/mail system is part of a longer and greater history of data's diffusion, a story of evergreater citizen empowerment and access. It is the story of evolution wrapped in revolution, of a changing society whose slowly advancing technology continues changes that began hundreds of years ago. Indeed, the landscape of electronic data incorporates cultural landmarks representing older technologies—the mail, libraries, the telephone—that are as familiar to us as the coastline of France.

This evolution has pointed toward a single goal, public access to public information, for more than three centuries. Electronic information continues and extends the slow, hard-won advances that have carried us from the birth of popular writing more than 230 years ago into the present day. The truly wonderful thing about these resources is that they marry the best of our past achievements into a single, integrated package. They combine into one complete system the storage capabilities of the old-fashioned library, the density of mass-produced books, the permanence and detail of the written message, and the immediacy of the telephone.

High-speed printing, international mail service, the telegraph, library science, the telephone, and television: each assured in its own way and in its own time increasing access at a decreasing cost to the wealth of potentially available public data. All had as their goal evermore comprehensive communication among members of a geographically expanding community. Computerized access to data and communication facilities takes its place in this history as the latest tool in the long fight to wrestle control of shared knowledge from the privledged few. What they offer is what we have always sought: A "citizen news" that places privileged data and the general tools of communication in the hands of normal people. The amazing rapidity with which society has accepted electronic data services is testimony to our communal desire to have history's promise of a *vox popular* fulfilled.

This is not the first "information revolution." Step by step, over several hundred years, a number of technologies combined to create the context that allowed the new computer-based technologies to unfold. What is remarkable is the degree to which today's fears and complaints about the "information explosion," concerns about the difficulties of controlling this new medium, are cautions we have heard before. For more than 250 years, aristocrats of one or another stripe have worried that then-new technologies would drag the general population into dreaded trouble and perhaps even sedition.

"A lumber house of books in ev'ry head," grumbled the British writer Pope. "Forever reading, never to be read," he wrote at the start of the second printing revolution, that period which wrested literature and publishing from royalty's control into the public domain of commercial publishing. Guttenberg created the moveable-type press, but it was only when faster presses and cheaper materials allowed inexpensive print runs of news and books that the real revolution occurred. And so, by the eighteenth century, a profusion of materials was being prepared not for the old market of aristocratic readers, but for the average citizen. For perhaps the first time in our history, inexpensive books and periodicals—the means of knowing—were available to everyone. As a consequence, the business of public writing was born as a legion of publishers, writers, and book- or news-sellers strove to provide popular books, articles, journals, newsletters, periodicals, political tracts, and religious treatises to an everexpanding public.[4]

That was radical! The very idea of a public press was unimaginable before mercantilism and new printing technologies combined to give us the resources we take for granted today. Had royalty known that the printing revolution would loosen its once iron grip on the control of information (and thus on power), Europe's hereditary rulers would have banned the faster presses and broad distribution system that brought the world of print to the common man. It never occurred to them, however, until the process was irreversible. A lumber house of books indeed! Pope saw only the beginning of what became, in the nineteenth century, the broad and very public dissemination of both new knowledge and new ideas. Diderot's *Encyclopedia* was an attempt to organize and summarize the whole of expanding knowledge gained from new science, new philosophies, and from legions of explorers who sailed the world and brought back evermore exotic tales of foreign lands and foreign peoples.

Thus began the global information age. No nation had a lock on knowing. No people had a monopoly on advancing knowledge. New ideas needed to be captured, disseminated, published, discussed, and cataloged. These changes made themselves felt in innumerable ways. New knowledge fueled new research, new experiments, and ultimately new sciences. More prosaically, settlers in Saskatchewan read Sir Walter Scott's works in inexpensive, British editions shipped on ever faster boats across the ocean to a new and eager audience. Americans in Kansas read the country's news, first in weeks-old newspapers from Boston, and then in local newspapers linked to the greater world by the telegraph. Travelers and explorers from many countries described their adventures around the globe to ever larger and more interested audiences with access to evermore ubiquitous and progressively less expensive magazines, periodicals, and journals.

All of this was but the first part of a process that resulted in an ever expanding volume of data being made available to the general public. Access to at least a part of this printed wealth became a necessity for every community. As a result, the public library movement began as a way to provide local repositories large enough for at least a portion of the evolving whole. The sheer volume of available materials required not only a system of warehousing, but also a system of cataloging that would allow anyone to find a single book or critical article. The information specialist was born in the person of the professional librarian.

In their struggles to tame the wealth, Dewey decimal–style hierarchies were brought into being.

As people traveled and explored, moved to the then New World and across its continent, new technologies provided another boon: the mail. Distanced, separate, isolated people wrote letters to stay in touch with those they had left behind. Explorers reported their findings, sons greeted their mothers, lovers promised to reunite. Settlers in Kansas wrote relatives in Ireland, knowing that a system of message transport and delivery would see their letters to a distant home. Letter writing was the first interactive, interpersonal medium. The magic of the mails gave birth to legends of its own—from those of the Pony Express riders to St. Exupery's early adventures in air-mail delivery. This was the personal side of the technologies that gave us travel, adventure, books, mercantilism, capitalism, and libraries designed to record it all. Mail carried books between continents, newspapers between cities, and letters between everyone.

Then, at the end of the nineteenth century, Alexander Graham Bell added the telephone to this expanding mix of different technologies of storage and communication. Despite the worries of traditionalists, and the hopes of futurists, the telephone did not replace mail. Introduced as a medium for the exchange of data, it was assumed that the telephone primarily would be a tool for businesses requiring the timely exchange of information, not a gossip machine linking the whispered confidences of housewives or lodge friends separated by distance. But from its inception, the telephone was seized upon as a primary instrument of personal and interpersonal communication, a means by which people might convey not only information but also emotion, whatever their distance and however unsophisticated their taste.

The telephone brought distant lands within reach of the individual voice, unifying areas geographically distanced. Its power grew as it entered more and more businesses and homes, welcomed from the start by a multitude of eager users. It was seized by users whose overwhelming numbers determined the messaging and communication system telephone companies provide today. Like books and periodicals, the telephone has become an omnipresent part of society, a means of allowing evermore frequent access to evergreater numbers of fellow human beings around the world. It was a part of the first information revolution.

All in all, this evolving history of printing and libraries, of private mail and telephone technologies permitted a scale of data collection and human interaction that would be otherwise impossible. People living at great distances were linked together, and the news and entertainment of the world became accessible to all. Writers and researchers around the world knew of each other's work. New industries, new art forms, and new systems of interpersonal interaction were the result.

This is the context of modernity's advances, the history that explains our current events. Computer-based communication marries the popular power of the printing revolution, of data stored for common use, with the sheer connectivity and presence of the telephone's common touch and nuance. It allows for easy retrieval of vast libraries of written data through the marriage of digital computers and the omnipresent, user-friendly telephone system. But the whole still is driven by the interpersonal message, the electronic request or query by one person of another for relevant data. We may call it e-mail, but it is still the hoary, personal message that ties the whole together. In a real way, electronic information systems join the weight of print with the ubiquitous ease of the spoken word, melding together two strands of the evolution in communication and knowledge whose modern phase began in the 1700s. It is thus another and perhaps the final step on the long road from official restriction to popular, perhaps universal, access to public knowledge and another step toward the democratic ideal of popular access to public data.

From this perspective, current battles over system access, control, and development make perfect sense. From the start, the history of this long evolution has been a popular struggle to wrestle control from official sources. Officials and their bureaucrats have always attempted to dictate the pattern of their growth while limiting access to the official few. Inevitably, however, citizens take command of emerging media, defining the pattern of their development through the sheer weight of public demand. The same thing is happening today in the evolving electronic world. Users, not owners, are determining the shape and form of the evolving, online world. For more than a decade, those whose interests range from aviation to zoology have been organizing online "forums" and "conferences," for example, bending these new technologies to their own, shared needs.

Most new technologies go through an introductory period in which they are seen as interesting oddities that are neither economical nor practical. During this period, they are usually difficult to use and costly to maintain; they are "gadgets" rather than necessities. But within a few years, those that survive become both increasingly efficient and evermore accessible to all. That is what is happening today in the maturing environment of computer-based data and communications systems. In the early 1980s, they were the exclusive preserve of the highly educated and specially trained. In a bit more than a decade, however, all of that has changed. The arcane formalities of disk operating system command lines have given way to Macintosh-style icons with "mouse-driven" point-and-click commands. Information systems like Internet have progressed from complex, UNIX-based machine-language systems to increasingly intuitive graphic interfaces. Ever faster processors and larger storage disks have opened the door to voice-activated commands ("Computer, find a file . . .") of increasing power and sophistication. At the same time, what was once a text-only resource is rapidly becoming a dense data field incorporating sound, graphics, and moving pictures. Multimedia and hypertext are rapidly becoming new standards for the whole.

Inexorably emerging from this process is an increasingly inexpensive and intuitive means of communication and public access. While it is based on older technologies, the evolving system has developed economies of scale and complex interrelations all its own. As a result, while the number of users has been increasing at a phenomenal rate—doubling every two years since 1987—the cost of online access has dropped by more than two-thirds over the last ten years. Nor has the rate of user growth slowed. In the first six months of 1994, for example, the number of users of the three main commercial online systems—CompuServe, America Online, and Prodigy—grew by more than 10 percent in the United States. By September, 1995, to use another example, there were more than 6.6 million Internet host systems, computers with their own Internet numerical addresses. While the vast majority of these were based in the United States (4.8 million at the beginning of 1995), the system was internationalizing rapidly. In China, for example, the Xinhua news agency reported that the number of Internet users increased from 3,000 at the beginning of the year to 40,000 by August, 1995. Chinese sources predicted that, by the end of the year, there would be 10,000 computers and 100,000 Chinese users accessing the 30-million member Internet.

The evolving technologies of online communication and data storage complete history's promise, advancing the ideal of popular access to personal communication and public information. This occurs not only through the acceptance of radical new technology, but, more importantly, through the reconstruction of older, seemingly distinct information systems in a new synergistic whole. The organization and structure of today's databahn is based on the best tools of our shared past: on the telephone's immediacy and informality, mail's specificity and privacy, the variety of the popular press, and the library's system of structuring volumes of data. Their union offers a broadly egalitarian, user-driven system of data storage and retrieval whose individual parts are both comfortingly familiar and available to all. What is rapidly emerging from this evolution, like a photographic print from the darkroom's chemical bath, is a democratic portrait of needs and desires that will, in the end, shape the final form of the maturing, changing technology people are now using evermore adroitly.

The result of these changes is a system that offers everyone, wherever they may live, both the accumulated expertise of our best researchers and the accumulated body of our shared experience. This book is a report on those changes; it is a field manual for those interested in using online systems to gain the data they need to construct the information required to control their personal lives.

All of the digital world's apparently distinct venues share, in the end, a number of characteristics, including a single logical structure and a general organizational approach. Thus the task of mapping the world of digital data is simplified considerably through reference to the constants that tie them together. An "electronic library" is still a library, organized hierarchically and logically. A federal database filled with census data is still a hierarchical collection whose logic needs to be understood before it can be accessed successfully. An electronic message is still a letter, a medium within a medium carrying news of hope or despair. It is in this mix of old and new, of traditional and unique, that the flavor and balance of the evolution-at-large can be found. There, too, is the logic and pattern that drives the whole. This is important because the process is not completed, it is simply underway.

In the mid-1990s, as formerly exclusive, on-line domains rapidly merge into a single, unified entity, understanding the similarities between electronic domains (and their print-based competitors) is especially important. The distinct venues (Internet, CompuServe, AOL, etc.) that previously inspired strong and exclusive user loyalties are in a period of rapid consolidation which, within a decade, will result in a single electronic storage and communication network. Just as in the nineteenth century separate railroad companies joined their tracks to create a national rail system—or, in this century, distinct telephone regions seamlessly merged into a North American communication network—online resources are in a process of unification that will render the idiosyncrasies of any one part irrelevant over the power of the whole.

The medium is not the message. That my electronic letter is carried from an Internet service to a CompuServe user's electronic mailbox— or from a Prodigy mail program to an America Online subscriber's mail site—makes no more difference to the process of communication (or to the content of the message) than the location of the post office mailbox has to the old-fashioned letter I mailed this morning. If what is needed is data on aseptic meningitis and its long-term effects, it does not matter to me whether data on that subject are found in an electronic conference dedicated to medicine, KRI's electronic library, or via a home-page link on the Internet. What was learned is what is crucial because, for most of us, the message is king.

The greatest impact of this evolution is in the greater access it allows everyone to previously privileged domains of public information. I call this the birth of "Citizen News," a system of dissemination that places the range of public data at the service of the average citizen. Citizen news is far more than the narrow, restricted forms of thinking and presentation currently taught in journalism schools. It is more than modern journalism and its daily assemblage of attributed quotes uttered by the elected officials or their experts on any given day.

From this perspective, a citizen's news includes all that has changed across our knowledge base: the complex of facts, assumptions, presumptions, and surmises that we may wish to learn about on any given day. It is built from the perspectives we exchange with one another without the mediation of reporter, editor, or producer preparing either broadcast tape or a printed page. It also includes a vast body of official data and research that are in the process of becoming as accessible to us all as what the mayor, president, or prime minister said at a press conference yesterday afternoon. After all, a newsworthy advance is only as important as the distance of its conclusions from those in volumes already resident in our libraries. Past records are the crucial benchmarks that define the "new," and thus the news. The more important a new truth, the more central was its predecessor to our world.

In all of this, the message is the medium that informs us, entertains us, and simultaneously assists us in facing the questions and crises of our lives. However it may be accessed, it is data we seek in the hopes that information can be formed which will bear on the problems we wish to solve, as individuals and as a society. The battle for public information is an old struggle that has been aided time and time again by first one and then another new technology. Once again, new methods of storage are available to all, and with them come easier methods of data access. But in this evolution certain things have not changed; they remain our individual need for data, our communal desire for access to public data, and the struggles that need and desire engender with those whose older privileges see our advances as a threat.

The world of data and information is changing. But change almost always occurs in response to an older, existing system's deficits, and online information is no different. Journalism, as we think of it today, was created during the first printing revolution as a means of assuring general access to public data. The foundation of popular knowing and an educated citizenry, it has served us well. But it always has been restricted by the limits of print publication, old systems of dissemination, storage, and retrieval. It is those limits that these new technologies are expanding day by day. And as we will see, the result is that a true, citizen-based news, one that is truly answerable to its subscribers, is in the process of becoming a reality.

NOTES

1. See, of course, his early work to remember how absolutely obtuse *it was*. "The Medium Is the Message" was the title of the first chapter of Marshall McLuhan, *Understanding Media: The Extensions of Man*. New York: McGraw-Hill, 1964.

2. "What Are We Doing On-Line?" *Harper's Magazine*. August, 1995, 36.

3. Currents section. *Utne Reader*. July–August, 1995, 35.

4. This is a short summary of a complex history. Those interested in knowing more about the progression from royal to democratic control of information, and about the evolution of print in general, would do well to read Alvin Kernen, *Printing Technology, Letters, & Samuel Johnson*. Princeton: Princeton University Press, 1987.

2

Old News: The Necessity for Change

If online resources were not useful, people would not spend the money for the equipment and accessories that access requires—computer, modem, fees for a data provider—or the time that it still takes to learn the mechanics of digital surfing and data diving. Were we perfectly content with our old ways of knowing, why would we so eagerly embrace the evolutionary new? Thus, before exploring the evolving world of online communication and data, its resources and its reality, it makes sense to take a moment to ask a simple question or two: Why are we so eager for the new? What is the difference between digital and traditional resources?

A partial answer can be given quite clearly. Unequivocally, the evolution of data from print to digital storage and electronic distribution is a significant advance. It is faster, more efficient, and at least potentially more accurate than older means of data storage and retrieval. Evolution advances the past's limits, and the migration of news readers and information users online is testimony to the degree that new technologies improve upon older, somewhat limited venues.

It is distance that fractures the many parts of our world, the villain who demands that we find tools of integration. Our homes and work sites are simply too far from those of the friends and relatives, the colleagues and researchers with whom we wish to be in touch. It is distance which requires that we find a better way to keep abreast of other researchers' findings, a politician's proclamation, a sick friend's condition, or an absent loved one's call for help. All of these things impact upon our lives in different ways, and any of them can occur thousands of miles from our individual homes. In a similar vein, we are all separated from one another by the obstacles of race and class. And yet, it is because of that distance that we want to know more about the social world of others with whom we work and live in our urban cities.

If distance is the divide we all must cross, new electronic technologies offer a means of overcoming it. To see their strengths, the reasons for their use, it first is necessary to perceive the limits of the old. And in this area, more than any other, the focus is on news, the system assigned the task of binding us together across continents and the world. And so, in understanding why online data delivery is becoming so popular, it is to news—old and new, private and public—that we first must turn. When it is personal, relevant only to family and friends, it is done by letters hastily written around Christmastime, or late-night phone calls when the news is critical. If the news is public, however—political, social, scientific—the process is part of the official system. Since the time of the town crier, through the early years of the printing revolution, across the nineteenth century and into the twentieth, journalism has been the glue that has held us together. First it was print; then pictures were introduced, bringing images to bolster the writer's words. Then came radio and finally television, which put moving pictures to the radio's sound and newsprint's words.

Periodical, magazine, newspaper, newsletter, news hour, and newsbreak—the content of the news, and thus of public information, has always been tied to the pronouncements, interpretations, statements, and proclamations of officialdom. The form of the news evolved over two centuries, from the discursive essay appearing months after an event, to immediate reports written in the modern style. Reporters in this century are trained according to the gospel of the famous five W's—Who, What, When, Where, Why—but they remain chained to the necessity of attribution. Each story is based on an official statement or an expert quote, to the style of "he said" or "she said." In the main, journalism translated official statements into the public domain, whatever medium one read, looked at, or listened to.[1]

It has to be this way because reporters are not presidents, physicians, politicians, police officers, or professors. They lack the knowledge to critically evaluate an official's interpretation of events in question. How can a reporter with a general education challenge a physician's evaluation of a surgical procedure? What will allow a commentator to critique a police chief's insistence that crime will diminish only if more police are added to his force, and more jails are built to hold the suspects the law finally convicts? "We have to trust them," Walter Lippman wrote of public officials in his book, *Public Opinion*, "because the books and papers are on their desks." And so, for decades, studies of news content have shown that between 70 and 90 percent of all news stories are based on the statements of government officials or official experts.

This is as true of television and radio reports as it is for the newspaper or newsmagazine story. Just as in the 1930s, when people assumed that news pictures could not lie and thus conveyed a greater truth than words alone on the printed page, a generation later everyone assumed that television's visual format offered us all a portrait of reality. Over the years, however, most have come to understand that the medium is not always the message, and television has been a false revolution. Its pictures offer a sense of immediacy but no greater depth to the news. The sound bites and 15-second clips still are based on the scrum's brief quote, on an official's arrogant statement. He said. She said. Like those working in other medium, TV journalists are still bound to a form that relies on the official proclamation, defense, or justification. Most reporters remain today what they have always been: conduits carrying largely unconsidered and unexamined data from the desk of officials and official experts to the general public's eyes and ears.

Until recently, that was sufficient. Nobody expected more. The expectations of viewers, readers, and listeners were nicely matched to the presentations of radio, TV, and print reporters. We trusted our officials, and we therefore trusted the journalists who reported on them. "That's the way it is," Walter Chronkite insisted each night at the end of his hourly TV show. And we believed him. But then, people also believed without question their elected presidents or prime ministers, trusted their senators and legislative representatives, and accepted the word of academics and paid experts who were given a public platform by journalists seeking appropriate quotes. News anchor and nation's president, news reporter and city official—in our innocence we accepted the match of speaker and reporter as offering a mirror reflecting the reality of the world, and not a shallow version of it. What is sometimes called the "Fourth Estate" has always been the first bureaucracy, the medium by which all others promulgated announcements and thus carried out their rule.

But in the last 25 years things have changed. The journalistic equation of statement and report that with each new technology seemed evermore precise gradually has become, in the end, suspect and maligned. The public's reflexive belief in officials and experts eroded over the years. As a result, people began to suspect not merely the public message, but also the messenger who carried the bureaucrats' words in a style and form that gave them weight. As a consequence, trust in journalists and journalism has declined in tandem with the growing public distrust of officialdom. In opinion polls measuring public faith and respect, politicians now languish below the levels accorded pharmacists and sanitary engineers. Not surprisingly, the journalist messenger stands only slightly higher than politicians in those measurements of public esteem.

The decline of news readers and news viewers thus comes as no surprise. As late as 1970, newspapers reached 97.9 percent of all American households, as did the newer forms of broadcast journalism. But by 1990, daily household penetration had dropped by more than 30 percent to 66.3 percent. Nor has there been any indication of a reverse of this trend. To the contrary, news circulation shows every evidence of a continued and irreversible decline.[2] Because newspapers are a commodity purchased, week by week and month by month, it has been the hardest hit of our modern medium. But others have similarly suffered at the hands of public disdain. Radio journalism, once a vibrant medium with a huge audience, has become a ghost industry reduced in most places to canned, 2-minute taped spots at the top of the hour. Even TV journalists are discovering growing viewer dissatisfaction that is translating into disaffected viewers. The news? Grab that channel clicker! Thank God! There's a rerun of "M*A*S*H" on Fox.

Some see this as a dangerous trend, a symptom of the death of democracy and a thoughtful, informed society. Neil Postman, a principal defender of old times and old ways, assumes that, in turning away from traditional media and old means of communication, we are *Amusing Ourselves to Death*. I, on the other hand, believe it to be a hopeful trend affirming the intelligence of an increasingly perceptive electorate. People have not stopped reading. They have simply stopped reading newspapers. They have not stopped learning, they have merely found other venues where data are better presented, less tainted, more accessible, and more complete. Changes in reader and viewer habits are not the death of democracy, the end of literacy, or the termination of an informed citizenry. In fact, they may signal a real democratization, an increase in literate communication, and the first opportunity we have ever had for an informed and perceptive populace.

At least since 1927, and perhaps for far longer, the percentage of the U.S. Gross National Product (GNP) allocated to mass media has remained relatively constant at between 5 and 6 percent.[3] What has happened in the last decade has been that money flowed away from traditional venues and into other information sources. Increasingly, people are applying monies to electronic resources that once were dedicated to traditional media. By 1993, about 25 percent of all North American households included a computer that was being used, increasingly, as a venue for retrieving data from one or more online computer services. In 1994, there were 65 million personal computers using Windows, one of four popular computer operating systems available, with an additional 2 million being added each month to the worldwide total.[4]

In the first six months of 1994, the number of U.S. households subscribing to commercial online computer services jumped 10 percent to nearly 3.9 million people, according to the Washington, DC–based *Information and Interactive Services Report*.[5] That is almost 350,000 more homes hooked up to Prodigy, America Online (which gained 130,000 users in this period), Dow Jones News Service, CompuServe (up 16 percent in 1993), and other, similar online resources. This phenomenal growth rate does not include the millions of people using other electronic services, such as the free bulletin board services (BBS) available in every city that connect to the Internet, which in 1994 had more than 22 million subscribers.

When disaster struck in the old days, newspapers put out an extra editions and folks waited impatiently for it to come to their doors. Maybe they turned on the radio or, later, the TV. But it was to the newspaper everyone first turned. It seemed solid and immediate, a physical truth that could be weighed in the hand. People trusted the news in a way that, from today's perspective, seems touching and quaint. More recently, in the event of catastrophe, people turned to their TVs to catch the images on CNN. Increasingly, however, they turn on their computers, using online resources—including CNN—to search for facts that make sense of what we once called the news.

During the minicrash of 1987, for example, when North American investors thought they were facing a full market meltdown, newspapers were ambiguous in their reportage. TV, radio, and newspaper reporters carried empty assurances by bureaucrats that nothing was wrong, nobody need panic, that nothing unusual was happening. What the effect of that crash might have been for any individual stock or stock group was difficult for the small investor to discern. After all, the *Wall Street Journal* did not care about Josephine Normal's college fund or Ralph Everyguy's mutual fund. Nobody knew what to make of the minicrash, or what to do. And stockbrokers were not available, even if they did know. Panicking investors who tried to telephone their brokers found telephone lines that were jammed for days by the exceptional volume of worried callers seeking advice, reassurance, or action.

The traditional system of voice communication and print news broke down. There were no delays, however, for investors using the then new online information and stock purchasing services. Dow Jones Information Service (DJIS) and CompuServe Information Service (CIS) offered their members a range of both "news" reports and analyses that tracked the market as a whole, by stock sector and individual issue.

Market quotes could be tracked across the day to observe the effect of the crash on a single portfolio. Not only could investors assess the damage to their portfolios, they also could buy and sell stocks online at any time and with no delay. Investors with online accounts used a range of news and analytic services to try to make sense out of the almost panic that filled the general media's reports. There were online meetings in CompuServe forums where people discussed the raw data received online, working together to make sense of what seemed to some to be a market meltdown, and to others, a buying opportunity.

The 1987 minicrash was a watershed event. Online usage during the week of uncertainty increased tenfold, and has been growing ever since. In subsequent years, the pattern became commonplace and familiar. In a disaster or in a crisis, the computerized information resources become a central source of data retrieval for online aficionados. As communications expert Joe Harris put it, "When the shuttle blows up, CompuServe will get so busy it will get jammed, which is really hard to do . . . [online] you get a lot of interesting tidbits from ex-NASA people or NASA itself . . . there's no [similar] place in either radio, TV, or newspapers or magazines where you can get instant reaction and in-depth answers to your questions."[6]

After the 1993 Los Angeles earthquake, Prodigy, another online vendor, ran a North American TV advertising campaign explaining how people could use their service to gain information on friends and relatives in the quake-effected area. During the 1994 winter Olympics, CompuServe had special forums set up for devotees of specific sports who wished to follow and discuss the action in Norway. Later in that same year, the O.J. Simpson case spawned a series of dedicated user forums, conferences, and online user groups dedicated to both the trial and the issues it raised for many people.

These new resources are in direct competition with both the traditional news organs and the time-honored definitions of public "news." They represent a more flexible and more complete alternate source of information on everything from automobile models and exotic flower purchases to the latest data from the worlds of zoology, medicine, and business. I no longer need a newspaper to read the stock quotes or business analyses. I can bypass third- or fourth-hand news reports and get primary—or at least secondary—data on my home computer. I no longer need a reporter's story if I want to learn about a researcher's scientific breakthrough. I can read the press release from his university or company on *PR Newswire*. I can read articles by that researcher online, often before they are published. I have access to better and more complete data than the traditional reporter whose function, in theory if not in practice, was to fill me in on the world we share and to explain its changes to me.

Computerized data and information challenges the old equations between writer and attributed subject, the basic assumption that news writers record what officials say. Simply, old-style news cannot compete with the new and evolving online information services. It has failed utterly to provide what Robert Maynard Hutchins once described as a full and fair, "forum for the exchange of comment and criticism."[7] It does not and cannot in any way offer a "representative picture of the constituent groups of society." News today is what it has always been, a vehicle for the opinions, conclusions, and perceptions of bureaucrats, elected officials, and their experts. It is largely a collection of facts without substance, of data without information. People have come to understand this, and more and more frequently they go elsewhere to learn about issues that concern them.

A hybrid of electronic data and traditional reportage, "digital news," is currently in its infancy. It is disparaged by journalism professors and old-style editors who still insist that the old ways are the best, that nothing really needs to be changed. "I want my reporters out interviewing, talking to people," the editor says. "Not playing with computers." If reporters have to research the context of a story, others complain that it will "slow down the news-gathering process and bury the reporter in data."[8] The assurances of a president, the declarations of a senator, the campaign promises of a mayor are faithfully repeated; who needs more? News is what someone says, and the demonstrable truth or falsity of those statements is largely irrelevant to the business at large.

To see why people are turning away from old-style news, and how electronic resources can change it, see Example 2.1: It is not an unusual or exceptional piece. "All Surgery Risky" is neither better nor worse than scores of stories that are broadcast on news hours or published in newspages every day. In reading it, view it with the immediacy of a person who believes that the information it contains may mean the difference between life and death. Assume that you, or someone you love, is scheduled for surgery in the coming weeks.

"All Surgery Risky, Doctor Says." No one is to blame. According to Dr. Raymond, surgery is as dangerous as walking across the street. There is danger everywhere. Disturbing as that conclusion is, the story offers a measure of comfort. Physicians are vigilant, and working to make things better. The government's inquests are making recommendations that will make our world safer. Hospitals are reading the reports offered by the coroner's service. Experts like Dr. Raymond are on the case. Newspeople make sure that the public is aware. Alas, there is little substance behind these assurances, or behind the facts of the news report.

Dr. Raymond is right when he says that the world is a risky place in

Example 2.1
All Surgery Risky, Doctor Says: 19-year-old Patient Died from Lack of Oxygen, Inquest Finds

SouthamStar Network

OTTAWA—The way Dr. Raymond Matthews sees it, major surgery is a lot like crossing a road. There's always a risk something can go wrong.

Matthews was assigned by Ontario's chief coroner to assist the investigation into the May 1993 death of 19-year-old Natalie Young at the Montfort Hospital.

A coroner's jury spent four days last week hearing evidence about Young's corrective dental surgery and the post-surgery complications that led to her death.

"It's a major operation," Matthews said in an interview from His Kingston home Saturday. "And with any procedure, there's a risk."

The operation, called a maxillofacial osteotomy, was performed to realign Young's upper and lower jaw. It took more than five hours to perform the operation which involved numerous incisions that included bringing Young's chin forward.

The inquest heard that the operation, performed by oral surgeon Dr. Gary Cousens, was successful. Young was given a perfect 10 out of 10 rating when she left the hospital's recovery room and was transferred to another ward.

She stopped breathing and went into cardiac arrest about six hours later. She could not be revived. The jury concluded her death was due to prolonged lack of oxygen to the brain.

Matthews, now retired, was the head of the Queen's University anesthesia department and a member of the Ontario coroner's advisory committee.

He said he's aware of only one Ontario death after a similar dental operation. That occurred several years ago in a hospital in London, Ont. But Matthews couldn't recall if the incident involved an oral surgeon or a plastic surgeon.

The maxillofacial osteotomy has been performed at the Montfort since Young's death.

But the inquest was told that an internal investigation of the incident was done before the surgery was allowed to resume. Various hospital committees looked into the use of anesthesia and resuscitation techniques, especially for people who have small airways.

And only one significant change was made: Patients are not allowed to have the operation unless they can be guaranteed a bed in the hospital's intensive care unit afterwards. If no bed is available, the surgery is postponed.

Young's mother, Suzanne, said she was assured her daughter would be given an ICU bed. But the inquest heard that none was available, so Young was transferred to a regular ward and left with a special care nurse.

After hearing lengthy and detailed testimony, the jury concluded that Young's death was brought on by "complications arising during postoperative surgery."

The jury was told that Young complained at least four times to her nurse, Judy O'Brien, that she was having trouble breathing.

O'Brien attributed the complaints to anxiety. She did not report the breathing problems to Cousens.

• The Jury's recommendations were directed at ensuring better post-operative care for patients like Young. The recommendations include:

• That oral surgeons provide "in-service training" for nurses and others on the special requirements of patients like Young.

• That medical and dental staff be made more aware of the many causes of "post operative restlessness."

• That if an ICU bed isn't available, the patient's vital signs be continuously monitored by a machine called a pulse oximeter. This machine gives a readout of heart rate and the level of oxygen in the blood, Matthews said.

Cousen's lawyer, Michael Birley, said in an interview that the oral surgeon is hopeful "these recommendations will . . . be of some assistance in preventing this type of occurrence in the future."

Matthews said the recommendations will be distributed to Ontario's 200-plus hospitals and circulated among staff. Health care officials usually take such recommendations quite seriously, he said.

---

which things go wrong. Earthquakes destroy buildings. Floods inundate cities. Lightening can strike the barn during a summer storm. Not all risks are preventable. But when a truck hauling dynamite speeds through a red light, barrels the wrong way down a one-way street, and slams into a pedestrian crossing the street in a hospital zone, we do not say, "Well, the way truck drivers see it, walking is risky." We ask if the signs were evident, the driver licensed; we ask what it was which led so dangerous and powerful a vehicle to behave in such an irresponsible and dangerous manner. The question unanswered in this story is whether Natalie Young's death was a random event, like lightening striking a baseball player. Or was it a preventable error, a mistake that should not have happened? According to the news service, Dr. Raymond says this death was, if not unique, then nearly so. But as the inquest recommendations make clear, this is not a story about maxillofacial osteotomies. It is about death resulting from anesthesia, and those are not uncommon. In recent years there have been scores of anesthetic-related deaths reported across Canada and the United States, many of them following dental procedures. Reported cases can be found in news reports, court documents, and medical journal articles dealing with anesthetic "mishaps" and "misadventures." The death of Natalie Young is in fact one of a very large class of similar and equally preventable deaths occurring across North America. The single conclusion in virtually every case was that these deaths are preventable.

No newspaper will send a reporter cross-country on the basis of a single inquest. But computers collapse distance, they make it as easy to search the files of a Vancouver or California newspaper as it is to search one's own in Ontario. In addition, they allow reporters to sift through reports of court trials and medical journal articles to define the causes of "anesthetic mishaps" beyond a general "Surgery Always Risky" story. Both the courts and the medical experts are in surprising agreement. There are, they say, generally three preventable causes in cases of anesthetic death: medical professionals prescribe incorrect anesthetic dosages, they fail to correctly monitor their patients during and immediately after surgery, or physicians fail to implement appropriate emergency procedures when problems first manifest.

The inevitable conclusion is clear. Unavoidable and unexplained deaths are extremely rare, about .09 deaths per 1000 procedures. If physicians and medical personnel follow established procedures, the risk to patients is minimal. If they do not, however, receiving anesthesia in surgery can be like standing in the middle of a busy intersection and having the traffic lights break down, showing a green light to all directions.

Coroner juries reviewing such cases have, in the past, typically recommended that during surgery physicians use patient monitors like the pulse oximeter, a small and relatively inexpensive piece of equipment that measures the pulse through the finger and translates that data into audible sounds and visual records. It is an early warning detector of respiratory and cardiac failure. This is not, however, new information. In 1986, for example, a Harvard Medical School study reported in the *Journal of the American Medical Association* that the use of appropriate patient monitoring (with tools like the pulse oximeter) radically decreased cases of patient "complication" both during surgery and in the postsurgical period.[9]

And in 1988, a group of U.S. physicians writing in the *Journal of Clinical Monitoring* argued that the use of the pulse oximeter and other monitoring tools would pay for themselves in 6 months by decreasing the number of patient deaths and the lawsuits that are their nearly inevitable result.[10] In other words, the use of such tools is a generally accepted and professionally recommended procedure. Failure to monitor is exactly like removing the traffic lights from an intersection where pedestrians may walk.

One need not be a medical researcher to know this these things. I am neither a physician nor a nurse. To access these data, a person needs online access to one or another service that offers medical journal articles, newspaper files, and law journal reviews. In the past, these were specialized areas of knowledge. It could take months to find the appropriate newspaper clip, and the resources of a library researcher to track down a journal article or a legal case. Now, however, these resources are as close as a computer and modem. And so they are as available to me as they are to a reporter from the *New York Times* or, for that matter, the *Kennebunk* (Maine) *Journal*.

The data retrieved from all these sources, whoever the searcher, are clear.

Surgery becomes risky when patients are not correctly monitored during surgery, when inappropriate levels of anesthetic are administered, and when patients are not watched for postoperative complications. We can assume that Natalie Young's physicians, and the hospital, knew this literature. After all, Mrs. Young had been assured that her daughter would be put into an intensive care unit bed where patient monitoring is standard operating procedure. We do not know whether the nurse assigned to Ms. Young was instructed in how to physically monitor her patient, or why she did not credit her patient's complaint about early respiratory distress. Nor, frankly, do we know why Ms. Young stopped breathing. We do not even know the type and dosage of anesthetic, or whether it was appropriate for a person of her age and size.

What we do know is that the story gives false impressions based on inquest testimony, and that the reporter did nothing but repeat what he or she was told. On examination, this story really tells us nothing about the death of Natalie Young. Its reassuring surface tone belies the hidden message—repeated deaths following anesthetic administration occur despite numerous inquests—one that should give any surgical candidate cause for concern.

Why was the story presented in this manner? Southam is a newspaper chain that stretches across Canada. The *Star*, Canada's largest urban paper, boosts a huge news budget and a mammoth news library. Together, these companies have resources galore. Material on this subject is not hidden. Anesthetic-related cases like this one have been covered by Southam or *Star* newspapers at least since the 1980 Vancouver inquest into the anesthetic-related death of a child named Darcy Leo after dental surgery.[11] At least two books on journalism have reviewed this material, with an emphasis on the Canadian case histories.[12] In addition, popular books on medicine have been at pains to report on this type of preventable death.[13] Further, there are scores of medical journal articles on the subject of the need for monitoring patients following anesthesia. A collection of the titles and abstracts from this collection can be located in any medical library, or downloaded at a cost of a very few dollars.

Why didn't the Southam reporter—or any other local reporter—take an hour to put this inquest into a context that would make even moderate sense? The answer is simple. That wasn't the job. The reporter was not assigned to cover the death of a young girl but to report on an inquest, to capture and allow to be published what was said by witnesses under oath. Who was responsible for Natalie Young's death, its relation to other similar occurrences, and what all of this means for normal citizens was irrelevant to the journalistic mission.

Alexander Cockburn says that there is in journalism an almost complete division between act and consequence, between an event and the things that caused it to happen: a child dies, a bus falls over a cliff, a war starts; that these events may be the result of prior actions or decisions is simply outside the boundaries of contemporary news. Think of it as a series of levels or states that stretch from knowing to not knowing. Journalism typically exists at a level that reports on some official statement or function. In this case, it is the inquest, the public stage where facts already filtered through official investigations are presented.[14]

At this level, many things already may be covered up, forgotten, or inadvertently excluded from the public view. And because the reporter is bound to write about the inquest and the attributed conclusions of the official investigation, the story cannot concern itself with it's supposed focus: the death of a girl after surgery. It gives the impression that it is describing that event, promising to provide information on its cause. But to do this, the reporter would have to look at what happened during surgery and at the quality of postoperative care. To understand the relation between that and Natalie Young's death, one has to look to prior events, to the body of cases, case histories, of legal precedent and medical knowledge that existed at the time of the surgery. It is here, in the context of the past, in cases that have been determined and procedures outlined, that the heart of the matter can be found.

This is the difference between data and information. "He said," "she said," "in the words of the Prime Minister" . . . each statement is a datum without context or means of verification. The doctor says "surgery is risky," and that is what the reporter writes. Put enough individual datum together, however, and a picture of the world that reduces uncertainty and clarifies the world at large may emerge. But those data must come from the world of prior occurrence. Old news is simply data masquerading as information. News as we know it functions at the level of the official report, of what was said by an official or an expert. Only rarely does it focus upon the real question: "What happened?" or "what *has* happened in the past?" The story that links fact and consequence, prior occurrence to horrible event, is rare indeed. News reporters rarely critique inquests or officials' stories, both because their job is to report what is said—not to investigate it—and because they rarely have the knowledge, background, or personal resources to do more than translate official statements into the public domain.

Paper records are clumsy things that require time and training if they are to be turned into effective tools. News libraries in Ottawa and Toronto are filled with local but not necessarily regional and national story clippings. "Coroner Inquest" is a large, thick envelope filled with old stories of past inquests involving boating accidents, hospital deaths, police homicides, fires, and drownings. To sift through them all would take hours, and then the only common denominator among that wealth of largely unrelated data is the fact that some deaths, whatever their cause, were reviewed by a coroner's inquest.

Even if the folder holds stories similar to Natalie Young's, they will be Toronto stories, with a few wire service briefs suggesting that something similar may have happened at one time in Vancouver, Winnipeg, and Montreal. A diligent reporter then would have to call coroners in those cities to learn enough to make those cases even minimally applicable to the task at hand: the death of Natalie Young. Distance takes time to surmount, and for reporters—or for any of us—time is a precious commodity.

Similarly, to check the medical evidence would mean going to a university library's special collection section where medicine journals are kept. Articles on anesthesia, maxillofacial osteotomy, and postsurgical care are buried in single issues of esoteric journals stored along shelves somewhere in large library complexes. To find the appropriate article in all of these journals, one first must use a master index, organized by subject, to find the titles of potentially relevant papers. Finding a promising title, and assuming that it is in a journal the library collects, the next task is to find the referenced article in the library itself, an oftentime consuming task. If the correct volume is being used by another, is lost, or is damaged, well then you are out of luck. Then the process starts again, a new hunt for another article in another journal stored two floors up and across the way, somewhere else in the library.

All of this takes time, training, and patience, resources that are foreign to most modern journalists. Editors are reluctant to grant "research time" when one can just as easily "report" an inquest or trial, file the copy, and then go home. And, to be truthful, patience—a requirement for research—is a personal attribute that is not highly valued in the business at large. Nor are reporters assigned to an inquest or court case expected to be investigators. Their job is to repeat, with appropriate quotes or clips or sound bites, the statements of inquest characters. As a consequence, readers and viewers are presented, day by day, with blatantly false truths like this one, stories that are correct in their attributed particulars but obvious fantasy when viewed from any other, more grounded perspective.

The problem is one we all share to the extent that we want our news to present some resemblance to reality, and because the reporter's obstacles to knowing confront everyone who needs to know how to act or what to do in a critical situation. Even if an article or news story is good, finding it when it is needed is typically an arduous and time-consuming task. You know you saw an article detailing questions to ask a physician before going into surgery. But whether it was written in the local newspaper, the *Toronto Magazine, Homemakers,* or some periodical read in the doctor's office two months ago is a fact forgotten long before its importance was clear and its need compelling. Somewhere you saw a piece on repetitive strain injuries and how ergonomically designed furniture might diminish the possibility of hand and wrist problems resulting from computer use. You read it last year when you still worked in an office. Now they have downsized and you're struggling with a laptop computer perched on the kitchen table. Your wrist hurts and that data is needed. Where to look? It might takes hours at the public library, using the *Periodical Guide to Popular Literature* in search of a reference, and then in search of the article itself.

Or one simply may go online, tapping into the wide world of citizen news. One need not be a physician or a lawyer to use these resources; most are designed for people with no prior training. Anyone can use them to turn stories like "All Surgery Risky, Doctor Says" from puffery to potent, from meaningless data to meaningful information. Online resources allow easy and immediate access to data at *every* level of the information tree, from the inquest's public report to the scientific evidence on which testimony may be based. Want to know about news stories linking anesthesia or anesthetic and death? The Dow Jones Information Service's TEXT library has five Canadian newspapers and more than 70 U.S. newspapers available online. All can be searched simultaneously with the words "anesthetic" and "mishap" or "death." With equal ease one can use that same phrase to search for articles on the antecedent context in an international medical library, like the ones housed on Knight Ridder Information or CompuServe. Legal journals have published learned articles on "physician responsibility." They are online, too.

Day in and day out, more and more people are using online resources in this way. Librarian Susan Robishaw, for example, suffered from idiopathic dilated cardiomyopathy, a disease that was destroying her heart. She had the good fortune of living near Philadelphia's Temple University, which has a first-rate transplant team, and had the even better luck of a good transplant organ becoming available. The operation was a success and approximately two weeks after her new heart was in place, she went home to Danville, Pennsylvania.

Like all people with organ transplants, she was required to take an immunosupressive drug whose job it is to prevent the body from rejecting what is fundamentally foreign tissue. Like many others, she was given a drug produced by Sandoz Pharmaceutical. She took 1000 milligrams a day of Cyclosporine to suppress the autoimmune system, the body's defence mechanism against foreign objects. This class of drug is what makes transplants possible; it is a crucial aspect of surgery's modern miracle.

After a week of drinking the drug each day, however, Ms. Robishaw began to experience an allergic reaction. A body rash developed, her throat became swollen, and breathing became increasingly difficult. She was hospitalized with all of the symptoms of anaphylactic shock, of a physical reaction to foreign chemicals, whether they be from bee stings or any other agent. She was admitted to the hospital and the reaction was controlled. But the problems did not end there. Each day, after drinking her Cyclosporine, the problem returned with evermore serious, life-threatening severity. Neither Temple University doctors nor Sandoz, the manufacturer, had ever heard of this type of reaction to Cyclosporine. All they knew was that if something was not changed, Ms. Robishaw would probably die.

Her sister, Janet Robishaw, was a medical doctor who frequently used an online medical database called PaperChase to research patient conditions. She was not a specialist in transplant medicine, but she was concerned about her sister. If others had suffered similar reactions, there should be a record of the case, she reasoned, somewhere in the international records of collected medical journals. And so she looked for information on Cyclosporins, the class of drugs used to prevent reactions, and drug hypersensitivity, a term describing reactions in general.

Dr. Robishaw found a Dutch case in which a man who had received a transplant suffered an allergic reaction to Cyclosporine administered in liquid form. However, when he was given the drug in capsule form, the article said, the adverse reaction to the drug disappeared. Dr. Robishaw brought the paper to her sister's physicians, who eventually put their patient on Cyclosporine in capsule form. It worked, and Ms. Robishaw recovered. Since then, both the drug company and the Temple University physicians have warned other transplant teams about the potential problem, and suggest the capsule as opposed to liquid form in cases of allergic reaction.[15]

Ms. Robishaw's physicians can be forgiven for not having known of a Dutch patient whose adverse reaction to an important drug was similar to those of a patient in Pennsylvania. Every nation has medical journals pouring forth literally thousands of articles each month. It is one of the great boons of these tools that they allow anyone to sift through mammoth amounts of potentially useful but actually extraneous material to find the one fact, the one antecedent, which may be of use in a situation or crisis. In medical searching, it helps to be a doctor or medical professional. But it is not necessary. These tools are easier to use than an old-style library's card catalogue.

PaperChase was developed by Boston's Beth Israel Hospital to facilitate staff searches of the National Library of Medicine's collection of more than 7 million references to journal articles in the fields of medicine, dentistry, nursing, and allied health sciences. The system includes a simple menu-driven system of searching designed for people with no computer training. It proved so successful that the hospital licensed its use to CompuServe, where they assumed that it would be used by physicians and medical professions in other areas, people like Dr. Robishaw. But to their surprise, it also has been used heavily by people facing medical crises, by nonprofessional folks who want to know more about their own illnesses and appropriate treatment protocols.

The electronic library began as a specialist's tool, but it has been appropriated by everyday folks. Barbara Harris, for example, is a 69-year-old woman who asked for help online in understanding a disease called temporal arteritis. The vision-destroying illness was affecting her older sister, Margaret, who at age 71 was going blind because of an illness neither woman understood. They wanted help in finding people who could help Margaret Harris learn to live with visual restrictions, who could explain temporal arteritis, and talk about different treatments.

Margaret's sister logged her question onto a "forum" on CompuServe, a meeting place for people with questions. A visual lab technician gave her information on the illness and a brief discussion of its treatment. Ed Madara, director of the computerized Self-Help Clearing House, came through with a toll-free number for a foundation that provides help and support for the visually impaired. His organization has in its electronic files the names, addresses, and telephone numbers of virtually every self-help and support group in North America. Others came forward to offer the names of articles on living with sight impairments, or explained how to find references to temporal arteritis and its treatment in the PaperChase library. People with sight impairments came forward simply to assure both women that having low vision did not necessarily mean a restricted life.

At no other time in history could a person facing a personal crisis find so wide a range of support so quickly. Nowhere else in the country or in history could the broad array of technical and popular literatures, of personal experience and clinical expertise be accessed so readily by someone in need of help. It is the flexible, plastic, communal nature of these services that allows each person to use them to fit his or her own needs, to seek the appropriate newspaper, magazine, or journal references which, with the help of experts or others with experience, combine to answer personal questions. This happens in every field and every context.

Physicians, lawyers, business people, politicians, and their experts have been using online sources for years. For example, U.S. psychologist Michael Sheridan was asked by the West Virginia courts to help determine if two children who had been living with their widowed grandmother should be returned to the parents. The father had been in jail, and during that time the mother had been unable to look after them. So the children had been living with their grandparents. But the father was paroled and the biological parents wanted their children back. The grandmother said that she did not believe that they were ready to become parents again, and that taking the children from her would be bad for them.

Michael Sheridan's job was to determine what would be best for the kids. As a relative newcomer to this kind of court-ordered assignment, he wanted to be prepared. To figure out what was best for the children, Mr. Sheridan did the same thing as Dr. Robishaw and Ms. Harris when they needed background and advice. He used an online legal forum to ask if anyone knew of relevant precedents, if anyone could suggest how he might best handle his job performing the court-appointed evaluation in this tricky case. Reams of advice poured in from U.S. attorneys from several states. They suggested strategies and ideas, and cited relevant, legal precedents that might be of use to the psychologist. Mr. Sheridan knew psychology, but not the law or the tricks of testimony. With his report, the psychological evaluation, he took into court a printout of their messages to make sure, he later said, "It was clear that I'd done my homework."[16] When questioned, he showed them to the judge. Not surprisingly, Mr. Sheridan's recommendations were followed. The grandparents got to keep the children, and the parents were encouraged to visit their offspring more often.

His was not an unusual experience. I first became aware of these resources in the early 1980s, when a lawyer from the small town of Corinth, Mississippi, wrote my newspaper in Vancouver, Canada, to ask for copies of stories I had written on the subject of anesthetic deaths caused by a specific type of equipment malfunction. I was flattered, of course, but did not understand how a small-town Mississippi lawyer had learned of stories in a westcoast, Canadian newspaper. With the requested clips I therefore included a note asking the lawyer where he had learned of my work.

He replied that he had done an electronic search for information on the type of mishap on which I had reported. My stories showed up in that digital search and were, he later said, a factor in the generous settlement awarded his clients. My stories showed general, public knowledge of a problem that his search demonstrated was also well-covered in medical journal articles. In law, he reminded me, prior knowledge meant greater responsibility. My story demonstrated that the technical malfunction which killed his client's spouse was one well described in the general as well as the popular literature.

At that moment I understood for the first time, the potential of the past and the potential of antecedent events to affect, not merely the outcome of a trial, but also, the whole of what we call public information. News that simply reported what was said at an inquest or a court hearing, the comforting pronouncement of a physician, or the promise of some bureaucrat now could be interpreted by the average person who sought the underlying base of experience that would either support or critique those arguments. The world I had been trained for was ending, I decided, and a new technology was creating a universe whose order would be vastly different. The potentials of these tools seemed to me glorious, important, and beautiful—a boon for us all. And so it is, glorious and informative at an unimaginably vast, unprecedented scale.

Across the distance of our lives, old equations have been broken. Journalists are no longer the only conduit we have to the greater world. Data are offered in many venues, only one of which is the old-style newspaper or news journal. As the tools and resources of the electronic medium grow in power and sophistication, new potentials are expanding for us all.

For several years, companies like the Dow Jones Information Service and CompuServe have offered electronic self-directed "clipping" services to subscribers. These allow users to list the subjects they are interested in, and have an automatic reader peruse news wires and other data sources for items that answer those subject headings. Why wait for a local newspaper to edit a story on multiple sclerosis, for example, when the computer will assure that the original story, and the report that it was based on, are automatically held in an electronic file? Who cares what a local movie reviewer likes or dislikes when one can immediately survey the opinion of reviewers like Siskel and Ebert? For those who like the old-style feel of the printed page, an $80 software program, the *Journalist*,[17] electronically tracks a person's subjects and then automatically "downloads" that material on command, transferring it to a newspaper-style page.

Old names have new incarnations in the electronic universe. *CNN, US News and World Report*, and smaller publications like the *Detroit News* now sponsor electronic sites where users may access the organization's electronic libraries and communicate with writers, editors, and other readers. In early 1995, for example, each week more than 50,000 users—one can no longer call them passive "readers"—accessed the online CompuServe site for *US News and World Report*. Some simply read new stories, others used its electronic library of past stories. Still others used the forum as a place to log a question, like Mr. Sheridan's, or to critique a story previously presented. Distance between a reader and a writer, a researcher and a subject are no longer insurmountable obstacles. This is the beginning of the new age of electronic journalism, one that frees provider and user alike to search far and wide for the best answer to a problem at hand. It is the first step toward a new balance between information seeker and data resource. The old equation was static, with fixed roles up and down the lines of transmission. The new balance is dynamic and fluid, defined by the new electronic conference center and library described in the next chapter.

NOTES

1. Tom Koch, *The News as Myth: Fact and Context in Journalism*. Westport, CT: Greenwood, 1990.

2. Joseph Ungaro. "First the Bad News." *Media Studies Journal*. Fall, 1991, 100–113.

3. Rogert Fidler. "Mediamorphosis, or The Transformation of Newspapers into a New Medium." *Media Studies Journal*. Fall, 1991, 115–125 (p. 118).

4. Jeff Ubois. "The Karma of Chameleon," *Internet*. October, 1994, 60.

5. Reuters. "U.S. On-line Subscribers Rise." *Toronto Star*. November 1, 1994.

6. Cathryn Conroy. "News You Can Choose: Nonstop Global Coverage Delivered Online." *Online Today* 8:1 (January, 1989), 16–21.

7. Robert Maynard Hutchins. In: *A Free and Responsible Press*, Robert D. Leigh, Ed. University of Chicago, 1947; reprinted, 1974.

8. Fredreic F. Endres. "Daily Newspaper Utilization of Computer Data Bases. *Newspaper Research Journal* 7:1 (Fall, 1985), 34.

9. John Eichorn, et. al. "Standards for Patient Monitoring During Anesthesia at Harvard Medical School." *Journal of the American Medical Association* 256 (1986), 1017–1020.

10. C. Whitcher, et. al. "Anesthetic Mishaps and the Cost of Monitoring: A Proposed Standard for Monitoring Equipment." *Journal of Clinical Monitoring*. January 4, 1988.

11. Martha Robinson. "No Guidelines in Boy's Death." [Vanocouver] *Sun*. May 30, 1980.

12. Tom Koch. *The News as Myth*, Ch. 4. Also see, Tom Koch, *Journalism for the 21st Century*. New York: Praeger, 1993.

13. Charles B. Inlander, Lowell S. Levin, Ed Weiner. *Medicine on Trial*. New York: Pantheon, 1988, 50–66.

14. This argument is made at length in Tom Koch. *The News as Myth*.

15. "Group Account Manager Undergoes Heart Transplant And Experiences Adverse Reaction To Medication." *Paperchase Pulse* 3:1, 1990.

16. Cathryn Conroy. "Making a Solid Case for Common Sense." *CompuServe Magazine*. December 8, 1991.

17. *Journalist* software, an automatic clipping program that uses multicolumn, news-style pages for the delivery of data, is sold by PED Software Corporation, Cupertino, California.

3

Everybody's Resource: The Knowledge Center

There is no information highway. Even the idea of the "databahn" is a misnomer, an inappropriate metaphor, and an engaging lie. Highways link distant places, but in the world online there is no distance. One does not surf across the links of a network or hunt between its various computers. In the online world, distance is a foreign concept, and so the idea of a physical highway linking disparate sites is spurious. To be in one database is to have potential access to all of the databases online. From the perspective of the user, any two points in the digital world are separated, perhaps, by a few seconds wait. It is like the time between floors defined by the elevator's hushed travel. But in the world of electronic data, the user does not move between floors. Wonderfully and magically, the resources on those metaphorical floors come to you.

In attempting to imagine this evolving medium, think of the best reference library in the world surrounded by an enormous conference center. Either the library or the conference center can be entered by one of a number of doors, magic portals that are available to anyone with a computer. (See Figure 3.1.) Each door has a name: Internet, Dialog, CompuServe, LEXIS-NEXIS, America Online, Prodigy, etc. Through these doors you can instantly find groups of experts—lawyers, physicians, scientists, politicians—or simply people interested and involved in issues that may be of concern to you. Many people in

Figure 3.1
The Online Library and Conference Center Have Various Points of Access,
Online Services, and a Variety of References Available

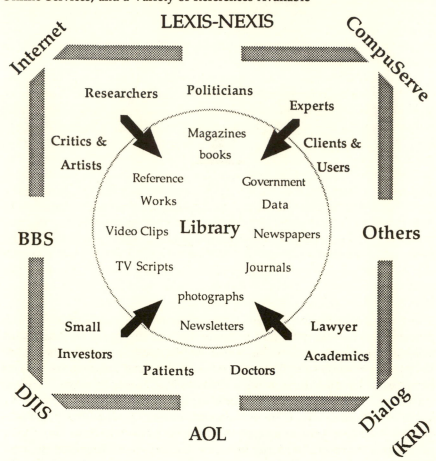

the conference center are familiar with the library's holdings, and will advise you on anything you want to know about it, too.

Both parts of this center cum library are designed to bring you data that can be used to answer any question. Let us look first at the library. It is usually called a database, a phrase I avoid because of people's tendency to confuse it with computer software programs, like FoxPro or Reflex, which are designed to filter and manipulate large amounts of factual data. And, frankly, calling it a library allows us all to perceive these new technologies not as something wholly different, but as a transformation and extension of resources we have used since childhood.

And it *is* a library, a place where articles, papers, magazines, journals, newsletters, pictures, directories, and even whole books are stored. That is all a library is, after all—a place for the storage of things others have written or drawn, a collection of maps and writings organized so that anyone with reasonable skill can find the pertinent piece of writing or the appropriate graphic that is needed to answer a question.

But this library is different from all of the others, from either the U.S. Library of Congress or the school libraries where we learned as students. In those old-fashioned, print-based structures, everything was on one of seemingly endless rows of shelves, and the trick was to find the shelf that held the book or article which offered the best chance of answering a question someone had. The most efficient way of finding the name of an article or book was by using a card catalog that held the names of all of the books and journals in the library, the names of all of the book authors, and listings referenced to broad subject categories. Each card carried a series of numbers that corresponded, more or less, to shelf locations in the library. After finding the name of a potentially useful book or magazine, one attempted to match the number to a single row and shelf. In this search one hoped but could not assume that the book would not be checked out, lost, defaced, or shelved inappropriately. If it was, well, tough luck.

Say that, as a child, you wanted to know more about Roy Rogers' horse Trigger. But when you asked the librarian, or checked the card catalog, there were no book's called "Roy's Horse." Unfortunately, neither Roy nor anyone else had written a book just about Trigger. So you looked up the more general subject of Roy Rogers, and then of "cowboys and horses." It was a first lesson in looking for specific data by searching general categories. Because this was an old-fashioned library, the catalog carried only the names of books and magazines, but not a listing of articles in collected journals. Those were stored elsewhere, and it would be years before anybody explained how to use the *Periodical Guide to Literature*. There were books on "cowboys" if not "cowboys and their horses," and so one roamed across the shelves, flipping through different books, browsing their contents for data that might answer the questions about Roy and Trigger which, to an 8-year old, seemed pressing and important. Perhaps one even asked the old lady who smelled of lavender. She was the librarian, a person who always laughed at our queries and sometimes even helped, when she had the time and inclination.

The electronic library is different. Simply, it is magic. Nothing is ever misshelved, defaced, "on loan," lost or "mislaid." Whatever the collection, it is always and wholly available to you. No need to wait your turn because every user is always first in line. Even better, the whole vast collection is dedicated solely to the subject you, its user, are currently most interested in. There is nothing else in the library but material that bears on the question you are asking at this minute. The digital library's vast collection of newspapers and magazine articles from around the world, its newsletters and specialty journals, the encyclopedias, directories, official notices, and reports by experts, even scripts from TV broadcast news and entertainment shows: all arrange themselves until the entire collection is focused on whatever subject you are interested in at this moment. Video excerpts of Roy Rogers' TV show are stored there, too.

One does not need to search through tiers of extraneous data because, vast as it is, everything you might want on any subject is right in front of you, on the computer's screen. Nobody in the electronic library walks down kilometers of hallway, traipses up and then down across separate floors of the library to find the data they seek. All related items, whatever their source, are on the same shelf in this library; and that shelf is always right in front of you. At the left are popular journal articles. Above them are materials from TV shows. Below them are medical, legal, and other technical journals. To the right are things by social scientists and economists. Somewhere, someone has written a doctoral dissertation on Roy Rogers, for example, and that is also in the conference center library, awaiting your collection. Should you need them, there are, as well, collections of debates by "just folks" who share your interests and concerns. They are fans of the cowboy, fans of television, and a group whose particular interest is that paragon of the West, Roy Rogers himself.

What makes this library cum conference center truly grand is that this enormously committed resource base changes, magically, to mirror any person's immediate field of study and interest. If you are interested in, say, an airplane like the AIRBUS, the library magically alters itself to reflect that interest. If the next subject is SAILBOATS, well, then that is what the whole system focuses itself upon. It can bring up reports on a type of business, a specific industry, or the performance of a single company. Material on consumer products, animals, home improvement, or health is available. All anyone needs to do is ask a question and the holdings of the library shelf will change to accommodate that interest. Aviation, aerospace, automobiles, bats, baseball, chimpanzees . . . all the way to vivisection, zoology, and xenophobic reactions to foreigners.

Another difference between the magic library and the one of our youth is that this library catalogs newspaper stories and magazine articles, including in its references stories that appear across the range of daily and monthly writing. Book titles are here, just as they were in the old catalog. So are book reviews and detailed book indexes. But the books themselves are not, usually. For them one still may have to visit the old-style library to withdraw a printed volume. Online and thus immediately at hand, however, are magazine, newspaper, and newsletter collections. The bits of potentially interesting data collected in this wealth of writing are vast, explosive, encyclopedic, seemingly endless.

It is all the fallout from the much discussed and badly named "information explosion." Actually, it is a data explosion. Knowledge reduces uncertainty in the face of chaos. It thus remains the rarest, most precious and vital thing in the world. Data are facts that may or may not reduce uncertainty, which may or may not even be true. Information is built from data, which are constructed from tests, facts, and incidences that can be joined, by us, to make something useful. What are stored in the computer, and in libraries, are largely data. Making information from them is always the hardest task we have to face.

Call it what you will, but the amount of material being stored in the center's library is growing at an extraordinary rate. It just gets bigger and bigger. That means that there is evermore potential information bearing on the problem at hand. That is irrelevent, however, if one cannot find the relevant datum, the isolated fact, an antecedent report, or at the least some person whose experience can make sense of whatever it is one needs to know. Fortunately, the expanding size of the electronic library does not hinder this task because it comes with an incredibly sophisticated, easy-to-use system of data sorting and retrieval. The bigger the library gets, in fact, the easier it is to tame its size and complexity by asking pertinent search questions.

That is the library, the resource core available to everyone. Like its print predecessors, it takes some getting used to. A latter chapter, "Finding It," is dedicated to the trick of finding things within its onmipresent and almost infinite collection. It is being used by people from all walks of life who need a crucial bit of datum, a single fact, a new angle on an issue or crisis. Users include physicians researching medical treatments, bureaucrats creating official policy, entrepreneurs checking up on their competition, kids doing school projects, lawyers researching antecedents in malpractice cases, and patients seeking more information on treatment of their individual conditions among others.

Print libraries lack the personal touch. The data they present are always one step removed from the experience of our fellows. One can read all of the articles in the world about alcoholism and still be an alcoholic. Kicking the habit for most of us means Alcoholics Anonymous meetings and the testimony of other drinkers, the personal support recovering alcoholics give each other. Because traditional print sources are impersonal, the library is not a great place to get another's unique point of view, or individual history. And so the electronic library is surrounded by the great conference center. Here is where people meet to exchange news, information, personal tragedies, private hopes, opinions, research, and references. In the center are aviators, business experts, children and grandchildren, doctors, therapists, alcoholics, lawyers, salespeople, scientists, parents, teachers: folks from every walk of life who may have a handle on the subject under review. Whatever your question, if others have asked it or are interested in the problem it represents, a portion of that online population will be available to talk about it, and point you to other referees or to sections of the library that may be of use in understanding or dissecting an issue.

How vast is this resource? Well, at present, the Toronto Hospital for Sick Children's computerized bulletin board service (BBS), Ability Online, fields an average of 1000 calls a day from its local members. Among them are people interested in the disease multiple sclerosis, mostly patients and family members of those afflicted by the disease. In Toronto, that means that there may be several hundred people with this interest who are online through this service. Ability Online, however, is a very small part of a greater collection of independent conference centers linked together through a net, a collection of BBSs joined so that people in many cities sharing this interest can discuss their experiences together. Participants in this "local network are in fact located anywhere, from Toronto, Ontario, to San Francisco, California, from Birmingham, Alabama, to Vancouver, BC, and perhaps on to Europe or Japan. Each part of this disparate web or net contributes several hundred interested persons, until the number of participants is in the thousands.

In its turn, the bulletin board system to which Ability Online belongs is a very small element of the online whole. There is for example the "mega-net," the Internet, whose more than 24 million members are linked to Ability Online through electronic mail service. And then there are commercial variants, like CompuServe, which have their own MS conferences as well as Internet access. And their members are also linked to Ability Online through e-mail. Whatever system one uses, however, and however it is tied to the whole, what happens is that a personal message or query is seen by hundreds or thousands of people, all of whom may have a point of view or an expertise that can be of enormous help.

Example 3.1 is a message received on CompuServe in a conference I administer on Family Health. It is a typical example of how personal and technical questions get answered in the library/conference center.

When Barbara Harris messaged members of CompuServe's Health and Fitness forum, a collection of people entering the conference center through that service's center door, it was as if a neighbor gathered up everyone in East Toronto and asked them if they could help her with

Example 3.1

> Re: Temporal Arteritis   To: All
> From: Barbara Brofmann 7720,6614   Section: The Doctor's Inn
> 10:35.26 a.m. August 18, 1995
>
>   My sister, age 69, was diagnosed with Temporal Arteritis in
> May, 1990. It was not diagnosed correctly for at least one month,
> at which time she was given a high dose of Prednisone. After
> two years, she has finally eased off the Prednisone since her
> SED rate is normal, but she retains the loss of sight in one eye
> and has only partial vision (peripheral on right side) in the
> other eye. Not enough to read or write. Neither she nor any of
> our family have ever known or spoken to anyone else with this
> disease. I wish there was a support group for affected people who
> are in recovery so they could share their coping mechanisms,
> adjustments, adaptations, etc. for living a very different life. If
> you know of a category or forum on CompuServe into which this
> need might fall, please contact me, as I can be her eyes.
>   Thanks to anyone who can help.

a personal problem. Those who responded to her query did so like
ideal neighbors: with concern and offers of assistance. That the respondents happened to be scattered, in real geography, across North
America was irrelevant to both her need and their desire to help. Just
as the electronic library focuses the vast resources of a mammoth library collection for any individual, so, too, the conference center focuses a wide and geographically dispersed community for the questioner. Distance is collapsed in the conference center. The result is that
anyone interested in a single subject—be it temporal arteritis, multiple
sclerosis, or Roy Rogers' horse—can share that interest and their experience with others.

Certainly, that is what happened in this example. Within hours of
posting her query she received a number of replies. People living with
low vision responded, using their own experiences to suggest ways in
which Ms. Harris's could help her sister, describing their own adapta-
tions to life with visual impairments. More technically, a medical technician working at a vision clinic wrote in to explain what temporal arteritis is and how it is treated. In addition, a physician offered to help
Barbara Harris find articles on the subject of her sister's disease in the
online library. He explained how to search its resources for items on
temporal arteritis and its treatment. He even offered to get articles for

Example 3.2

Re: Temporal Arteritis   To: Barbara Brofmann
From: Ed Madara 7420,6515   Section: The Doctor's Inn
11: 26.15 a.m. August 18, 1995

Dear Barbara,

   Very sorry to hear about your sister's loss of vision. One place
you or she may want to call is the Lighthouse's National
Center for Vision and Aging in New York City. They are open
9 to 5 weekdays and have a toll-free number: 800-334-5497.
   They have information on support groups across the country,
which your sister could call to learn more. They also have
information on vision aides which may be of help. If you do call,
kindly mention that you learned about them from us here.
   Take care and hope,

Ed at the Self-help Clearinghouse

her if she had trouble with the library. No need, she said. His instructions were sufficient, and she found the data she needed.
   In Example 3.2, Ed Madara, Director of the New Jersey–based,
America Self-Help Clearing House, provided the toll-free line of an
agency dedicated to helping people with vision problems adapt to their
environment. The Clearing House is an enormous electronic directory
that has cataloged virtually every self-help, support, or referral agency
in North America. If you need a local Alzheimer's Disease chapter, the
telephone number of the MS Society, or a support group for the bereaved, their catalog provides that information for you. In recent years,
Ed Madara and his Clearing House have become a first stop for thousands of people seeking help. Seemingly effortlessly, the resources of
this extended community—library and conference center—came forward to offer assistance, support, background information, and personal experience.
   This happens thousands of times a day, through one or another door
and in one or another area of the online conference center. Whatever
one's interest, whatever one's need, there is a conference, forum, or
user group whose members are interested in and knowledgeable about
the subject of your interest. Thousands of local bulletin boards exist
across North America. Many of them are dedicated to specific subject

areas, and, increasingly, all are linked by electronic mail to the conference center-at-large. A handfull of commercial companies, for example, America Online and Prodigy, offer larger accumulations of potential assistants. There are, for example, at present more than 4 million people using the "forums" that comprise CompuServe Information Service's (CIS) door to the conference center. And Internet user groups can boost a total potential membership of five times that number. At present not every online resource is available to all online users. Barriers remain, depending on equipment and host server. Still, an advice pool of even 100,000 knowledgeable and concerned people is an exceptional resource.

Whatever service one uses, library and conference offerings are joined through a series of connectors linking the resources of individual electronic entry points to the whole. These are called "gateways," and what they do is assure that, for example, CompuServe members can talk to Prodigy users, participate in Internet forums, and exchange mail with Ability Online participants. They assure that the resources of the U.S. Bureau of Census can be accessed by users wherever they enter the system, irrespective of their geographic location. Think of a huge sports stadium with different doors and groups of people entering through each one. Once they are in the stadium itself, seated and waiting for the game to begin, the door they used to affect an entry becomes irrelevant to their status as fans. It is their unified presence that counts. Online members are like those sports devotees, all coming to the electronic conference center through different doors, all together, however, at the game itself.

This was not the case several years ago. Through the 1980s, each center door only opened onto a restricted area in which members were separated from the whole, like moviegoers entering a multiplex theater with its many separate screening rooms. CompuServe users had their resources. Folks on Prodigy had others. So America Online users, for example, could not visit Internet user groups, talk to CompuServe, or download files from the Internet library core. And for their part, Internet folks could not use their protocols (FTP) to visit CISOU AOL, and their sometimes splendid forums.

But as the number of center doors increased, so did the gateways that linked these resources. The whole has in recent years became evermore accessible. Increasingly, people are recognizing that any one library section is rarely exclusive, and people entering through one door, CIS for example, can access materials from another section's collection. In the magic library/conference center, the available collection therefore includes not only what is in one's own library, but also all that is in the greater system's other libraries. By the mid-1990s, Internet had become the common mail carrier linking all of the sections of the conference center. Bulletin boards, commercial services, and Internet members could all connect to one another via electronic mail. More important, perhaps, the Internet itself has become a gateway to and from other, once exclusive domains. Commercial services developed connections that gave their members access to both Internet pages and user groups. Knight Ridder Information, for example, developed a "home page" that allowed people to access its resources (for a fee) through the Internet. It is as if a rooming house had been renovated and the artifical partitians between formerly small quarters knocked down, leaving only a few large, open, serviceable areas for huge congregations of people.

There are still areas of exclusivity in the commercial library/center. Some barriers remain. But as a later chapter explains, these barriers are rapidly falling as the whole system matures. Similarly, everything is not yet online. This is an evolving, growing knowledge system. The public wing of its library has been open for barely a decade. And the universal conference center, while open for business, is still very much under construction. With both, things are evolving rapidly, not by the year or month, but day by day. In a few more years, if present trends continue, the system of online storage will be so developed that everything will be available from every entrance to the library/center, and the conference center will allow every user, whatever his or her gateway, into the largest of common rooms. But, today, there are still occasional glitches, differences, and gaps in the data available at any door.

Not everyone is interested in every subject, in every query that comes forward. So, whatever service one uses to enter the conference center and its library, the next choice is who you most wish to talk to. One can decide this based on subject matter or user expertise. If the subject is business, do you want to speak to corporate spokespeople, small investors, company customers, or someone else? If the subject is euthanasia, you can meet with health-care professionals, family caregivers, the physically challenged, or ethicists. If the subject is an aviation disaster, there are pilots, mechanics, airline officials, and customers online. If you want to talk about the news, there are journalists and readers from Finland to Japan, all able and sometimes eager to discuss whatever issue you may raise. And, of course, there are news professionals willing and anxious to let others know what they think of a particular magazine, newspaper, news story, event, or writing style. Just as in the library one can sift through the available data to focus on a single question, here one can pick the membership of a group to whom one most wishes to speak.

Others have called this the "virtual community" and sung the praises of its interpersonal warmth and cohesion. There have been stories of people who met online and then in person, who fell in love and were married; of extraordinary support given by online friends to people in trouble. But in my experience, electronic acquaintances are rarely a community, virtual or otherwise. Rather, the whole is a pick-up group of similarly interested peoples, like a self-help group whose members are focused on a problem that they all share, or membership in a university course where one works intensively a semester with others in the class. Community implies not merely geography, but sustained interaction over time. Online associations tend to be intense, but focused and brief. People come together to discuss an issue, review a problem, exchange data, or assist another in a search. But a neighborhood or community online, where associations are ongoing is usually narrowly defined by the subject at hand.

Thus, the people one meets in the center are determined, in large part, by their areas of personal interest and individual expertise. For example, because of my experience in elder care, I moderate a discussion group that explores these issues. Most days, I spend some time in that area helping others find references, answering some questions and referring others to the library, or to other experts I know online. As a working writer and sometime journalist, I also periodically log onto the journalism forum to review new postings by colleagues in that field. When I have software problems, I visit the forums and conferences maintained by software companies (Microsoft, Boreland, etc.) whose experts are online to answer questions from technical illiterates like me. And recently, I have been meeting online with legal researchers to discuss issues evolving out of my work in elder care. When something happens that I do not understand medically, I go to a medical forum whose members are doctors and nurses experienced in the field of gerontology.

Those are my interests. Others visit very different groups within the center at large. For example, an acquaintance of mine talks almost daily with other small stock investors who trade news, views, and techniques for maximizing their personal income and stock portfolios, holdings that grow bigger as they work together. They all use the library core to check prices, corporate reports, and arcane economic indicators which, they insist, will predict financial futures. Another friend, a medical researcher, is also a martial arts fanatic who belongs to a variety of forums created for those involved in Karate, Judo, Aikido, and so on. But since he makes his living as a professor of opthamology, he also works online with other scientists involved in his area of research. Everyone can find online a mirror to their unique mix of problems and strengths, interests, and expertise. They use the library when researching data, and compare their findings with others in the center. How much time they spend on any one item or in any section depends on what they need to know, how much they value the input of others, and the amount of time that they have to spend on research and in conversation.

Let me give you a news-based example of how others have turned the conference center into a resource, and a personal-data gold mine.

In early 1993, a ten-passenger airplane carrying South Dakota Governor George Mickelson and seven other people crashed into a brick silo in the state of Iowa. All on board died in the crash. Obviously, reporters from South Dakota and Iowa were on the story immediately. But past the fact of death, which meant writing obituaries and stories about grieving families of the deceased, the question was, "what happened?" Why did this plane with a supposedly experienced pilot crash into a brick silo rather than coasting gracefully to its destination?

The plane was a new one, the Mitsubishi MU-2 twin-engine aircraft. Well-trained and conscientious reporters in Iowa and North Dakota looked for stories in their local news files on the Mitsubishi, and found nothing. It was the first time most reporters had heard about the plane. Reporters immediately talked to Federal Aviation Administration investigators, who said what officials always say: "I'll do an investigation, make my report, and you'll hear from us in three weeks or three months."

Mark Anderson, one of the crash-site reporters, worked for the *Rapid City* [Iowa] *Journal*. He also is a subscriber to the CompuServe Information Service. CIS, as it often is called, has a huge array of data libraries and a broad spectrum of "forums," places where people with specialized interests, knowledge, and expertise trade gossip, data, and sometimes even information.[1] Mr. Anderson logged onto the Aviation Forum, a place where airplane pilots, engineers, and specialists congregate, and posted a message that asked if anyone knew about problems with the Mitsubishi MU-2.[2]

Airline pilots messaged back that there indeed had been problems with the plane. In fact, they said, the National Transportation Safety Board had requested earlier that the Federal Aviation Administration ground all MU-2s until the possibility of cracked hubs could be inspected. It seems that there was a structural problem with these things, whose job it is to hold the propeller blades in place.

Anderson and the *Rapid City Journal* were armed with a crucial datum, with the statement of prior problems with the Mitsubishi MU-2's hubs. It was not a smoking gun, iron clad evidence of what brought the plane down. But it was a clue to the shooter. If the data relayed in the forum were correct, it would mean that there had been previous incidents of failure, previous federal reports, perhaps old lawsuits that would be listed in either the newspapers or court report files. Evidence of those events were potentially available, of course, in the electronic library.

In the end, Mr. Anderson and his paper did not have to go there.

They had a hypothesis that could be confirmed or denied simply by checking with official investigators and FAA officials. They asked first if hub failure was a suspected cause of the crash. They then asked the officials about past problems with Mitsubishi MU-2 hubs, and reports on it. They checked with the National Transportation Safety Board to see if it had, in fact, requested that FAA officials down all MU-2s. Voices from the conference center had, in short, given them the ammunition for their interviews, and had pointed them towards where reports might be stored.

The *Journal* then ran a story about past problems with the Mitsubishi MU-2 hubs, noting the National Transportation Safety Board's antecedent but until then unpublished concerns about the part. They did not say this was the cause of the crash of the plane leading to a state governor's demise. They did, however, suggest that it was something being investigated as a very good bet. A few days later, they smugly published a second piece confirming government investigators' suspicions that the hubs were responsible for that specific crash. Within a week, they ran another story on the decision by the FAA to ground all MU-2s until the problem, now confirmed, could be corrected.

Like Barbara Harris, Mark Anderson needed an expert voice to direct him toward the data that might answer his question: What about those Mitsubishi MU-2 airplanes? Had he gone to the local airport and hung around the small plane pilot's hanger, he might have waited days to find someone with knowledge about the Mitsubishi MU-2. At the airport, pilots would have been busy filing flights plans, doing preflight checks, and tending to their customers. They might not have had the time or inclination to talk to him. People entering the electronic conference center are there because they want to talk, trade information, and exchange views. Thus they are predisposed to answer the queries of others. And online, the number of people he can communicate with is vast—thousands of pilots rather than 10 or 20. Like Barbara Harris, who needed data on a disease called temporal arteritis and information on living with low vision, Mark Anderson sought the advice and experience of others. And they responded.

That is what the conference center is, a system for serving up people willing to share special knowledge and personal experiences in answer to another's query. Time and again, what the center does is give a point of view, a hint of prior occurrences. It takes us from the official diagnosis, definition, or statement down the ladder of fact and context to a level that allows all of us to start asking meaningful questions. Its parts are linked by the conference center citizens who use the library, who know how to cross from the experiential to the technical and back again. Together, the evolving whole frees us from the past's absolute reliance on official points of views and timetables.

How good are the data returned from the center? Simply, they are as expert as the persons whose views are presented. They are as detailed as the articles that are stored in the library. They are as good as the experts quoted on any TV show whose script is stored online. The articles are no more or less accurate than the state of knowledge of the researchers and writers who crafted them. Because it is online does not necessarily mean that it is true. But then, the statements of our human sources are never verities. Because a physician or expert says that something is so does not make their declaration a gospel. In sifting fact from fancy and surmise from superstition, electronic resources have one enormous advantage over old-style libraries and interview resources. Because of the enormous range of material online, it usually is possible to get to the truth by searching up and down the scale of potential data.

This is something that has not changed. Skepticism is the rule, whatever the medium. I do not take as gospel the statement of the fellow on the next bar stool. Similarly, why would I assume that his words are verities simply because they are presented in an electronic format online? Because a statement is in the newspaper does not mean that it is true. And because a report is stored digitally does not give it added weight. Online or by traditional means, everyone must evaluate the data received. The only difference in the conference center is that if I like what is being said, I can make a copy of the statement by printing it out if I need to study it later. That is something one cannot do in a bar if one's neighbor is saying something intelligent.

There are several ways to communicate with the library and the conference center. At present, most ways involve typing on a keyboard, although voice systems are evolving so quickly that, experts say, by the year 2000 the keyboard may be an anachronism and speech is all anyone will need to participate in the online world. Whatever the future, typed messages are currently the easiest way to access the whole. Messages typed into the system are either posted on a bulletin board for others to read, sent privately to one or more other conference center members, or exchanged in real-time. One can have real-time conversations typing back and forth to one or more other people, each taking his or her turn in the "chat" mode.

It is something like the old days of citizens band radios, where people broadcast messages on assigned channels, and others could choose to answer or just listen to the chatter of others. Sometimes the airwaves became cluttered with too many voices, and people wishing to talk privately then would switch to another channel where they could converse in relative private. People on Internet's IRC or CompuServe's CB service—which are different names for the "chat" mode—can do the same. Whatever service one uses, in the center the "talk" function is like a huge CB radio-style party in which everyone types.

But because not everyone can talk at once—or wants to—messages, queries, and observations are more usually posted in a conference for future comment by others. Barbara Harris' question about temporal arteritis, for example, was typed into CompuServe's Health and Fitness Forum. Others read it over a period of a day or two and left their replies. In this manner, a "string" developed, a linked set of questions, answers, and responses. Barbara Harris' original message eventually spawned a string of 13 messages, which I saved, both for the information it contained and as an example of how these systems work. If you want to read those messages today, sorry. You are out of luck; they are not online anymore. Just as most people throw out letters they have read, conference center computers typically discard messages after a time if nobody has asked that they be permanently saved. The system "scrolls," slowly erasing the oldest messages unless otherwise instructed to keep them.

Because of this, most conferences maintain small library sections of their own. These often include important strings, user information, and frequently asked questions (FAQs), queries most commonly received in that section of the center. These are specialty, branch collections of the online library, and their purpose is to assist a specific center conference's members.

FAQs have become so common that the center's Usenet wing has a special file called news.answers that contains lists of FAQ and their answers from different subject-oriented, Internet user groups. Is this a formal library or a conference center service? Well, it is both, a dedicated library file that is part of a user conference section. Usenet interest groups—there were more than 6000 at last count—can be accessed these days through most doors to the conference center. It is best known through its Internet connection, however. In fact, some people think of the Usenet collection as the core Internet resource, although it is actually a totally separate system of conferences and special-interest meeting groups linked through that system. For those who wish to know more about Usenet, its groups, and resources, look in the library for a series of articles on the Usenet and how it works, news.announce.newusers. How you access it will depend on what door you enter through, of course: Internet, CIS, AOL, or some other service.

Everybody knows how to get to the local library or conference center in the city where they live. In Toronto, for example, I take the Queen Street streetcar to the Young Street subway, which I then ride one stop north to visit the Metropolitan Toronto Reference Library. If I have a question about library references, I can simply call its information desk and enlist the aid of a librarian. The telephone number for that service is in the phone book. To visit the Toronto Convention Centre, I take the Queen Street streetcar to Carroll Street, where I change to the #304. Then I get off at John Street and walk south to the SkyDome, where the Blue Jays play baseball. The Convention Centre is next door.

The ease with which I can visit or telephone either site masks the awesome complexity of these transportation and communication systems. The streetcar and subway schedules have developed over years of intricate planning and study so that cars and trains meet near transfer points but do not collide or intrude on each other. The telephone's ability to reach across the city or around the world masks a system of cables and lines and routing computers that send the number I dialed through one of an uncounted number of possible paths until it reaches its destination. What appears easy is an illusion carefully created by generations of engineers who have worked to create complex systems that seem intuitively simple.

Because the online universe is new and evolving, it has yet to mask fully the complexity of what it presents. Therefore, in order to use it, one needs to know a few simple things about the system at large and how it can be accessed. That is the bad news. The good news is that if one can use a telephone, one can join the online world. Anyone who can find a book or magazine in their local library can become an expert in the electronic library, where ever vaster resources are stored. For those who are new to both of these electronic tools and their potential, a bit of background is offered here.

When someone asked Albert Einstein about how a telephone worked, he thought a minute and then replied: "Well, assume that you want to speak to Los Angeles and you're in New York. Imagine a giant cat which stretches across the continent, with its tail in New York and its head in Los Angeles. You pull the tail and the head meows." That's all you need to know, he said. And, really, that is all anyone needs to know about these evolving technologies. Online computer communication, at one level, is a computerized cat. The tail is a personal computer, like the one this text is being written on. At the other end of the line is another computer. Perhaps it is one that is owned by a huge Internet provider, one of the University of California monsters, for example. Or it could be a PC owned by a friend to whom I want to send a file. It does not matter how big or small that computer is. What does matter is that both ends of the conversation have access to the telephone. Access is built upon the back of the telephone network, which is rather like the nervous system of Einstein's cat. After all, for its head to feel a tug on its tail, there has to be something that carries the message up its body to its brain.

Unfortunately, computers speak a language called "binary," a peculiar form of speech that telephones do not know. Just as cats do not see certain colors, the telephone does not actually understand computer speech. And so, for the whole thing to work, computers at both ends of the cat need translators that take their chatter and make it into telephone talk. The translator is called a *modem*. The proverbial "black box" (which may be beige or green or polka dot) hooks the computer into the telephone lines and allows them to carry its message to whatever number is dialed by the phone.

Unfortunately, all of the parts of this system are individually stupid, mute, and incapable. Whatever speed a personal computer may achieve (a 386 MHz, a 486-DX4, a zippy Macintosh with a fast Motorola board)—and however much memory storage the hard disk promises—it is still not smart. The computer needs to be told what to do. And modems, while good at the tasks they were designed for, are even more stupid. But then, no individual telephone has ever received a Nobel prize. They are dumb, too. Telephones do not know who to call, or how to route a person's voice to the neighbor's machine down the street or another telephone half-way around the world. All of that takes lots of engineering, a lot of programming, and careful design by experts who created and continue to modify the system at large.

To tell both the computer and the modem what to do—what number to dial, what speed to send the message, and how to cooperate with the computer at the other end of the cat—requires a specialized but inexpensive piece of software. It holds instructions for the computer and the modem, comes on a small floppy disk or as part of the computer's basic software package, and is run on the computer itself. The software, and there are many different types, bosses the computer, modem, and the telephone that links them both to the world. The modem is told what speed to speak at and what "protocol" to use when addressing its distant fellow. It is instructed in dialing the telephone and how to send and receive data. All in all, telecommunications software is the hero of the show, and like the computers it works with, these programs are getting ever better, faster, smarter, and easier to use.

Most online vendors have special software designed to ease a user through its door and into the library cum conference center. Internet, for example, has the new Mosaic program. CompuServe has the CIM (CompuServe Information Manager), while the Dow Jones offers its Text Retrieval program to make using its library almost easy. America Online, Prodigy, Dialog, Westlaw, LEXIS-NEXIS: All of these have special software instruction packages that facilitate using their own online systems, keys to the door promoting integration between you, your computer, and the vast online world.

A brief example will show how this works. I use a general program called SMARTCOM on both my Macintosh and IBM computers to connect to several sections of the library/center. Because the computer's operating systems are different, I need different versions of the software for each machine. Silly, I know. But as I said, computers are still rather stupid things. In the main menu of the program is a menu bar on which there are a number of headings including "connection," which lets me set the telephone number I am to call, and "settings," where I tell the software what it needs to know to help my computer at the cat's tail to talk to another at its head. Under "preferences" is a box of choices whose parameters set my telecommunications terminal. How big a message packet would be sent (the bits)? What speed would the modem send that at (the baud rate)? Would there be parity? How did it handle "stops"? Choosing among the many possibilities used to be a complex task because everybody used different settings.

Increasingly, however these are becoming standardized. The most common settings are shown in Figure 3.2. In ten years, nobody will need to set these things because they all will be a common set, in the same way that most railroads now use standard gauge tracks so that everyone's cars can roll along. But today, people using standard software still must ask conference/library door keepers what speed they should use (Tip: If one lists "maximum," then the home computer will use the fastest speed agreeable to both machines), the dress the data will be sent in (bits and stops), and what error protocols are to be used, if any (Xon/Xoff).

For those using dedicated, system-specific programs (America On-line or Dow Jones Information Service for example), one does not have

Figure 3.2

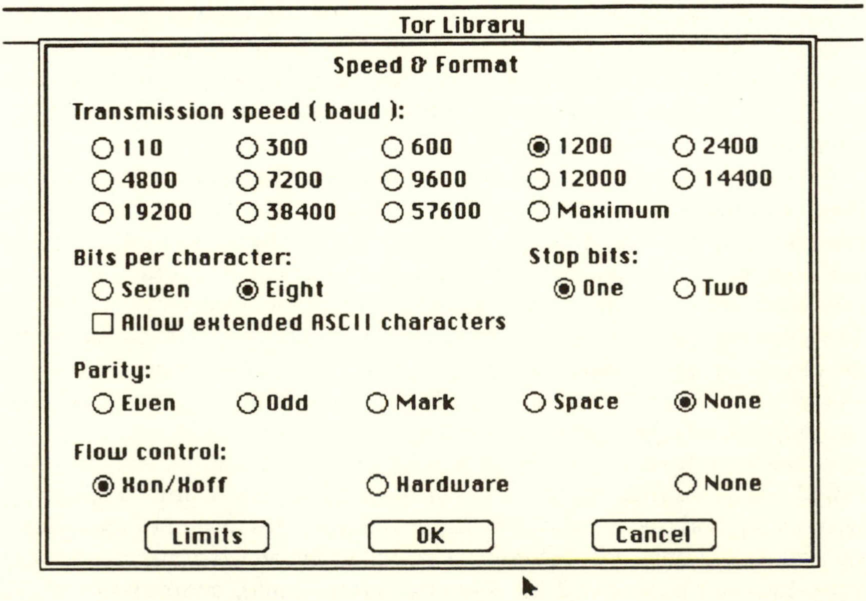

to set these things. They are built into system specific software designed to access a specific door to the conference center/library. Typically, one still has to tell it what telephone number to dial, however, and the modem's baud rate. But everything else is as automatic as a fax machine, which can send a printed page to another machine anywhere in the world.

To access the Metropolitan Toronto reference library's computers from my home, for example, I have to type the access number into a SMARTCOM pull-down menu "phone connection." Then I type in a conversation speed or baud rate (1200) and general communication directions (8 bits, one stop, no parity). Then I click the "dial now" command. The software tells the modem to dial the number, and together they listen for the familial whine which says that the computers on both sides are able and willing and ready to talk to each other. Once the modems make their "handshake," the library computer shows my computer a menu that includes ways to search the electronic card catalog (by subject, author, keyword, etc.), to reserve books, to check my account ("That many overdue??"), and generally do everything but read a book online. This is a new way of using old, familiar resources. The local system of access is not strictly part of the center's electronic library, but a window from there into the local, hard-copy, old-style resources that I have used for years.

I also can enter local doors to the conference center—CIS or the Hospital for Sick Children's BBS Ability Online, for example—using this same software. In each case, I give it the correct telephone number, of course, and check the other parameters of computer-to-telephone-to-computer speech. And, for many gateways, I have to use a password that identifies me on the system at large. Alas, most systems require a password. That is how they charge, regulate users, identify mail, and generally run the system at large.

Entering all of this information every time I wish to access one of these resources would be irritating, so most software programs allow users to save such data as a "script" or "log," which can be used again and again. These instruction sheets are the same as the letterhead saved by my word processor, or the "redial" mechanism in my fancy home telephone. In this case, however, the program "remembers" the telephone number, computer parameters, my password (if I ask it to), and so on, so that the next call will be automatic. I say to the computer, "get me into Ability Online (or CompuServe or Internet, etc.)," and it does the rest.

Some believe that, in a decade or two, everyone will have a single access code that will allow all users access to the whole of the center and its formidable library. In the same way that we have only one telephone number, and need just one credit card to do all of our shopping, there will be a single access password and identification for each online user. In fact, users will need only a single number to allow them to dial into the conference center library at large. Perhaps, but that is for the future. Because this is an evolving, changing technology, however, today's reality is a variety of services, access numbers, gateways, and protocols.

The best way to learn what parts of the centre cum library are suited to any individual's particular needs is to begin at the simplest, least expensive level and slowly expand one's degree of access and power. Local bulletin boards are usually free and offer wonderful opportunities for informal exchange, but they typically do not offer the advanced research library resources a person like myself may need. At the other end of the scale are services like the enormously powerful and specialized library gateway called LEXIS-NEXIS, which costs several thousands of dollars a year. Most people choose other less expensive gateways entering library sections that are more than adequate for their general use. Between these two polls are intermediate and less expensive commercial services, compromises with formal libraries that, while extensive, are less complete than the LEXIS-NEXIS collection. These intermediate collections include the Internet, CompuServe, America Online, Prodigy, Dow Jones Information Service, and other less well-known names.

Whatever gateway one uses to enter the library/center, all online systems share the same, general organizational structure. While the navigational commands may differ, and different software programs may be used to facilitate the use of one or another gateway, the similarities between them all outweigh these temporary differences.

NOTES

1. Alfred Glossbrenner. "CompuServe's Sigs: On the Frontier of Civilized Searching." *Database Magazine*. October, 1989, 50–57.

2. Andrew Nachison. "Reporting from Cyberspace." *CompuServe Magazine*. November, 1993 46–48.

4

The Essential Tool:
Electronic Mail and
Messages

The "news" is more than what is printed in the morning paper, broadcast on the radio at noon, or pictured on TV's evening report. It is, in its broadest sense, what we know that has changed from one day or week to the next. It is new data, new surmises, experiences, or facts that occur somewhere in our community. News is the accumulation of what has happened which changes our world. It is, simply, the accumulation of shared experiences and ideas. Old-style news covered a thin portion of this total; online news offers a far broader spectrum.

It used to be that something passed slowly, person to person, as data discovered by one were eventually shared along the spoken grapevine with the community at large. Later it was transmitted through public tales told by storytellers and, later yet, broadcast through the village by real-time, real-voice announcers. In those days they were called "town criers." Only in relatively recent times, beginning perhaps a bit more than 200 years ago, did public information become a common print artifact. It became "news," carried in a letter or disseminated on the public pages of a periodical. And now, of course, it is also pictured on television, broadcast on the radio, transmitted by telephone, or carried across the electronic net. But however it is presented, "news" is about changes that should be noted. It is, in the end, about data and ideas, the thoughts we have about ourselves.

Nothing is more potent than an idea or more vital than an opinion to be defended. Good ideas take on lives of their own, traveling from person to person, or group to group, and then across communities in a way that always has seemed mysterious, almost magical. It is the ability to communicate, to share and trade concepts, emotions, aspirations, and histories which makes our magic work. Indeed, it is the ability to exchange thoughts which, many say, makes us human. As Lewis Thomas put it: Humanity is *A Fragile Species* known, "by the property of language and its property, the consciousness of an indisputable, singular, unique self."[1] Without the ability to communicate, we are nothing. As importantly, without a way to save and preserve our exchanges, to write them down so that they can be shared with others, the communicating consciousness that we so prize would be a shifting, ephemeral, sometime quality that is easily lost to time.

There is nothing to compare to the sound of a friend or colleague, to the nuance and cadence of the spoken word and the facial expression that accompanies it. And yet, sometimes we need to see those words, to hold onto them and think about what others say. The mail system gave us the ability to direct or redirect those personal words to whomever we might wish to address. The best of our complex ideas are preserved in books and articles stored in bindings on library shelves. No longer does the best we can articulate depend on the memory of a single listener. It is all held in vast warehouses of books and magazines, or in personal letter archives, preserved on one or another printed page.

The combined electronic conference center and library focuses and preserves communication in a way that is remarkable, a true merger of voice and print. Its nervous system is the telephone network, and its model is the mail. In fact, what these new technologies do is give the written word the range and power of speech itself, assuring that within seconds our questions, queries, and responses will reach the appropriate friend, colleague, relative, resource, or adversary. And if we need to know what has been said previously on a subject, the electronic message is the medium by which we can retrieve past writings (books and journals, after all, are only very long messages), or communicate with librarians who may help us in our research tasks. And so, in a real sense, what the conference center does is marry the oral and the written into a single medium, utilizing the best features of both.

The medium that ties together the evolving system of electronic research and communication is the electronic message, the old-fashioned letter transformed into digital form. It is called *E-mail*, the electronic letter cum message. Like its print-based predecessor, its power comes from an ability to extend through the written word the power and range of our personal statements by translating them into a new medium. E-mail carries our thoughts to the greater world in a new and more flexible manner than the postal system or even the voice telephone ever could.

Many people love E-mail because it is extremely fast, enormously efficient, and supremely cost efficient. As migratory peoples who move, on average, more than once a decade, we seem always to be seeking a faster and more personal means of recapturing associations lost to distance, to maintain connections with people we have left behind. E-mail is the best of all worlds: Mail, telephone, and the old-style library's most durable attributes are combined in this new communications system. Nor is this surprising, because each of those more traditional technologies collapsed space in its own way.

Mail and the telephone brought distant friends and distant ideas closer to our personal lives. It is the sheer magnitude of the library and its ability to hold thousands of ideas against the day we may need one that makes it so important to us all. But it is the immediacy of the telephone, its ability to carry a reassuring voice almost instantly to the nearest telephone phone receiver that makes it such a powerful part of our lives. Mail does this as well, albeit at a slower rate. Its advantage has always been one of physical permanence, the power of the written word, which can be considered, studied, and saved. In the old days, it was the only way to assure the exchange of ideas and personal stories between people facing the fact of physical separation.

Even a century a go, a letter from the Old World to the New was a long drawn-out and cumbersome process. A letter from London was carried by horse-drawn cart to the sorting center. From there it went by train to the docks, where it was loaded onto a boat bound for New York, Boston, or Halifax. Once on the continent, it again traveled by horse to a sorting center, where employees put it in an appropriate bin. Then it went into a train or horse cart to journey overland toward wherever we immigrants had finally settled. While print-mail is far faster today, it still requires an enormous staff using expensive equipment to take that British letter, route it through the sorting house, get it onto a plane to New York, Boston, or Toronto, resort it for local district delivery, and then carry it to a person's door.

Within the electronic system, however, physical distance becomes irrelevant. Unlike letters, these messages are virtually instantaneous, as immediate as an idea whispered in a loved one's ear or a picture drawn by a child in pride to give to an absent uncle. We are all just nanoseconds from all others with whom we may wish to communicate. Not only are these messages immediately personal connectors between two people (friends, relatives, business acquaintances, or colleagues), but with a keystroke command they simultaneously can become open letters directed to hundreds of people.

That is because the online system carries data at tremendous speeds along telephone lines. Electrons and not horses carry the post, bringing voices, messages, articles, and books to our desktop. A letter or article still travels, of course, but it does so at digital speed, zipping through the interchanges of Internet computer services, in and out of the gateways of CompuServe and America Online, back and forth across the conference center, which has expanded to include all electronic addresses, contracting real distance between any two users.

To reach someone by voice, one needs to have telephones linking both sites, and a telephone number that will ring near the person being called. To send that same person a letter, one needs a postal system capable of carrying one's message, and an address which assures that the person, company, or organization we designate will receive the letter we write. These requirements do not disappear because the message being sent is electronic. Both the sender and the receiver need to share a technology, like the telephone or an integrated mail system. Both need to have an address from which a message can be sent by one and received by another.

This is true whether one is messaging a friend, sending inter-office mail, or querying a library about a book, article, or news release. Example 4.1 is the heading of a letter I received on CompuServe from the mother of a friend, an 11-year-old boy with cerebral palsy. It was sent the evening of November 23, 1994, and available to me anytime after 8:45 P.M. In fact, I read it two days later when I next turned on my machine. Carla, her son, and I all have CompuServe accounts, so this is an "internal" message, one in which both users share the same postal system.

All Carla had to do was fill out the mail header, which includes the

Example 4.1

From: Carla Elrond, 7140,2162   Subject: re your book
To: Tom Koch, 71600,1123   Date: Wed, Nov 23, 1994, 8:45 PM

Tom,
   I got your book today and we read the first chapter. What's really astounding is that you discuss many themes and issues that my son has been working on with his father (I'll let him explain that to you more fully later).
.
. the rest of the letter . . .
.
Carla

addressee's name (Tom Koch) and his or her computer address (71600, 1123). "Subject" is a brief statement for the receiver's use, a note that says what the accompanying mail is about. When Carla writes "re your book," she is telling me the general subject of her note or letter. The mail system automatically stamps the whole with a time, date, the sender's return address (7141,2161), and name. At the end, the mail system automatically lists "Distribution" because, many times, people send multiple copies of letters to a group of people. This is like the older "cc:", a courtesy in cases of multiple copies to let addressees know they have shared a communication.

That's the CIS system, and it is not very different from those of either local bulletin boards, competitors like America Online, or the many parts of the Internet. In today's standardizing but not yet standard environment, what the apparent simplicity of the CIS system hides is the complexity of routing and paths that any message must travel as it climbs from one computer through the telephone network to a computerized storage and sorting facility, and finally to its designated receiver's electronic mailbox. On the Internet, however, the complexity of that passage is more overt.

Example 4.2 is the mail information automatically entered at the top of a letter from an Internet friend, Mark Ridgley, who works at the University of Hawaii in Honolulu. All in all, it says a lot about the current state of electronic mail and the system by which it transfers messages from one person to another. This message traveled from his personal computer to the University of Hawaii computers uhunix3 and relay1 and was sent from there to the CompuServe computer system's arl-ing-1. Once in the CompuServe system, it was routed to my mail box, whose number is 71600.1123, were it awaited my logon. All this information is automatically stamped on the top of the message. It is as if an old-style letter mailed from Honolulu, Hawaii, to Toronto, Ontario, was signed off by every postal substation, sorting system, and airline that carried it between those two locations.

Because our mail crosses back and forth between Internet and CompuServe mail/message systems, our online addresses for each other must always include the name of the home system. When I write to him, for example, I use the following address:

INTERNET:*ridgley@unix.uhcc.Hawaii.Edu.*

My mail address, the one he uses to address his reply, is my CompuServe identification and location number: 71600.1123@compuserve.com. In the world of Internet mail, the destination occurs after the @ sign.

"Unix" is the type of computer that receives electronic information

Example 4.2

From: Mark Ridgley
INTERNET:ridgley@uhunix.uhcc.Hawaii.Edu
To: Tom Koch, 71600,1123　　DATE:　　11/15/94 12:13 PM

Re: +Postage Due+paper references
Sender: ridgley@uhunix.uhcc.hawaii.edu
Received: from relay1.Hawaii.Edu by arl-img-1.compuserve.com
(8.6.4/5.940406sam) id PAA29696; Tue, 15 Nov 1994 15:11:31 -0500
Received: from uhunix3.uhcc.Hawaii.Edu
([128.171.44.52]) by relay1.Hawaii.Edu withSMTP id
<11381(5)>; Tue, 15 Nov 1994 10:04:15 -1000
Received: by uhunix3.uhcc.Hawaii.Edu id <148515>; Tue, 15 Nov
1994 10:04:01 -1000
Date: Tue, 15 Nov 1995 10:03:45 -1000
From: Mark Ridgley <ridgley@uhunix.uhcc.Hawaii.Edu>
Subject: paper references
To: tom koch <71600.1123@compuserve.com>
Message-ID: <Pine.3.89.9411150938.C8271-0100000
@uhunix3.uhcc.Hawaii.Edu>
MIME-Version: 1.0
Content-Type: TEXT/PLAIN; charset=US-ASCII

Tom,

Here are the paper references you requested ....

　Mark

---

on the Hawaii campus, the one his personal computer goes to when it wants to find mail or use the electronic system. "Uhunix" is the Unix mail receiver, the university's postal station for incoming mail. "UHCC" is the name of the other machine being used on the UH campus as a mail sorter. It holds this message until Mark Ridgley turns on his computer and receives it. .Edu is the suffix for educational institutions. Other address suffixes include .Com for commercial, .Gov for U.S. Government computer sites, .Ca for Canadian locations (*not* Californian!), .NL for Dutch computer sites, and so on.

This is very reminiscent of what telephone service was like in the 1920s. A host of independent regional telephone companies, each with different equipment and procedures, cobbled together the potential for national and international phone service networks. Local calls were easy to make. Regional calls took a bit of time. International calls required operators speaking different languages to join their resources over tenuous, long-distance telephone cables. It used to take hours for folks from, say, New York's Bell Telephone system to connect a call to their counterparts in Japan, Holland, or Mexico City.

The Internet in particular, and interservice communication in general, is something like that today. There is a loose federation of systems using different languages, procedures, equipment standards, and protocols. The whole works, but, like the old international telephone system, it is neither standardized nor seamless. Here, however, the added time required to port a message across any one system, or between systems, is measured in seconds, not hours. Because the whole is so fast, users often do not realize that what seems instantaneously simple is actually cumbersome and complex.

One thing which makes electronic mail so fast is something called traditional *packet switching*. A letter or message sent by normal mail is placed in an envelope and dispatched as a unit. Everything travels together. Everything arrives at the destination as part of the whole. Electronic messages, however, travel piece by piece in data "packets," each packet traveling by the best available route. And then, at the final destination, the whole is reassembled for the receiver. It is as if one wanted to send a jigsaw puzzle to a friend. Rather than mailing the box of pieces as a bulky parcel, however, each piece would be mailed independently by one or another courier service. And then, at the friend's house, a "gremlin" would magically collect and assemble the pieces one by one. All the receiver would see is the completed puzzle. Packet switching allows the electronic mail system to route different parts of a message or letter by the fastest available route. However, each goes with a code that describes its place in the whole. In this way, the system does not have to wait for a free line that can carry, say, 15K of data as a single block. It can send the data bit by bit. And because this is electronic rather than physical mail, the whole seems almost instantaneous. What takes hours and days in the physical world requires in the electronic universe only seconds.

Fortunately for us, neither Mark Ridgley nor I needed to concern ourselves with these myriad details of routing, packets, and system design. Our respective online organizations do the work automatically. But then, in writing letters we do not normally think of the many sorters, carriers, and substation attendants involved in transporting a letter from a Toronto mailbox to an address in Hawaii (or California, or England). We just scrawl the traditional data (name, street address, city, country, and postal code) on an envelope and trust it to the postal system. With electronic mail, we just type the address and assume that the complex of computer linkages will carry our words back and forth.

It does not matter if letters are sent from the U.S. Postal Service to the Japanese post, or visa versa. It also does not really matter anymore if our mail is carried by CompuServe, Internet, Prodigy, or a combination of those systems. All we see in the end are the messages in our mailboxes; and the only trace of their complex, digital passage is the material stamped automatically in the letter's header.

E-mail and messages are used for more than just personal notes between acquaintances. They are the central medium of the library system, and the engine that drives the exchange of information across the conference center. E-mail serves as the online world's library runner, the medium by which we can retrieve materials from the center's library shelves. It thus allows us all to query the shared knowledge base. In the old days, library searches were limited by the physical collection of the specific library we visited. One filled out a call sheet asking for a journal issue to find a specific article and its attendant datum. A runner went into the bowels of the building and—if the material sought was not lost, misplaced, in use by another, or previously stolen—eventually returned with the requested material. Now, however, we send an E-mail to the center's library core asking for the specific journal article and it appears, as if by magic, on the computer's screen.

Electronic mail is so easy that some people have created mailing lists for the free dissemination of stories, articles, or reports. There are thousands of lists available across various services, each list serving a specific subject or user group. Folks at the CompuServe Journalism Forum, for example, send to interested members a weekly announcement detailing background on new stories in science and medicine. Those of us interested in this service sent the Forum SYSOP (system operator) a message saying: Please, I'd like to receive future copies of this list. And now, every week, we receive a four- to ten-page electronic mailing with information on new advances, previews of major new research, and descriptions of upcoming journal articles.

This is called "subscribing" to a list, and there are literally thousands of them available in the electronic universe. Whatever one is interested in, there is an E-mail tip sheet which covers that subject. These are not areas for chat and discussion, but newsletters sent to all from a central source. Organizers of this and other lists have a master address file of subscribers who each week automatically receive copies of the finished list in their mailboxes. What they get, however, is not like a mimeographed or xerographic copy. In the electronic universe, to copy something means that a user's host computer—its main system switchboard—gets a message that an original is available, and if addressees want it, they can peek at the original.

Think of a hall of mirrors in which one image is reflected many times. That is exactly what happens with an online list. The computer has addresses of users who will be allowed to see the mirror, to peek

Example 4.3

Sample Page from CIS Journalism Forum Science Wire List

From: Jim Cameron, JForum WizSysop, 76703,3010
To: Tom Koch, 71600,1123   Date: Sun, Nov 27, 1994, 8:33 PM
Subject: SciWire for 11/27/94

_____SCI__WIRE_____

This digest of leads is from files uploaded in the past week. Use
it for a quick off-line scan of files at the top of the library, ending
Sunday Nov. 27. This list of leads is divided into Medical and
Science. You may receive all or only Medical or only Science as a
weekly e-mail message by sending a message to Roger Johnson
[72600,3411].
MedNews Leads

TIPS.JHM Bytes: 5214, 23-Nov-94
Listed below are story ideas from The Johns Hopkins Medical Institutions: "False memory" conference explores beliefs about
abuse; Catch bone problem before it becomes serious; Diet may reduce dialysis deaths; national study evaluates childhood asthma
care.

PEPI.NHB Bytes: 6531, 22-Nov-94
In the first major clinical trial to examine the effects of sex hor-
mones on heart disease risk factors in post menopausal women,
scientists found that all four of the hormonal regimens tested produced significant increases in the levels of HDL or good
cholesterol.

DOGPAI.NCS Bytes: 6434, 22-Nov-94
Researchers at North Carolina State University's College of Vet-
rinary Medicine have demonstrated dogs often have pain after
surgeries such as spays -- even if they don't show it -- and that
pain medication helps them recover more quickly.

APNEA.NIH Bytes: 3384, 22-Nov-94
Story on a study of 800 people and the effect of smoking on sleep
apnea.

PSYHOL.DUK Bytes: 3958 21-Nov-94
A study of emergency room records supports the idea of a "Christmas effect" that increases the number of patients seeking mental
health care just after the holiday season.

at an original document stored online. If that person wants to save a copy rather than just read a reflection, he or she can copy it onto the personal computer's hard disk. This is called *downloading*, taking the image held by the computer and making it one's own. By requiring only mirrored images of the original rather than individualized copies, the whole process is speeded up enormously: one list, one document, many receivers. Whenever a user logs onto his or her computer, the current material will be waiting, along with a system message that says, in effect, "Hey, dummy! Check the mailbox. You have stuff to see electronically."

Often, these "lists" refer to other online resources, pieces of the library that have new data or information. They are like tip sheets in which each entry refers to materials in a forum or conference's own library, a section of the conference center where discussant files are stored, sometimes permanently and sometimes only for a few weeks or days. So if I am interested in an item like PSYHOL.DUK, an announcement of research findings by Duke University psychologists, I need only go to the Jforum's library and retrieve the whole story.

This type of service is not unique to CompuServe. In fact, lists are one of the strongest features of the Internet service. Whatever the subject, lists exist for the sole purpose of assuring that interested parties receive identical information packets. Some are study courses; others are announcements, like the Journalism Forum science list. There are, for example, master listings, or directories of list resources, in one or another area that can be searched like library directories. One example for health-related resources that has been described by John S. Makulowich is: bit-nic.educom.edu list.[2] To search it for lists and groups on a single topic, one sends an E-mail message to the following Internet address:

listserv@bitnic.educom.edu

and in the body of the message one types:

list global/<keyword>

where "global" is a command that says "show me whatever you have" and <keyword> describes the subject that you are interested in. So, in his example, because Makulowich wanted to know what lists and groups were available in the general area of medicine, his message to the bitnic.educom.edu computer read:

list global/med

(translation: describe for me all resources in your list that include the prefix "med" in their titles). In response, he received an electronic letter listing 30 conference groups and data resources covering a range of medical discussion groups, data resources, and specialized information lists.

Besides library-style lists and resources, the online world is filled with news groups and discussion groups—electronic sites that pass E-mail from individuals to congregations of people interested in a single subject. Some of these focus on general topics, like bicycling, while others are designed to provide a forum for those interested in extremely esoteric subjects. MEDFEM-L, for example, is for people involved in research on feminism in the Middle Ages (*jrondeau@oregon.uoregon.edu*). Others carry an equally narrow focus on more popular topics. For example, there is the RRA-L—Romance Readers Anonymous List (*jlangend@kentvm.bitnet*)—and Mayberry, another dedicated to the life and fictional times of Andy Griffith's famous TV show, "Mayberry RFD" (*amillar@bolis.sf-bay.org*).

Lists and news groups sound similar. The difference is that the former is a predetermined mailing. It is automatic. News group participants, however, must logon to a specific news group site to see what is available. There one finds a menu of available topics that can be individually accessed for discussions on specific topics of interest. Unlike mail, it isn't sent automatically. Rather, one goes online to find individual subjects of particular concern. News groups let users follow and participate in certain discussions while avoiding those that seem uninteresting to them. What both news groups and lists share is the ability to bring people who share an interest together. Choosing one or the other is a matter of preference, of time available for subject research and of respect for the quality of material carried in either form. A list written by Nobel laureates would probably be of high general interest. One written by paper airplane devotees would be of less interest to most people.

The essential characteristic of these resources is that all require a critical mass of similarly interested people. Their geographic location does not matter because the medium collapses distance, allowing folks from many places to interact. What results is a method by which similarly inclined people can share information and discuss issues as if they were in a classroom or lounge together. That is fortunate for those interested in uncommon topics. It would be hard to find many people in a single neighborhood, or city, who are interested in feminism in the Middle Ages. And while most people have a vague awareness of "Mayberry RFD," few are interested enough to have studied old episodes, or to have memorized the minutiae of that fictional world. There are fanatic fans and dedicated scholars interested in almost any conceivable topic. But they are rare birds who are dispersed across the country and sometimes around the globe.

In the old days, the few who might know of others sharing their interests would write, one to one, in a loose and easily broken chain of communication. But because the online population is enormous, the potential for finding others of similar interest is increased many-fold. And because communication online is simplified and virtually instantaneous—one to one and one to the many—the type and range of materials that can be exchanged are almost unlimited.

Think of a university or high school where there are not enough people to support a single course offering. Two or three people want to study this topic, but that is not enough to qualify for allocation of the resources a course requires. Online, however, there may be hundreds who share that interest. Linked by mail, messages, and lists, a constituency is born that may span the globe. In fact, some universities are creating online courses and programs for potential students who cannot attend classes in person. The University of Tennessee in Memphis, for example, now offers an online degree program in journalism through CompuServe. It includes a series of six-week online courses, each worth three semester credit hours. Each course includes written materials mailed to students by the faculty, student projects mailed back to the instructors, and online discussions in the conference center. Mail, mailings, and conferencing are combined.

Whatever the subject, the procedure is always the same. Someone creates a single, master copy that contains specific data or information and sends it to a central depot for distribution. The host computer then "explodes" that message by duplicating it and sending copies to central computers where they can be "mirrored" to each subscriber. One letter, many receivers. For example, in 1994, a member of the CIS Journalism Forum, Marci Newmann (ID 74637, 145), posted a message online informing us all that there was a course available online for those wishing to develop better Internet skills. "You sign up for it like a listserv by sending mail to address

listserv@ualvm.ua.edu

with a message of

"subscribe roadmap <your name> in the body."

I decided to take her advice and sign up. So I sent a letter to the Internet address she gave, a direction which in itself carried a good deal of information. "listserv" is the prefix for the command station of any subscriber service. It is where one asks to be put on or taken away from a mailing list, where one requests files, sends orders, and so on. UA1VM is the name of the list's computer. It is the human equivalent of a "port address" that is also found in Internet headers; it is a series of numbers that designates the sender. However it is designated, as UA1VM or by its numeric equivalent, the computer is located at "ua" (short for the University of Alabama), an .edu (educational) institution.

My subscription was accepted and I became one of 66,000 people from more than 75 countries who took Patrick Crispen's third, month-long course on Internet techniques. We were all on the list, and that meant that the University of Alabama computer made sure that all of us received, day by day, a copy of the materials which had been loaded into its memory banks. I was one of ten CompuServe members receiving the lessons. The others were on Internet or other systems. Whatever door we used to enter the electronic center, the process was the same. UA1VM shared its master lesson with another, in my case CompuServe's, which in turn informed its subscribers that mail was waiting for each of us on the subscriber list. (See Example 4.4.)

The CIS computer did not have to take 14 copies of the daily lecture, one for each of us however. That would have been inefficient. It mirrored one copy for all of us and then whenever any of us logged on, each of us was told that we had personal mail waiting. It was a computer lie, or perhaps a computer truth. The system made us all think that the one copy was ours alone. The header for each course included all of our CompuServe ID numbers, but not our names. Those are human and not computer necessities; all the CIS computer had to know was that it should personalize the address 71600,1123@compuserve.com (ID number at site compuserve.com) for client Tom Koch. We all like the personal touch.

Of course, it did the same thing for the other list subscribers on other systems, telling each reader that it had material just for them. And so the list materials were directed around the world to host computers which then addressed that material as "personal" mail, with copies to

Example 4.4

From: Patrick Douglas Crispen,
INTERNET:PCRISPE1@UA1VM.UA.EDU
To: Tom Koch, 71600,1123 (unknown), 72073,2557, (unknown),
74364,2605, (unknown), 74631,61, (unknown), 71277,245,
(unknown), 100102,2057, (unknown), 74164,1271, (unknown),
73324,3617, (unknown), 71035,2401 (unknown), 74071,3436
Date: 11/15/94 9:44 PM

Re: ROADMAP15: FTPMAIL

each list subscriber. When we downloaded a lesson to our personal computers, those copies became our own in fact as well as computer fiction. This ability to store one copy for many saves enormous space, something that is often at a premium on large as well as small computers. The fiction of "personal" copies, when in fact one receives personal headers on group copies, is a means to efficiently maximize the available storage area.

Those interested in taking this online Internet program today through CompuServe or any other center door are out of luck. "Roadmap" was a victim of its own success. What started as an altruistic aide to a few became so popular that it quite literally began to overwhelm both Mr. Crispen and the University of Alabama's computers. In late 1994, when he was forced to discontinue the offering, he stored all of the individual courses in the UA1VM computer, making them available as library files for students to refer to.

Since we all received copies of the syllabus, we are able to use the commands he taught us to go into the University of Alabama's computer and retrieve copies of lessons missed and lost. The procedure for doing this is the same as that of getting any material from a listserv address. For example, when I accidentally erased the answer sheet to the course's first quiz (yes, there were tests), I sent a message requesting a new copy to

LISTSERV@UA1VM.UA.EDU

with the following instructions:

GET QUIZ1A LESSON POP QUIZ ANSWERS F=MAIL

"Get" is the computer command that tells a receiving computer to retrieve a specific file, message, or article. To be retrieved, the item has to be located by name within the computer's hierarchically ordered storage system. Fortunately, the Roadmap syllabus included a list of filenames and "filetypes," the category of data required; so in this case I told the computer to get (filename) "Quiz1A" from (filetype) "Lessons" with the title "Pop Quiz Answers." F=MAIL told the computer that I wanted that material mailed to my online address.

Had I not known these names, I could have E-mailed the Alabama listserv address for a directory of all its Roadmap holdings in the same way that John Makulowich asked another listserv to locate files dealing with medicine (the command would be: list global/Roadmap), then reviewed that direction until I came to the material I needed. Finding filename and filetype is like looking up a telephone number. One has the name (Koch, T.) and the city (Toronto) and perhaps the street address. With the name, one can locate several Koch, T's from among the millions of Metropolitan Toronto telephone subscribers. With the address, the alternatives are winnowed down to one. Filename and type are the name and address data that allowed me to find a single file among the more than 30 Roadmap course listings, which themselves are among thousands of files stored on UAV1M at UA.edu.

Those interested in Patrick Crispin's workshop will not find it at the University of Alabama these days. It has migrated to a new address online. Because so many were interested in this least expensive of online tutorials, it has been permanently archived at

gopher.anes.rochester.edu.

In the menu of that holding select: Roadmap Internet Training Workshop. For those unfamiliar with Internet regions (gopher, ftp, etc.), chapter six offers a primer on those resources and their locations.

Everything online is organized in a lock-step, top-down manner. The whole universe of electronic data, which may be accessed by electronic messages, is structured hierarchically in the same general manner as the old-fashioned print library. This is not surprising, since our society organizes most of its data in this way. Just as in a library one searches from the general subject to the specific book title or journal article required, here too one goes from the general (UAV1M holdings) to the specific (Roadmap holdings) to the individual (filename/filetype). What this means for data searching will be explored in detail in a later chapter. But for the moment, the important fact is that while the message is the medium carrying requests, queries, and data, it does so in a universe whose logic is direct, hierarchical, and traditional.

Conference center mail, like library storage, is also hierarchical. My message to Mark Ridgley went to a single system (Internet), to a sorting location in that system (uncc.Hawaii.edu), to a computer in that system (uhunix), and finally to an electronic address (Ridgley).

If I had mailed a personal request for the missing lesson, it would have been carried, by normal mail, to a person (Patrick Crispen) at a location (Tuscaloosa, Alabama), at his mail address there (the university). Again the hierarchy appears. But that letter requesting a copy of Roadmap lesson Quiz 1A would have taken several days to traverse the distance between Ontario, Canada, and Alabama, USA. He would have had to find the lesson, make a copy of it, put it in an envelope, and address it to me before sending it back by post. It would have taken weeks if every student losing a lesson had to be answered in this individual manner. The post would take a week or so, but the human effort to find and physically copy material might have required a month or more. Electronically, however, the whole was handled automatically in less than an hour.

Impressive as this is, the electronic messaging system really comes into its own when people use the conference center to develop interpersonal dialogs on a single subject. In CompuServe "forums," bulletin board "conferences," and Internet's Usenet "newsgroups" alike, letters are not sent to the listserv administrator, but instead are posted electronically to a single computer address where they are mirrored for public review by all interested discussants. These forums/user groups/newsgroups—the name differs depending on the service door used to enter the library/center—are the heart of the conference center cum library. They are subject-oriented, electronic sites designed not only for directed information—lists and lessons—but as electronic sites encouraging and facilitating communal interaction. In them, people log-on to give and receive support, and exchange experiences, information, library files, and reports.

Conference center forums and user groups are not ideal sites for searching out a single datum. They are, however, terrific places to ask the essential question that will lead to more detailed explanations. Wendy Venderhope's posting in Example 4.5 is a good example. There have been hundreds of stories on Lyme disease in scores of newspapers, and none of them are immediately at hand, however, now that she needs some help. She may have a vague memory of reading something, but now she needs data, not memories. And more specifically, she needs data that will allow her to help her aunt in Florida, the

Example 4.5

From: Wendy Venderhope, 94203,221   To: All
Topic: LYME INFO NEEDED!   Msg #451221
Section: Family Health Forum: Health & Fitness+
Date: Mon, Nov 08, 1995, 10:15:13 PM

Anyone:

 I have an aunt who suffers from Lyme disease. She recently
moved to Florida, and needs the names of physicians who
specialize in Lyme disease. She lives in Leesburg, which is about
halfway between Ocala and Orlando.
 Also I'm sure she could use any info on support groups, information
clearinghouses, etc.
  Thanks.

Wendy

---

woman with Lyme disease, to find help and support. Rather than visiting the local library and searching through the *Periodical Guide to Popular Literature*, she filed her query online in the conference center magazines.

A few hours after posting her open message, several people responded to her query. They included a man named Frank Wisner who referred her to a book on the illness by Denise Lang. A good reference, Wisner said, and its appendix included a valuable listing of Lyme disease support groups in the United States. That list included groups in Florida, of course, where the disease is prevalent. If that book was not in her local library and she needed help immediately, Frank included in his message the name and telephone numbers of the Lyme Disease Foundation (203-525-2000 or 800-886-5963). Simultaneously, Ed Madara, director of the America Self-Help Clearing House, offered the same information. This is what Wendy needed and wanted, a location in the hierarchy of stored data and potential references that could help her help her aunt.

This type of quick, direct answer to a specific question represents perhaps 40 to 50 percent of the online traffic I monitor day by day. It allows people to receive directions to library and other data sources within hours of formulating a problem. The message is one of need; it's medium is the written word. Sometimes questions are framed not in a formal posting, but on "chat" channels, which are parts of the conference center that are set aside for real-time, simultaneous conversations. Like a telephone conversation using TTY systems for the deaf, computer chatters speak to one another by typing in their comments and reading what others reply on-screen. In the near future, these may become fully spoken exchanges with text used as a method of archiving, rather like printed scripts of radio shows or records of testimony in a legal court. At the present, however, whether on Internet "IRC" channels, bulletin board "chat" bands, or the citizen band–style sections of commercial services, messages are typed back and forth between two or more people simultaneously working at their own computers.

Example 4.6 is a recent "chat" I had with a man named Brian who asked if we could "speak" for a moment. It occurred on CompuServe in the Health and Fitness Forum, where I am an assistant administrator. Like all folks online, I was free to either ignore his request or refuse it. I signaled, via the computer, that I was available to chat and the conversation occurred, line by line, as we messaged back and forth via instant mail, rather like the conversations the hearing impaired engage in when using special telephone based machines.

It is really pretty simple stuff. Brian did not need lots of data. He did not want to do a major library search. He wanted reassurance. He

Example 4.6

Brian: Tom - are you there? Got a second? I'm looking for some
information on cancer.

Tom: Brian: What type of information?

Brian: Can a small thickening of tissue on your thigh (feels like a
lump) be a location for a tumor? The Doc isn't sure what it is. Know
anything?

Tom: A small lump can be a lot of things. I suspect your physician
may want to excise it, or at least 'biopsy' it and take a sample if
he's not sure. Right?

Brian: Yes, we will do this in about three weeks. He has given me
some antibiotics in the meantime. But it seems to be growing still.

Brian: Do you know of anybody who ever got a tumor on their leg?

Tom: Yes, but every case is different . What does your doctor say?

Brian: I'm just wondering if anyone has ever had tumors on legs. I see
your response says yes. OK.

Tom: A growth, as you know, is not necessarily malignant. There are
many types of benign tumors (growths which do not invade the
rest of the body). That's probably the case with your tumor, if
that's what it is. The biopsy should tell the tale. My suggestion:
get the biopsy and don't worry until after the results.

Brian: OK Tom. Thanks for the response. We'll wait and see.

Tom: Stay in Touch. Whatever you find out, drop us a line in the
family section of this forum. We can refer you elsewhere (i.e. the
Cancer Forum) if you need different online information. But at the
moment, I suspect, fear is the enemy.

Brian: OK. Thanks and bye for now.

Tom: Bye.

---

wanted to know if anyone had ever heard of a problem like his, or was
his affliction unique. Was he alone? Was he in danger? Was his doctor
behaving appropriately? Thousands of times each day, conference center participants participate in similar exchanges. The amazing thing is
that, almost always, people are willing to give their time to others.
They respond with "Sure. I'll chat. What can I do for you?" Curiosity
and the pleasure of being asked for help by another are motives
enough for most who spend their time in this manner.

The simultaneous "chat" mode is also used when one person wishes
to announce a new finding, a new product, or some recently discovered fact of interest to a range of people who can be expected to have

questions about it. And so one finds Microsoft's Bill Gates in conference, messaging about Microsoft's new software; U.S. vice president
Al Gore describing the current administration's policies; or a researcher
involved in chronic fatigue syndrome answering questions about the
disease. In addition, "chat" modes have become vehicles for self-help
and support groups of all varieties. Alcoholics Anonymous meetings
are held online in this manner, for example. Just as in face-to-face
meetings, there is a moderator who welcomes people, an AA member
who testifies, and a larger group who uses the interpersonal support
to maintain their sobriety for another day.

Not all problems are accessible to immediate reply or simple affirma-
tion. Sometimes they require a different type of dialog and discussion.
In those situations, bulletin board–style user groups, conferences, and
forums provide a better medium for the exchange of ideas, data, and
support. Chapter Seven demonstrates how complex emotional, medical, and social problems are resolved through written dialog over time.
In these situations, one writer poses a query or describes a problem
that becomes a subject of discussion for others, who write notes and
send references to the original sender and to other correspondents involved in the message dialog. That letter is posted for all to read, and
perhaps respond to. In this way a "string" of messages is built up over
days or weeks. This congregation of messages can be saved and archived in a user group library or by any single participant.

The following extract is part of a string begun by a man, William
Merced, after the death of his son.

> I had never let myself realize just how much I loved him, and
> now he's gone. I never ever would have thought that this could
> hurt so much, or that I would miss him so badly. My wife and I
> have seen a couple of different therapists and from what they
> say, after almost three weeks, we may still be operating in shock
> and this could get worse before it gets better.
>
> I'd like some insight into this shock business, and what it's like
> when it wears off and how do you know if it is wearing off, or if
> you're even in it. We've been told to take it easy and let this go
> at it's own pace, but isn't there something I can do to speed up
> the process?
>
> Any help would be appreciated.

The discussion occurred on CompuServe in the Health and Fitness Forum's "Family Health" section. Discussion groups, like lists, are organized hierarchically, rather like rooms in a house in a housing development. Imagine a housing project with hundreds of individual
dwellings. They correspond to the user groups on a single online sys-

tem: Internet, America Online, Prodigy, CompuServe, Ability Online. Each house has an address and name that describes its general theme. In this case, that name is the Health and Fitness Forum. Within the house are different rooms, specific addresses that detail specific subjects, each room representing a place where people interested in that subject will meet. Each room has a small library, chat system, and bulletin board of its own. In this case, William Merced, a project dweller, came to the Family Health Room in the Health and Fitness forum on CompuServe to both tell his story and seek the insight of others.

The Merceds' son had died several weeks, accidentally strangled in a bizarre Halloween incident while creating a "house of horrors" for other trick-or-treaters. It was "one of those things" in which nobody was to be blamed—a death without a villain. His original message described what had happened and then went on to describe the pain and anguish he and his wife were feeling. From Halloween until almost Christmas, others who had experienced the loss of a child messaged in to discuss their strategies for survival. This was not a formal support group. Rather, it was a coming together of people who, touched by the another's pain, were reminded of tragedies of their own. Some talked about how common such accidents are and how others had used their own losses to mount campaigns to help prevent similar deaths in the future.

At Thanksgiving, several people messaged the bereaved couple simply to say "This will be a hard holiday for you, but we're thinking of you. You can survive." Just before Christmas, others messaged to remind William and his wife that they were not alone, that people remembered their pain and were thinking of them. It may be that the act of messaging provided a measure of therapy for William Merced; the very act of participating in a dialog like this may have been itself a sign of healing. But the content of these messages themselves, and the fact that the "string" built over time encompassed more general issues of handling grief and tragedy, signaled the uniqueness of this form of dialog over time.

Poignant as this example is, it is typical of the emotionally charged dialogs that sometimes occur in the digital world as people from around the world focus in on another's plight. Not all forum discussions are so heavy, however. There are conferences devoted to jokes and comedy, to photography and photographs (with images stored in the section library), to professional interests and computer programming. In legal conferences, people may message to one another about cases cited on a single subject, assisting one another in building their legal briefs. In medical conferences, practitioners in isolated practices may ask their colleagues for suggestions when facing a set of peculiar symptoms. The range of subjects is limited only by human curiosity;

the potential for expertise is defined by the number of people who access the conference center.

My father, a misanthrope for 78 years, would have been relieved to know that the views and opinions of every "schmoo" were not indiscriminately saved forever. "Who cares what some other fellow says?" he would have asked. "Why should I want to talk to someone who is no smarter than I am?" We all possess oceans of ignorance. But what he often forgot was that most people also contain deep wells of expertise. The trick is to find the people whose knowledge and experience will help in any given situation, and to ask them for the help all of us, sooner or later, will need. In these pick-up communities, there is an extraordinary wealth of knowledge and experience that can make the difference, quite literally, between life and death, between despair and renewal. Even without the power of the online library, these electronic mail lists and conference center association forums or user groups are an enormous resource.

Chapter Seven looks at several strings from various sources in an attempt to explore more deeply how this system of communication works, and the degree to which the medium of electronic messaging in fact contributes to a person's ability to gain insight and quality data. The next chapter describes the logic of the system at large, and how to find appropriate sites for specific discussions within the vast conference center. Then the online library's ability to answer factual queries is explored, both as a distinct resource and in association with the conference center's many rooms.

NOTES

1. Thomas, Lewis. *The Fragile Species*. New York: Collier Books, 1992, 18.
2. John S. Makulowich. "Internet Resources on Alternate Medicine." 1994, available via URL ftp://ftp.clark.net/pub.journalism/altmed.txt.

5

Finding It: The Organization of Online Material

Damn. Where did I see that article on living wills? I know I read it a few weeks ago, but was it in the *Toronto Star*, or in a magazine at the dentist's office? Perhaps it was in *US News and World Report*. But then, maybe it was actually in *Time Magazine*, or *Harper's*. Now that I need the data it contained, well, the story's location is lost in the morass of "I forget," with only the fleeting of memory of "this is important" left behind.

That's the problem. We know things are out there which might help us in our personal lives. But where are they? How to find the data online, or resources that will lead to it, is a problem. After all, almost no one remembers every book, article, or reference work they have read. Even the fortunate few with photographic memories, those who can say, "Oh yes, it was in the *Wall Street Journal*, September 26, 1995, page 13, column 1" are not exempt. Their memory extends only as far as their experience, not to the wealth of published materials that they have not read but suspect are out there, bearing on an issue of personal, immediate concern.

In the burgeoning world of public knowledge, nobody is encyclopedic. There was a time, several hundred years ago, when one person could in fact know all that time and society had to teach. But in those days the Bible was the source of all wisdom, ancient Greek texts had the last word on science, and a royal library might include, at most, several hundred volumes. Today, on the cusp of the millennium, more than 40,000 new books are published each year in the United States alone. Between 1980 and 1990, more than 3000 publications were started in the United States. In other countries and in dozens of different languages, the pattern was repeated.

Nobody knows it all. Even the most dedicated physician cannot read every medical journal and pharmacology report that might pertain to a patient's condition. Not, at least, if he or she also wants to spend some time with patients. There is just too much being written and studied and discussed for any one doctor, no matter how conscientious, to know. In the same vein, no financier can read all of the data being published today on economic changes, corporate realities, developing industries, emerging markets, or product development. It would take years to read the daily literature; and by the time anyone had read it all, that much more would have been printed.

This is the famous but misnamed *information explosion*, the fact of evermore material potentially available to us all. It is data, however, not "information" which has expanded at so vast a rate. The two describe very different things whose characteristics may or may not coincide. *Data* are potential information, facts that may be true or false, statistics that may be relevant or irrelevant, opinions that may be profound or silly. In each case it depends on whether they can be substantiated, and whether or not they bear upon the issue at hand. *Information*, on the other hand, remains a precious and rare commodity. Built from data, it is knowledge of demonstrable validity that reduces uncertainty by describing the world in a way that is relevant and useful.

To find the data we needed as school children, we were advised to visit the library. That is still good advice. But today, the library is also in the conference center, and there one finds a wealth of resources. In almost all ways, the new digital library is patterned on the traditional print system of organization and hierarchies. It is, therefore, not hard to apply old knowledge to these new resources. In the world of print, card catalogs carried entries under general subjects (age or aging), author names (Koch, T), and titles of specific works. In addition, there were specialized indexes for census and specific directory material, phone books for instance. Perhaps one went to *The Reader's Guide to Periodical Literature* and looked up the subject or author there. If data on a famous person were needed, there was always a *Who's Who* somewhere on the reference shelves. And of course many newspapers published annual indexes to the stories they had printed across the previous year. There was even an annual directory called *NewsBank*, which catalogued, year by year, the titles of news stories from 100 U.S. newspapers.

Those resources have not disappeared. They are still important and useful tools, and they are available online in electronic versions. Internet users interested in the *Reader's Guide,* for example, can telnet to lib.uwstout.edu, and then log in with the password "library" (those unfamiliar with Internet terms will find them explained in the next chapter). U.S. Census material is available in many places, including CompuServe (FIND CENSUS), for example, and of course on the Internet. There, however, the address is a bit more cumbersome (http://www.census.gov/cdrom/doc/lookup doc.html). In addition, there are vast collections of full-text magazine articles, both general-interest and specialty collections for business, finance, science, and medicine.

An advantage of the online library over its print-based parent is that online collections are usually updated weekly or monthly. The U.S. Census folks can add new reports, new figures, and new data which, in print, would require months of preparation at the printers, and months more for normal mail distribution. Online resources are therefore generally far more current than their print cousins. It may take months for a journal, magazine, or book to be mailed from the publisher, cataloged at the library, and finally placed upon the shelf. But in the electronic library, they appear within days of formal publication. And because it takes only seconds to update a single fact in a computer collection, once digitized, data collections (phone, census, etc.) can be changed to reflect new knowledge that has appeared since the first publication date. In this sense, the online library is often more flexible, more current, and more encyclopedic than its print counterpart.

Consider the Internet as an example. There are, at present, scores of books now being published, each offering catalogs of online listings. There is the *Whole Earth Internet Guide,* the *Canadian Guide to the Internet,* and teaching resources like *Internet for Dummies* that offer online citations in their tutorials. These and other books are published year by year and are outdated well before they arrive in the bookstore. In 1995, a new Web address was added to the Internet every 20 minutes. Resource groups come and go on the Internet with rapidity, and on other services almost as quickly. The leisurely pace of traditional printing cannot keep up. To solve the problem of location online, one therefore needs an online directory and search system. Everything online is cataloged and cross-indexed several ways. That is what makes this system so efficient.

For example: Whenever a new address is established, its owner has to submit an application to InterNIC, which then includes it in its burgeoning online directory. Anyone can search this directory at its "Web" address (http://www.internic.net), or via older means of access, including Telnet (telnet to internic.net) and FTP (ftp to ftp.internic.net). For those who are not Internet users, these names and resources are explained in the Internet chapter of this book. The alphabet of online systems—KRI, CIS, DJIS, LEXUS-NEXIS, AOL, etc.—each has a directory that can be searched.

The difference between print and electronic libraries was illustrated by a recent experience. A television news report mentioned an article that appeared in the *Journal of the American Medical Association* (*JAMA*) in March, 1995. The article by a Canadian researcher, Dr. ????? Cook, the reporter said, swallowing her words, described a study of Canadian Health Care Workers and their divergent attitudes toward withdrawal of life support from critically ill patients. This was an article I needed to read because of a project I had been hired to complete. The University of Toronto library subscribes to *JAMA*, but it takes weeks or months before new magazines can be received, stamped, cataloged, and finally shelved for reader use. Similarly, the Metropolitan Toronto Library receives the journal, but it requires weeks or months before it can make a new edition available. Obviously, printed indexes will not include Dr. ????? Cook's article in the 1995 edition until sometime in 1996.

I found the article reference online with little trouble. On CompuServe, I went to PaperChase, a "front-end" bibliographic search system that updates its holdings week by week. It was created by Beth Israel Hospital in Boston to facilitate staff searching of the electronic medical library called Medline. Included in that digital collection is the journal, *JAMA*. Within a week of hearing about this article, I found the full citation by searching for "Canadian" and "Life support" and "withdraw or withdrawal." But this was only the citation, not the reference itself. For that I used Knight Ridder Information (formerly called Dialog), a service that collects the full text of medical journals, updating that collection every week. I entered the library through KRI, typed "MedText" to reach a collection of full-text articles, entered the author and title I learned about on PaperChase, and retrieved the article. Well, what I got was the "mirror" of the copy in the *Index Medicus* library computer in Washington, which was passed on to Knight Ridder Information's California-based computers, and from there to the computer on my desk. I then quickly downloaded a copy so I could read it at my leisure.

That was easy. I knew where to find the journal whose article I was seeking, the subject matter, and an author's partial name. But when there is a question without a specific target, a general query without a library location, the question becomes: How do I find it? Where to go for information on Alzheimer's disease, TPK Data, Inc., or the country of Brazil? When the correct resource is uncertain, professionals and amateurs alike must play the old children's game of "categories," better known as "Twenty Questions." One person has in mind an object, a person, or an event that the other player or players must not guess, but deduce. This is done by asking categorical questions which the first person must answer truthfully: Is it animal, vegetable, or mineral? Human or inhuman? Poet or warrior? Performer or writer? Living or dead? The game goes on until either 20 questions have been asked without revealing the subject, or the questioner finds the right answer. Last week I played the game with a 7-year-old friend who posed as my problem Jim Henson's famous muppet, Kermit the Frog. The answer came to me after eight category-narrowing answers: animal, definitely living, performer, living, singer and actor, movie and TV, not cartoon, muppet, frog or pig.

Print and electronic librarians alike play "categories" every time they engage a client in what's called in the trade the "research interview." When they play the game, however, they help the customer to define the problem in such a way that a single text or two can be named as probable solutions to the problem poised. Usually the process is so informal that nobody, not even the librarian, thinks to dignify it with a name. "I need something on the elderly," a person says to the librarian. Too broad, he responds. Do you want to know about elderly who are sick (caregiving, home care, local resources) or those who are well (buying power, demographics, political affiliations). If it is the former, is the client interested in general information, experiential accounts, or local resources available to assist in the care of patients with a particular disease? A quick trip to the old card catalog (paper or digital, the game is the same) and, Voilá! Look at this book by Tom Koch, called, *Mirrored Lives: Aging Children and Elderly Parents.* "An experiential account of caring for a fragile parent which includes a 'how-to' section for those concerned with or facing long-term care situations."

Whatever door one uses to enter the library/conference center—CompuServe, Dialog, Internet, America Online—the game is the same. Rather than asking a person for help, however, one sends an electronic query or E-mail saying, "I'm looking for x," and the automated system answers. In effect, one plays "Twenty Questions" with an electronic directory. But in this version of the game, one that is designed to locate the best data available, the questioning does not begin with "animal, vegetable, or mineral?" It starts with the question: "user group or library?" If the answer is user group, one seeks the name of a user group, conference, or forum whose members are interested in the subject you seek to address.

If the answer is library, however, the next question is "book or article?" and then, "popular or technical?" or perhaps, "database or statistical?" Online or off-line, to find a book one searches *Books in Print* for author name, title, or subject area. Every branch library has a copy of this resource, and it can be found in most sections of the online library as well. For more information, check out the digital version of *Book Review Index*, 1969–present. General magazine readers still can turn to *The Reader's Guide to Periodical Literature*, the old-style librarian's first line of defense in searching for popular articles. Digitized, it is available on CompuServe under that same name. Internet searchers need only telnet to lib.uwstout.edu, and then log in with the temporary password "library." The process is the same for old and new libraries. There are, however, new and better search tools available through many of the center's library resources than are available in print libraries.

The strategy for "Twenty Questions" online is

1. Find the general directories
   1.b. Choose a category
2. Find a general category
   2.b. Locate a more specific directory
3. Look for the subject
   3.b. Find a way to limit the search again.

Whatever tools one needs, whatever electronic door one uses, the game is still, however, "Twenty Questions." In searching for the answer to any question, begin with the general and search for the specific. Move from the broad category—the type of resource needed (book, journal, census, forum, or conference)—to the specifics of a subject (health, business, travel, language, recreation). Then step by step narrow the search (a specific journal among the many, books published in a single year, etc.), to an evermore focused query. All online library services are organized to facilitate this hierarchical method, which first identifies general online resource areas and then assists in selecting the appropriate resource to answer a single question. Whatever the idiosyncrasies of an individual electronic library branch, whether one is looking for an article, a citation, or a user group, the logic of the search is always the same.

That is the principle, but its execution requires a precise frame of mind. Sometimes it is best to search broad categories—looking for all references on a single subject—at other times only a narrowly phrased query will do. For example, friends suggested I look on the Internet for the Hawaii Bicycle League (HBL) home page where a book of mine, *Six Islands on Two Wheels: A Cycling Guide for Hawaii*, was mentioned. But when I searched for "HBL" and then "Hawaii Bicycle League" I found nothing. Perhaps I misspelled something, or the search system I used made an error. Then I searched "Bicycling," but found hundreds of responses; too many to sift through efficiently. Next I looked for "Hawaii," and found a state home page that included a subsection, "sports." Click, and then presto! Cycling, appeared with a listing for HBL. In this case, the specific was too specific, and the general category led to the individual online location I wanted to review.

Data searching is not just a lock-step procedure, but something of an art. Perhaps the best illustration of the art of "Twenty Questions," and how the whole of the center's library can be focused on a single question, is told by Barbara Quint in Reva Basch's book, *Secrets of the Super Searchers.*[1] The editor of *Searcher: The Magazine for Database Professionals*, Quint and her publication have been well-known resources in the little-known world of library science, data searching, and the evolving world of the center's library. Reva Basch asks her to remember a difficult search. In response, Barbara Quint describes what she calls, "The purest Zen experience I ever had."

I call it, "The Great Spit Search." It happened at the Rand Corporation, where for 20 years Quint was the think tank's head of research. Among her tasks was introducing the growing online resources of her department to researchers who often thought little of librarians. Convincing them of the researchers' expertise, and the power of their data systems, was a mission to Quint. But even she was taken aback by this query from a group of researchers studying the impact of drug education programs on teenagers from New York and Connecticut. To determine if their subjects were still using drugs after attending a drug orientation program, each student's saliva was collected and tagged for testing. The project was funded by the U.S. National Institutes of Health (NIH).

After collecting and testing hundreds of samples of spit, the researchers discovered that the NIH rules required them to store all samples collected during the work. None of them had thought about this when they wrote their grant. None had considered where and how hundreds of spit samples could be kept for the time required by the folks who had given them the money to do their work. And so they trouped into Barbara Quint's office to politely inquire if she could suggest a way to store saliva for an indefinite period of time. After all, she was the head researcher, and as part of her responsibilities she had visited corporation scientists to explain what her department did, what their resources were, and to invite folks to come to her office if they had a problem.

"What do we do with this spit?" they asked. She invited them to her computer terminal, trying to figure out how to deal with this bizarre request. As she tells it: "My mind was blank. So I thought, Let's see what we can do. First, they are asking for a service to be performed. Services are performed by institutions that sell services. That is a commercial services directory problem. But what directory? Well, storing spit can't be too big a business, so let's try the broadest directory, the

Electronic Yellow Pages (an electronic business directory created by Dun and Bradstreet).

"Okay. I've got my database selection, now what do I do? Well, what do I know? I know it must be in a specific geographic area. . . . The third thing I know is that they want something stored. So I entered all the terms I could think of for that concept—storing, storage, inventory, warehousing, and whatever. The last thing I know is what they want to store—spit. What is the nature of spit? A little voice came back and said, 'Spit is organic; spit spoils.' So how do you deal with something that's organic and spoils? You have to keep it from spoiling. And how do you do this? By making it cold."

That was the solution. Where (New York/Connecticut), what (storage warehousing), how (refrigeration, cooling). No problem! Quint is the name and categories is the game. It seems obvious in retrospect. When she searched the *Electronic Yellow Pages* (called Biz*File on CompuServe) for refrigerated storage facilities in the New York/Connecticut region, her computer returned the names, addresses, and phone numbers of three commercial warehouses. "Any other questions?" she blithely asked the scientists. No, thank you very much they said. Barbara Quint made it look so easy they left grateful, humbled, impressed, and wondering why they didn't think of this themselves.

Unlike most of us, librarians generally do not rely on informal data from others who may themselves have personal experience in the areas where we seek data. Their expertise is in hard data, not interpersonal information. They therefore rarely use the online conference center as a vehicle for gaining data in the search for information. But people in the center are not librarians. When faced with a problem, their reflex response is to ask someone for help, either in using the library or in strategies for coping with a personal problem or situation. In a crisis, nonlibrarians (and nonwriters) don't first think of the game "Twenty Questions." They feel panic. Losing the categorical reflex of cool logic, they also lose a handle on what it is they want to know. And so most people turn to others for help in regaining their perspective, in finding the strategies for problem solving.

Spitfire's message, in Example 5.1 is a typical call for help. At least once a month I see one like it on CompuServe's Health and Fitness Forum. Those who, like me, are involved in family care for the fragile elderly will see similar messages across the conference center. They are posted in legal, social, ethical, religious, and general discussion groups. People are afraid, they are worried, and they need not merely comfort, but data. Spitfire's message, for example, was posted in the Alzheimer's Disease Conference of Toronto's Ability Online Bulletin Board. For the sake of argument, assume that Spitfire was not lucky enough to be in Toronto where a service like Ability Online hosts a section called "Alzheimer's." How would she find online help?

Example 5.1

> Date: 08-22-95 (09:30)   Number: 237 of 245 (Refer# NONE)
> To: ALL   From: Spitfire
> Subj: RE: HELLO/Help Status: Read Type: GENERAL
>
> PUBLIC MESSAGE: Alzheimer's (241)
>
> My mother has been diagnosed with Alzheimer's. Her older sister died of it some years ago. Am expecting hell on earth. I try not to think about the future, because when I dwell on it, it gets depressing. All I know is that I'm afraid I'll be following the same path someday. Please supply information.
>
> "SPITFIRE"

The first question is: What type of help does she want? To simply express fear (or rage or joy or ecstasy), a forum, conference, support group of sympathetic souls is the perfect place to be. But in her message are two factual questions: "Will this be hell on earth?" and, "Since my mother has Alzheimer's and my aunt died from it, will I be a victim of this illness as well?" So she needs both personal support and the answer to some hard questions.

Everyone with a computer can access local bulletin boards like Ability Online. Because elder care is so common a worry, chances are there will be a section where Spitfire can find personal support. But to move to the online library, one needs a larger service. Whether it is the Internet, America Online, CIS, or something else does not matter. All of them do much the same thing, albeit with slightly different commands.

On CompuServe, for example, searching for resources that can answer a question is done through the command FIND. This takes a user through the service's resource directories, which list all of the forums and libraries potentially applicable to a question. It can do this because each forum and library area has set a series of *descriptors*, that is, subject categories that detail the broad expertise or holdings of each section of the conference center and library holdings available# through the CIS door. This is the general search, the initial step in finding the right conference or resource. If one types "FIND Alzheimer," the CompuServe menu turns up no matches. It is too specific a first query, like asking question five right off the bat in the "Twenty Questions" game. If one uses "FIND Health" or "FIND Medicine," however, a long list of potential resources appears. Both "Health and "Medicine" return lists that are almost identical. It returns a list of potential resources, "Match for: FIND 'Health' " (see Example 5.2).

Obviously, many of these potential resources can be eliminated without examination. Those dealing with other diseases, for example—AIDS News Clips, Contact Lens Supply, Diabetes Forum, IBM Clinton Health Plan, Rare Disease Database, and Sundown Vitamins—will not be of much help to Spitfire. HarperCollins Online is a resource detailing that publisher's books. It can be searched for references in this area. But let us assume that that has been done and the appropriate text is not found in their list.

Forums focusing on either general health concerns or those dealing with seniors issues are potential resources that she can use. They include the Medsig Forum, where physicians hang out online; the Retirement Living Forum, where issues involving seniors are discussed; the Disabilities Forum, in which information is provided on maximizing life patterns within the confines of illness; and the Health and Fitness Forum, where a variety of health issues are addressed. Spitfire could file her question on any of these forums. If she has not encountered them before, typing GO MEDSIG (or GO DISABILITIES, etc.) will bring up a description of the forum and its mission statement.

For harder data, FIND also returned several news-based references. They include the CNN Online Forum, which allows one to search old

Example 5.2

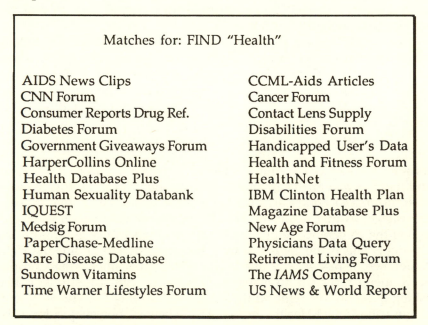

Matches for: FIND "Health"

AIDS News Clips	CCML-Aids Articles
CNN Forum	Cancer Forum
Consumer Reports Drug Ref.	Contact Lens Supply
Diabetes Forum	Disabilities Forum
Government Giveaways Forum	Handicapped User's Data
HarperCollins Online	Health and Fitness Forum
Health Database Plus	HealthNet
Human Sexuality Databank	IBM Clinton Health Plan
IQUEST	Magazine Database Plus
Medsig Forum	New Age Forum
PaperChase-Medline	Physicians Data Query
Rare Disease Database	Retirement Living Forum
Sundown Vitamins	The *IAMS* Company
Time Warner Lifestyles Forum	US News & World Report

news scripts; *US News and World Report*, with both a library of past articles and a forum for user queries; and *Magazine Database Plus*. In the first two, she can ask questions about Alzheimer's, and perhaps a staff writer will know of a story on the subject of either Alzheimer's research or Alzheimer's patients. Both forums include text libraries of past articles that their respective organizations have carried. Each can be examined with "search phrases" (Alzheimer's disease, Alzheimer's and treatment, Alzheimer's and home care, Alzheimer's and family) in the game of "Twenty Questions' " search for pertinent data.

Also in this list is PaperChase, a medical reference library, and The HealthNet Reference Library (GO HEALTHNET). Like the system as a whole, it is organized for those who like the game of "Twenty Questions." It offers a series of menus, each of which describes a category that leads to another category, which leads to another, which hopefully provides data that may help answer a question. Here is the main menu, the general directory where all HealthNet queries begin:

HealthNet Main Directory
    Introduction
    Disorders and Diseases
    Symptoms
    Drugs
    Surgeries/Tests/Procedures
    Home Care and First Aid
    Obstetrics/Reproductive Medicine
    Opthamology/Eye Care

The game of categories proceeds, step by step. "Introduction" describes the service at large, and warns that it is not designed to replace physician visits. The following sections (a list of categories) are self-explanatory. Disorders and Diseases describes diagnosed conditions; so for an overview of Alzheimer's, that is obviously where she should go. Choose that option (in bold here) and another menu appears, which breaks down the general physical category affected:

Disorders and Diseases
    AIDS/HIV
    Nerve/Brain
    Psychiatry
    Skin Diseases
    •
    •
    Urinary

Because Alzheimer's Disease describes a condition in which changes occur in the brain, which affects behavior, "Nerve/Brain" is the section that next Spitfire needs to choose. It is listed in bold type for the convenience of readers; in the menu, of course, it is undistinguished. Doubling clicking the control wand on that entry brings forward the following menu:

Disease of the Nerves and Brain
Dementia, Alzheimer's Disease
Stroke
Parkinson's Disease/Tremors
Multiple Sclerosis
Headache Syndromes
Epilepsy/Seizures
Peripheral Nerve Problems
Miscellaneous

The 1150-word essay on Alzheimer's Disease that follows is a model of clear writing about a complex medical subject. It includes a definition of the disease, the state of current research, diagnosis, treatment, and medication. It mentions the state of current research on hereditary Alzheimer's, which seems to run in families, as well as nonfamilial Alzheimer's. In addition, it covers the progress of the disease in general terms, discussing both how it affects the patient and that person's family. The following two paragraphs are an example of the material included:

It is extremely important to emphasize the importance of utilizing the support services of geriatric and other institutions. Home care, family counseling, day care centers, medical support and social services rendered in a comprehensive manner can enormously ease the burden of the disease for all affected. The personal physician should be asked about the availability and desirability of such resources.

In summary, Alzheimer's Disease is a profound problem which taxes the coping ability of all patients, their families and friends, health care providers, and social support services. Research is active, and medical and social treatment plans can offer significant benefits; yet we still have a long way to go.

OK. Not hell on earth, perhaps, but obviously living with someone who has Alzheimer's is no Sunday walk in the park. Armed with this background information, Spitfire now can search for information on "home care, family counseling, day care centers, medical supports, and social services." There are many ways to do that. She can use online forums to ask people what they know about local services, use the *Electronic Yellow Pages* to look up addresses, etc. Similarly, she can ask others who have lived with Alzheimer patients if they can suggest coping strategies for living with patients in the early stages of the disease. Or, those subjects can become category questions for another article search in, say Health Database Plus, a collection of popular magazine articles dealing with health issues, or the technical collection of medical literature that PaperChase represents. Online, she can also access her local newspaper's library, or general magazine directories, to search for stories on Alzheimer's that they may have published.

And if Spitfire needs to know about how others have lived with the disease, if she seeks information on support groups in her area, or if she requires data on finding financial assistance in any state, that is what people in the conferences, user groups, and forums are happy to provide. The game goes on, question and answer, forum to library, to library again, until she has the answers she needs.

That is how the game is played on CompuServe:

Find: Subject

First question: Forum or library?

Second question: If library, then news script, magazine article, database entry, or journal reference?

Third question: If magazine article, should it be popular or technical, etc.

The only commands one really needs to know when accessing the conference center library through this door are "FIND" and then "GO." Automated CIS directories do the rest of the work. This is why people pay commercial systems—for a range of resources ordered through easy-to-use, menu-driven categorical systems. It is what makes their broad base of resources accessible to the novice and the occasional user. The menus make it easy to get to a logical site, get the needed information, and then get out as quickly as possible. While time spent searching CIS directories is free, accessing services like HealthNet carries a modest hourly surcharge above the $8.50 monthly membership charge that all North American CompuServe members pay.

Like many other services, CIS is designed for the amateur who needs help in finding his or her way around the system and to the appropriate section. But every service, each door to the center and its library, is different. Many bulletin boards have no formal libraries, for example, while some commercial data collections have no forums or conference sites. The hard core of the conference center's library is chock filled with articles, data, and references to articles or data. Because they are designed for reference use and not for chitchat, they are not as user-friendly as CompuServe, America Online, or a local service like Ability Online.

Examples of these library-only services include the Dow Jones News and Information Service (DJIS), LEXIS-NEXIS, and KRI. As one might expect, Dow Jones is dedicated to business- and finance-related resources. That means that its data on, for example, Alzheimer's Disease will be filtered through that perspective. Search the Dow Jones for data on Alzheimer's disease and one is likely to find the financial details of nursing home companies with Alzheimer's clientele, projections by drug companies for new drugs designed to fight the disease, and discussions of the home care industry serving noninstitutionalized patients. This is all valuable information, but not what Spitfire is looking for.

Services like LEXIS-NEXIS and KRI offer enormous library reference bases that may be pertinent. Like CompuServe, KRI is a huge, international, multi-lingual service. Its library is more complex, and its searchers are a little harder. But for those who need data, it is a wonderful place to be. And, because it is international, there is usually easy access from anywhere, both to the service at large and to its professional searchers and customer service troubleshooters. In fact, KRI is now available on the Internet (http://www.dialog.com), and in late 1995 it became a "provider" through Microsoft's online service. What this means is that those with access to the Internet, or to the Microsoft Internet gateway, can access KRI not only through its dedicated telephone numbers, but from anywhere they have Internet access.

I like Knight Ridder Information, formerly known as Dialog, for detailed client searching. Because it is a dedicated library resource, it has most of the articles and citations carried on the CompuServe system, and more. Much more. For example: KRI has more than 4500 journals indexed; the full federal database of Security and Exchange Commission filings; the names, addresses, and officers of all U.S. businesses (American Business Information files 531 and 532); abstracts on pharmacology and chemistry; and worldwide patent information on all registered products now in development or on the market. Its collection contains the full-text libraries of more than 60 U.S. newspapers, five Canadian newspapers, and a slew of others from Europe and Asia. With a single query, users can search a single newspaper, a group of papers (for example, the major U.S. newspapers), or all can be searched simultaneously. In addition, it carries the full texts of articles from hundreds of general-interest and specialty magazines. They, too, can be searched individually, by general subject grouping, or all together. For a bibliophile and data maven like me, this is heaven.

Playing categories in this section of the digital library is not, however, as easy as it is on CompuServe. There is no simple "FIND" command. Instead, KRI has a menu-driven search system to help users find appropriate resources by choosing categories which, step by step, take the users through a game of categories until an appropriate resource is found. So in Example 5.3 one may choose "14. News & Full Text Publications," and then choose from a list of "U.S., Canadian, European, Asian, etc." references. If one chooses Canadian, one then can see the list of newspapers and news resources available. Then one finds the story being sought in the *Toronto Star*.

Professional searchers think of menu-driven searching in the same way that experienced bicyclists think about training wheels. But for most of us who make our living in other ways, help is always welcome. Training wheels may make the difference between riding and walking. A good, menu-driven search engine may be the difference between a successful and an unsuccessful search. "Command" searches, the advanced form of the game categories, allows users to play the "Twenty Questions" game in a faster fashion than the menu-driven system. Both methods search from the general to the specific to the individual resource required. Command searching requires user familiarity with online directories of the library's resources, and memorizing a few commands and key locations in the KRI library system.

In playing categories on KRI, for example, the first question is: Which directory should I use to find the best resources for my query? The menu system is one way to arrive at the appropriate "file," or library shelf. Another way is to query the system's directories directly. Those are still called "files," and each is identified by a name and number. The online directories include, by number and name:

> *File 411—Dialindex:* The general directory for all Dialog resources. It is where most general searches begin, especially if one does not know the file to address a query to.

> *File 415—Blue Sheets:* Descriptions of every library shelf in the electronic library, each containing data on subject matter, specialized search criteria, costs, special commands, etc.

> *File 410—Chronolog Newsletter:* The company's in-house magazine archive. It has articles that describe new files, search tips, announcements, etc. This service is updated ten times a year, which is how many times the newsletter itself is published.

Use of these online directories is free, which means neophytes can root around, stumbling, looking for the best source to address a query without having to pay a price for their inexperience. It is a substantial

Example 5.3

DIALOG MENUS (sm) MAIN MENU

Chose a subject CATEGORY by entering an option NUMBER.
Select a DATABASE by entering its acronym (e.g. PROMPT)
or # file number (#16).

1 Agriculture, Food & Nutrition
2 Biosciences & Biotechnology
3 Dialog Business Connection (sm)
4 Business Information
5 Chemistry
6 Company Information
7 Computers & Software
8 Energy & Environment
9 Engineering
10 Government & Public Affairs
11 Industry Analysis
12 Law
13 Medicine and Drug Information
14 News & Full-text Publications
15 OAG: Official Airlines Guide
16 Patents, Trademarks, Copyrights
17 People, Books, & Consumer News
18 Physical Science & Technology
19 Social Sciences & Humanities
20 DIALMAIL
21 Help in Database Selection
22 News/Rates/Help/Practice

Copyright 1992 DIALOG Information Services, Inc.
    All Rights reserved.
/H = Help   /L = Logoff
 /B <Dialog file no.> = Command Mode

---

savings for new users, as well as for those like me who, while experienced, find themselves caught and confused by a strange query or request. I frequently need to find data on a subject I had never thought
about, one whose very categories are not immediately clear. That is
when I search Chronolog Newsletter for references to sources in that

subject area, cruise through the Blue Sheets with search words designed to identify the appropriate and specific file, and use the main directory in an attempt to find general areas to which queries can be addressed.

In addition, there are specialized directories worth mentioning. If one needs data on a corporate entity, there is a file organizing the whole business collection by company name. And if one needs material on a single subject, another directory lists all journals by name. Finding the appropriate journal identifies the databases in which it is stored.

> *File 416—Company Finder:* A resource identifying all possible locations for data on a single incorporated company. In other words, a company name becomes the global search phrase, which builds the shelf of relevant data.

> *File 414—Journal Name Finder:* A master index to journals that KRI has online. If, for example, one is interested in water resources, search File 414 for "water" and it will find the available journals with that word in their title. It is updated quarterly.

In the library, it is important to note when a particular file is updated. Things change fast online. References updated only once a year are likely to be quickly overtaken by new research and events. Knowing how frequently a file is updated—the information is in Blue Sheets—is critical for those who need the latest corporate financial report, the newest article on research, or the latest wire story on some world event.

In its attempt to make things easier for the user, KRI also has organized its library in several interesting ways that allow the greater collection to be searched by general category questioning. Medtext, for example, is the name for all medical journals stored with full text; Papers, on the other hand, collects articles from all U.S. newspapers online; while Marketfull is a library of full-text market research reports. With these categories, and a few others, people needing not only citations but the articles themselves are assured of getting what they need and want.

Practically, all this means that simple questions can be answered conclusively in this part of the center's library. One can find precise answers to questions which, in old-style libraries, would be very difficult to research. For example, here is how I answered the CompuServe member's queries in Example 5.4 about Alzheimer's treatment and the disease's potential for familial transmission. There are two parts to Brian's query: first, What is the drug Cognex and how does it affect

Example 5.4

From: Brian P. McCouhlin, 87571,357
To: Tom Koch, 71600,1123
Subject: ALZHEIMER'S advice
Date: Mon, Nov 9, 1995, 1:45 PM

   My mother suffers from Alzheimer's, and is in the middle of
the second stage. Thankfully, she is beyond the point of real-
izing that something is amiss. I am the primary caregiver, and I
am very fortunate that Dad left her comfortable enough to be
able to live in an assisted living environment. Nonetheless, it is
hard. What is the medication 'Cognex'? I'd be interested in
more information on this. I worry that I will someday have this
disease. Does anyone else share this fear? In fact, every time I
forget something or a name I should know, red flags go up and I
wonder if....... Thanks for the shoulder.

   Brian

Alzheimer's Disease? and second, Will I get Alzheimer's because my
mother has it?
   To find data on Cognex, a drug used to fight Alzheimer's, I used
"Drug" as the category search phrase in File 415, the Dialog Blue
Sheets directory. Each "file" listed includes a description of subjects
covered in that section. Are there any resources on drugs? Yep. There's
Drug GMP Report (File 158), Drug & Cosmetic Industry (File 16), Drug
Store News (File 570), and File 229: Drug Information Full-Text. A
search for "Drugs" also brings forward Embase (Files 72 and 73), which
contain is current drug and biomedical literature. Searching there, one
finds a highly technical description of the drug that is of little use to
the layperson.
   Drug Information Full-Text, File 229, seemed a good place to ask
about Cognex. Blue Sheets informed me that this resource was created
by the American Society of Hospital Pharmacists. Using "Cognex" as a
search phrase in the file returned a long article that provided detailed
information on the drug. The crucial information, from Brian's perspective, followed the chemical and molecular description of the drug,
which is also known as Tacrine.

   Tacrine is used for the *palliative treatment of mild to moderate pri-*
mary degenerative dementia of the Alzheimer's type (Alzheimer's dis-

ease, presenile or senile dementia) . . . The rationale for the use of Tacrine in this condition is to potentially increase CNS (central nervous system) acetylcholine concentrations, which can be deficient in patients with Alzheimer's disease. Thus, therapy with the drug has been referred to as cholinergic neurotransmitter replacement. The current indication is based principally on 2 short-term (12 or 30 weeks), double-blind placebo-controlled studies in patients with a diagnosis of probable Alzheimer's disease of mild to moderate severity. (1,13,17) . . . Both studies demonstrated *clinically important but modest and variable, dose-related improvement* in cognitive function and clinician-rated global assessment of observed clinical change . . . there currently is no evidence from well-designed studies that therapy with the drug can alter the underlying disease process of dementia. [Italics added]

Simply, Cognex may increase needed chemicals that Alzheimer's patients seem to lack. Two studies have shown some improvement in some patients using the drug, but who will benefit, for how long, or to what degree are things that the experts just do not know. Cognex does not affect the long-term course of the disease, it just treats some of the symptoms, sometimes. The numbers in parentheses (1, 13, 17) refer to footnotes referencing articles and reports included with the full report. So those seeking more information know where to turn.

Addressing Brian's other question (My mother has it. Will I?) was a little harder. By searching the Blue Sheet's directory for reference to "health or medicine" files, potential reference libraries returned included: Health Periodicals Database 163, a collection of general-language articles on health issues; Embase; and the general category of MEDTEXT. A search for "Alzheimer's" in any of these resources would return hundreds of articles. To find out about familial Alzheimer's, one would have to narrow the field to look only for articles on: (Alzheimer's or Alzheimer) and (gene? or heredit? or famil?). When two or more words are strung together to create a directed search, the whole is called a *search phrase*.

The parentheses tell the computer to look for any article that includes either spelling of Alzheimer's *and* one or another of the following words. It is, in effect, three searches in one. Articles on Alzheimer's (or Alzheimer) and (1) gene? or (2) heredit? or (3) familial will be returned. The question mark is a device that tells the computer to look for words with these roots, and any other ending. So "famil?" tells it to search for Alzheimer's and family, or familial or familiarity, but only where it is associated with the word Alzheimer's. Whether the search is on CompuServe, Dialog, the Dow Jones, LEXIS-NEXIS, or any other service, crafting a good search phrase using appropriate category words is the trick to finding the desired information. The rule is: Use general words (health, medicine, business) in attempting to locate the section of the library, but use specific words (Alzheimer's, familial, genetic) when narrowing the field to a few appropriate articles or facts.

In researching heredity and Alzheimer's, I used a collection of medical journal articles called Embase. In my first pass, I found several hundred articles, far too many to review. So I next limited the search to review papers published in the years 1992–1994. This would, I decided, give the most up-to-date data, and, by adding "review" to the phrase, I would get articles that surveyed the best of older publications. Review articles collect and evaluate older literature, presenting it in a modern perspective. This narrowed the articles potentially bearing on Brian's question to a manageable few, including two whose abstracts are included here:

> *Title:* Breitner JC et al. "Use of twin cohorts for research in Alzheimer's disease."
>
> *Journal:* Neurology (1993 Feb) 43(2):261–7
>
> *Abstract:* The causes of Alzheimer's disease (AD) remain a mystery despite the recent identification of several putative environmental risk factors and the discovery of several linked genetic loci and point mutations associated with the disease. *Particularly uncertain is the generalizability of the genetic findings to the common forms of disease encountered in clinical practice or population research.* Twin studies of AD can illuminate causal mechanisms, both genetic and environmental. . . . *[italics added]*
>
> *Descriptors:* ⟨Alzheimer's Disease⟩ ⟨Disease in Twins⟩ ⟨Aged⟩ ⟨Aged, 80 and over⟩ ⟨Cohort Studies⟩ ⟨Human⟩ ⟨Research⟩ ⟨Review⟩ ⟨Review, Academic⟩

So, as of February, 1993, the best answer researchers could give Brian was that scientists had identified several risk factors which might contribute to Alzheimer's, including some of which are inherited. A 1994 study, published in a technical journal on Alzheimer research, expanded on the issue of Alzheimer's genetic base. In this case, too, the abstract provided the general data we needed.

> *Title:* "Technical feasibility of genetic testing for Alzheimer's disease."
>
> *Journal:* Alzheimer Dis Assoc Disord (1994) 8(2):102–15
>
> *Abstract:* This article examines the feasibility of using molecular genetic information for diagnostic and predictive testing in Alzheimer's disease (AD). The scope is limited largely to

early onset familial cases. . . . Age of onset and familiality have emerged as the most useful clinical features demarcating subgroups with common origins. The accurate use of genetic data in AD, for diagnostic, screening and predictive purposes relies on the most up-to-date knowledge of the transmission of the disorder in relation to mutations in these genes. The interpretation of genetic data is examined for each of the known early onset genes. In addition, we review the data pertaining to late onset disease and risk conferred by the APOE locus to both familial and nonfamilial cases.

Isolated cases of AD occur at all ages of onset, but no AD mutations in the beta APP gene have yet been identified in isolated cases.

Descriptors: ⟨Protein Precursor⟩ ⟨Apolipoproteins E⟩ ⟨Chromosomes, Human, Pair 14⟩ ⟨Chromosomes, Human, Pair 21⟩ ⟨Genetic Counseling⟩ ⟨Heterozygote Detection⟩ ⟨Human⟩ ⟨Middle Age⟩ ⟨Predictive Value of Tests⟩ ⟨Risk Factors⟩ ⟨Review⟩ ⟨Review, Tutorial⟩

The next question was to define the varying types of Alzheimer's disease mentioned in the article. A quick and inexpensive search ($2.50) on CompuServe's Healthnet yielded simple, plain-language definitions of the varying types of Alzheimer disease mentioned in the technical article. Not surprisingly, nonfamilial Alzheimer's is when the disease occurs without a family history. Familial means several older members of the family have been affected by the illness. Early onset and late onset refer to when the symptoms first began to appear in those relatives.

So, for Brian, the answer to his question ("Will I get it?") is . . . maybe. Data online are about the general case. To make them into information, he will need to know more about his family history, for example. Did his grandparents show symptoms, and if so, at what age? Was this a general (maternal and paternal grandparents?) problem, or limited only to, say, his mother's line? His personal family's history is not online, of course, but resources for researching genealogy are. Across the conference center there are a number of specialized conferences and forums on this subject. Maybe it will be enough for him to know that there are different types of Alzheimer's and different patterns that may or may not affect him. If Brian wants to *know* if he is at extreme risk for familial Alzheimer's, however, he will require genetic testing. Only evidence of the chromosomal anomaly identifying predilection to the disease will give him hard information. Should he go this route? Is it worth it? That is his choice, and one he can discuss with his family physician, online in Alzheimer's related forums, or in conferences dealing with "ethics."

CompuServe and KRI both returned similar but not identical article lists in companion searches in this area. This is not surprising. There is a vast redundancy online. One can find the same reference in a variety of directories, and through a number of different center doors. But this is to be expected. Many print libraries have copies of the same book, and it does not really matter which branch you borrow from if you want to read, say, *A Place in Time: Care Givers For Their Elderly*. Similarly, many online services share the same files, and whether one accesses them through CompuServe, KRI, or the Internet is a matter of user access, cost preference, and familiarity. After all, the "original" is actually stored in a single computer and mirrored to users through whatever door they use to enter the conference/library center.

Remember: Whatever *door is used to enter the conference center/library, the data being sought are the same*. In both of these cases, CompuServe and KRI functioned like reference librarians in a closed stacks library. They took my typed note requesting information to their respective directories, and then sifted through potential resources to find those specializing in medical collections. They then instructed library runners to retrieve relevant data in the form I requested: citation, abstract, full text, or all three together. The "best" service for any search depends on one's budget, the complexity of the question being asked, the type of data sought (statistical, official, newspaper, self-help group, etc.), and the detail required in that answer. Costs will vary considerably between different services. What may be free in one location can carry a hefty fee in another part of the center's library. If one needs to see a U.S. company's current financial statement, called a 10K, it is available on varying services, including KRI, DJIS, and CIS. Current records are free on the Internet. I use KRI when I need historical corporate data, the footnotes to a specific report, or in other special cases. But for a general glance at the 10K, well, why not accept a less expensive alternative? One advantage of having the keys to varying center doors is that folks with limited incomes can shop for the least expensive access to a specific resource.

Sooner rather than later, price and availability will be standardized across the greater center library. By that time, these digital resources will become commonplace, and knowledge about their use will be taken for granted. Already, most North American university libraries have electronic catalogs describing their collections and online resources providing access to the greater conference center/library's electronic holdings. The trend is almost sure to expand in the coming years. One can see this future, today, at the Los Angeles County Public

Library, where in 1993 Steve Coffman directed a staff of FYI librarians whose job it was to find online information for clients. A researcher whose work is described in Reva Basch's *Super Searchers* book, Coffman and his staff went online to find answers for library users who needed immediate and detailed help. The charge was hefty—$65 an hour plus direct expenses—but that included the searcher's time. Those who learn to play the game and use the electronic resources available online do not have to pay an expert for his or her time.

What was remarkable in the early 1990s was that a public library offered such a service at all. As costs decrease and user savvy increases, this type of service will become the norm. And, as more people learn the basics of simple searching, they will increasingly seek electronic rather than print reference materials. This does not mean the end of librarianship. The reverse is true. Expert searchers who understand the byways and crannies of the center cum library will be in demand for years to come. They know their resources. They know where to look. They know how to play the game, "Twenty Questions."

The most serious work, the best work, is always play. Elements of the game may change, but not the logic of its rules. Whether future users log into the library with a keyboard or use voice commands, point-and-click on hypertext, or search footnoted references, they still will have found the resources they needed by playing the game of "Twenty Questions." This business of categorization, of hierarchy and organization is, psychologists say, how we all order the world. It is the means by which humans make sense of the chaos around us. Expertise in the game will become increasingly important as more and more data are stored online, requiring everbetter questions in the search for a specific fact, datum, or opinion. There is no better example of this than the Internet in its current state of evolution. And so the next chapter focuses on it, not merely as a resource, but as an example of hierarchies, search patterns, and the evolution of these digital data/ knowledge systems.

NOTE

1.Reva Basch. *Secrets of the Super Searchers*. Wilton, CT: Eight Bit Books, 1993.

6

The Internet: Fact and Context

In the last few years there here have been thousands of English-language news stories about the Internet. In addition, this one door to the digital conference center/library has spawned scores of books, its own magazine (*Internet World*), a series of newsletters, and several television shows dedicated to teaching "newbies," new users, the intricacies of "surfing" the "Net." As a result of this enormous and uniformly favorable publicity, being online in the center at large has become secondary to being on the Internet. That the whole has been a disappointment for many of the millions who have tried it in hope and left in despair is a result of overblown promises, unrealistic expectations, and a general misunderstanding about the electronic universe in general (new! amazing! totally different!!) and the Internet itself.

Everything you have heard about the Internet is false, incomplete, exaggerated, inaccurate, and/or outdated. It is simultaneously a voraciously democratic medium, a vox popular, and an anarchistic system in which no voice or venue can dominate. It is historically elitist, benefiting academics and the well-to-do most of all, but it is becoming a general resource for people who use it through library-based hook-ups and "free-net" community access systems. Whatever else it might become, the Internet is an increasingly fertile ground for commercial enterprises and exclusive, sometimes expensive, vendors. It is hierarchically structured in its organization, and can be thought of as an information tree with more branches than the magnificent old Banyon that stands in St. Thomas Square in Honolulu, Hawaii.

Confused? Everyone is. There are dire warnings that the sheer number of users clamoring online will cause the imminent collapse of the Internet as we know it. Others assert that its greatest strength is the ever expanding number of people who have potential access to its resources. It is both a surfer's environment and a data diver's habitat. Most people, of course, exist between these poles. They are at least mildly interested in the medium and its "culture," if only because it is so much in the news. But they are more interested in this resource's ability to either advance or inhibit their search for answers to problems or questions of immediate personal importance.

To make sense of the evolving, changing structure of the whole, a few simple facts are helpful. First and foremost, the Internet is not the online universe any more than New England is the United States. In fact, what is called the Internet is exactly like a regional association, a part of the whole that shares certain characteristics with its neighbors. Conferences meet on its UseNet, for example, a state in the association at large. Think of it as Rhode Island. There are other states—FTP and Telnet, for example—that are discrete domains comprised of news lists and various libraries chockablock full of data. Finally, the Internet at large is also a vast library system with a huge array of census figures, business facts, medical data, news files, magazine articles, and other resources. This library is not distinct from the online world's greater collection, however, only a part of it. Think of the formal library as . . . Massachusetts.

Like CompuServe, the Dow Jones News Service, America Online, and others, the "Net" is a medium by which one enters the center where people discuss issues in user groups, read newsletters disseminated by listserv librarians, and access collections housed online for general use. There is even an area for "real-time" chat. And like those other services, the "Net" is a way into the online library, where books, articles, newspapers, and other data collections are stored. The Internet also shares the logic and structure of the greater conference center/library of which it is a part. Indeed, in its earlier incarnation it created the standard that has allowed the whole confederation to develop.

A bit of history may be helpful at this point. Whatever it may become in the future, the online universe's newest fad is also the electronic data exchange's oldest member. Its excesses, idiosyncrasies, and general structure evolve from its history. The centre's logic, and that of its individual parts, grows out of our recent, communal past.

In the early days of computers, America's cold war warriors assumed in the 1960s that a nuclear war was likely to occur within 10 to 20 years.

Because U.S. missiles targeted Russian's strategic information centers, it was assumed that Soviet warheads were similarly aimed at U.S. data concentrations, urban industrial locations with telecommunication facilities. The wheels of government couldn't go around, after all, if the hub was blown away. So the U.S. Rand Corporation, a cold war think tank *par excellence*, argued that the way to survive World War III was to create a communication and information storage system without a hub, a network in which no point was more central than any other. The whole had to be so constructed that if one part was blown away, taken "offline," messages normally routed through it could be delivered by a different path.

This is simple network theory. Its basic principles are familiar to anyone who drives a car or uses a telephone. Both systems are lattice-like structures that have been consciously developed to assure that the integrity of the system at large is not dependent on any one path between any two individual locations. Remember how, in Western movies, the villain always cut a telegraph wire to isolate the hero and his community? A single connection between two places or people is vulnerable. The modern telephone system's reliability is based on the many potential paths joining any two points across the whole lattice-like, honeycomb structure in which the whole is connected by more than one path. If Los Angeles is flooded, San Francisco is hit by an earthquake, or a volcano erupts in Oregon, a few lines may go down temporarily. As a result, a few "nodes" (homes, city blocks, neighborhoods) may have service interrupted (go "offline"), but the structure of the whole is maintained. Those interruptions do not seriously disturb the greater pattern of national and international communication that continues unimpeded across the larger network. Messages that would have been routed through the affected sites are simply sent by another, alternate path.

Drivers know how this works because the road system is a similar type of network. During the morning traffic jam commuters are continually switching from congested to less congested routes, seeking the best moving path on the lattice of primary, secondary, and tertiary roads connecting suburban home and downtown office. The more roads connecting A and B to other sites, the stronger the whole will be. If one route is clogged, take another. Temporary interruptions may occur in small areas, but the greater system of transportation remains in service. That is why, after World War II, the U.S. military strongly supported the building of the U.S. interstate highway system. It assured alternate routes for the movement of men and material on a continental scale. Even if one city or highway were destroyed, the military would be able to navigate across America by other, perhaps secondary routes. If there is only one line between any two points, destroying that destroys the connection. In a lattice-like, honeycombed system, however, many points assure the integrity of the system.

Today's Internet results from the military's desire to create a similarly dependable structure for the transmission of communications and data. In 1969, the Department of Defense Advanced Research Projects Agency connected four huge mainframe computers at the then enormous cost of 1 million U.S. dollars. Each computer was linked to all of the others through telephone lines so that if one was lost to war or misadventure, connections between the others would be retained by alternate paths. They were the large computers at the Stanford Research Institute, the University of California at Los Angeles, the University of California at Santa Barbara, and the University of Utah. A network was born. With only four "nodes" in the computer system, however, the whole was still vulnerable. Two direct strikes and the whole would collapse. And so more computers were added to what was then called ARPANet, and with each addition the system grew. After all, the larger the system and the greater is total connectivity, the more potential links and alternate paths there will be between any two parts of the whole.

Eventually, the network grew large enough to be partitioned into two distinct systems, albeit with connecting links. The first became an academic, research-oriented computer system and the second, MilNet, was reserved for military analysis and communication.[1] Over time, the academic network, ARPANet's successor, took on more and more semi-public nodes, and accepted more and more sites in its growing structure. The whole began to look like a lattice in which each computer "node" was independent, equal, and connected to all of the other sites by myriad potentially connecting paths. Because mainframe computers were both expensive and required expert technical support, these new nodes typically were centered at research centers and at universities. Academics used them for complicated computer-dependent studies and for professional communications.

From the early 1970s through the late 1980s, ARPANet's successor, the early Internet, was largely academic and research-oriented. Its library collections included ever increasing resources for scientific documentation. Everything worked in the way the military planners had hoped it would. Each site was independent. All were connected by various paths. No single hub made a convenient bomb target. There was no central site or directing node to bomb. To destroy the whole, every site, or at least all of the telephone lines connecting them, would have to be simultaneously and permanently destroyed.

Over time, the growth of the network expanded beyond exclusively American, or even North American, jurisdiction. What began as an

American military project inevitably became an international resource. Research is not a parochial business, and the need of academics and planners to communicate with colleagues in Canada, Britain, Switzerland, and even Russia made the expansion of this part of the original ARPANet an inevitability. And so, over time, researchers in other countries were invited in. They put a portion of their computing power into the whole, and expanded the network with their presence. The military still restricted their part of the whole, the old MilNet, but the largest network by far became a wonderland of academics and researchers interested in everything from anthropology to zoology.

Not surprisingly, across the still exclusive system, users wanted increased and broader access to their friends and colleagues, whatever their nationality. They wanted to talk about more than business. Many had gone to school together. They collaborated on projects, attended the same conferences, and, in the way of the academic world, rose in their professions by moving from one university (and group of colleagues) to another. And so, like friends everywhere, they had things to discuss besides work. Did you hear about Betty's husband? Where can I buy a good used car? How about those Mets? And so, inevitably, the computerized system first designed for the military and then co-opted by academics became a medium for its users' personal concerns, too. There was private mail between users, of course. But across the system, people sharing common interests began meeting together electronically, messaging to one another in unison. Because their creators were academics, these electronic meeting sites were called *conferences.*

Over time, these user groups became formalized and the UseNet was born. It is a system that operates across the Internet lattice but is theoretically distinct from it, much as the Dutch telephone system is part of the international telephone network, a distinct part of the whole. The computerized Internet lattice is now layered with old, new, and even newer parts incorporated together. There is the old and shadowy ARPANet, the military links that are still in place. Above that is the UseNet system of group messaging and communication. And then there is the Internet, the publicly visible darling of the 1990s. In addition, and evermore entwined with UseNet and Internet, is another level comprised of commercial providers (America Online, CompuServe, Delphi, Prodigy, etc.), which originally offered private clients similar but independent resources. Today, however, they are increasingly linked through the center to the Internet at large. At every level and through every door to throughout the evolving system-at-large, however, the essential medium is the marriage of computers linked by telephone lines. The effective medium, however, is the message, the typed note, request, or command.

The success of this originally military vision far exceeded the wildest dreams of the Rand Corporation's cold war warriors. But then, even they could not foresee the potential for today's inexpensive personal computers, each with more power than an old-style, oversized mainframe. With them, anyone can access one or another part of this system and enter one or another center door. Computers are no longer elite resources, but the means by which everyone can enter the center-at-large through any of its myriad nodes. So the lattice has expanded again, with each user able to enter the honeycomb network through any of the many available center doors, at any level of the hierarchy, using any telephone in the international communication system. The miraculous tool that first connected our voices to those of friends in distant places now allows everyone access to the nonplace of digitized data libraries and meeting places.

Today, the Internet is like a giant beehive, one of several that are so interrelated as to constitute a single, superswarm (the center). We individual users are like bees flitting in through one or another entry way, depositing pollen ("uploads"), seeking nourishment ("downloads"), or exchanging information together (in conferences).

Whatever door one uses to enter the conference center (CompuServe, Delphi, America Online, etc.)—whatever "host system" in computer-speak—everyone can read and respond to another's electronic mail using the Internet as a common carrier for electronic mail. Its mail address system has become the standard for intraservice communication, allowing members of private systems to message each other and all Internet users. Similarly, clients of most commercial hosts (AOL, CIS, etc.) can join UseNet groups, or access one or another section of the Internet's digital library in various ways. This increasing uniformity and interrelation means an increasing magnitude of user resources. In 1984 there were over 6000 groups on the UseNet. Since then the numbers have exploded. It does not matter if members participate through a university node, a commercial site, or a private carrier. UseNet is *not* the Internet. Nor is it the whole conference center. It is a part of the whole, an example of how apparently distinct resources merge into a greater interconnected system. In this case, it is one that is linked by the telephone, addressed by the mails, and stored digitally in library-style digital structures.

The increasing number of people using online resources—the number of people now online is believed to be more than 25 million—did not go unnoticed by business people. They saw the evolving concentration of users, the sum of the members of all of these increasingly interdependent systems, as a financial opportunity. So while private service providers like CompuServe began to develop ever better links between their systems and the many parts of the Internet, electronic data vendors began to market their resources to constituents across the evolving network. Smaller businesses of every shape and size also saw the increasing concentration of users as a market. I first sent flowers to my aunt in 1987 through an online FTD hookup. It was a radical, cool, amazing ability in those days. After all, I was in Hawaii and she was in Buffalo, New York. Now, everyone, from car manufacturers to a small deli up the street from my house, has online marketing and information sites. Everyone can find a place online to promote his or her wares to the greater digital world. The center thus has a new partner, commerce, and the library/conference center has become the library/ conference center cum bazaar.

This was not what Rand's think tank planners envisioned. They did not set out to create business opportunities, venues for desultory discussions, or resources for people like you and me. But since there is no single body or boss that can deny anyone access because of politics, race, or style, everyone is free to participate. The network is certainly democratic—of the people—and, at the UseNet level at least, anarchistic as well. Anybody can create a user group. All voices are equal. Anarchy, however, is not necessarily chaotic. Because there is no president of Internet Inc., does not mean that the whole lacks structure. In fact, each part of the whole is organized similarly in a logical, old-fashioned hierarchical manner. But because it is, despite the appearance of uniformity, still a confederation of independent networks and disparate services, users need to learn separate commands to access the "Net's" many and distinct, semiautonomous regions.

ACCESS

The Internet is a series of hierarchies, of smaller boxes fitting snugly into larger boxes. For example, there are three types of connectivity, that is, three ways to be a part of the whole. They are: through a gateway server, through a remote computer, or by direct access. Entering through a gateway server means using a provider like America Online (AOL), CompuServe, a Freenet, or even bulletin board systems (BBS) like Ability Online. These center doors provide "gateways" to other parts of the whole; they are bridges that allow members in one part of the lattice to move to resources that were created and administered by another section. In the early 1990s, this only worked for electronic mail interchange. But by the mid-1990s, remote access through gateway servers allowed users increasingly complete access to Internet-based resources.

Another way to connect with the "Net" is by "remote modem access" to a dial-up terminal connection. An employer (academic, governmental, or commercial) whose main computer is hooked into the Internet gives its employees or clients individual access through their personal computers. When the whole was dominated by academe and the military, this was really the only option. Now, of course, many different types of organizations are developing online nodes and resources, and giving their employees access as well. In Canada, for example, the Canadian Broadcasting Corporation has created a series of online sites for its staff's use. Viewers and listeners are regularly encouraged to message comments and complaints to shows proudly boasting Internet addresses.

Unaffiliated individuals can also get remote access through commercial companies who buy a dedicated, commercial link (direct access) and then sell access to that link, piece by piece, to those without other connections. A few years ago, in the rare cases where such service was available to the average user, it was extremely expensive. But as the online world has expanded, the cost of this type of user service has dropped rapidly from hundreds of dollars a year to, in some places, under $20 a month. With remote access, nobody is hooked to the center directly. Rather, their personal computers are linked through telephone and modem to a provider's mainframe. That computer is online and part of the lattice; one taps in and leaves like a bee entering and then leaving the hive.

It is a matter of mirrors. Everyone signing on believes him- or herself to be "on the net," directly involved in messaging, conferencing, and searching. But in fact they are *in* the net, in the conference center and library cum bazzar. The node computer that one dials to is the access point, the center door. It is one hexagon in the general lattice, one honeycomb in the greater hive. Building that door can be expensive. Patrick Crispen writes, for example, that in 1994 the University of Alabama at Tuscaloosa paid $29,000 a year for its dedicated Internet connection.[2] Direct access is what lets the mainframes at each node remain ready and willing to carry our messages and queries 24 hours a day. Direct access puts the designated computer directly into the lattice, one honeycomb among the many.

Networks

Choosing a provider and a level of connection is only the first of many choices potential users must make. Because it is anarchistic, a network comprised of independent nodes, each tenuously linked to the whole, each part of the Internet has its own language, hierarchy, and protocol. That means that finding any single resource is usually a bit more complex than typing FIND: "Medicine" in a uniform part of the online space like CompuServe. On the Internet, one first has to identify the computer to be searched, and then the language that computer speaks before even attempting to use its directory to identify potential resources.

Major Internet resource areas include, in a partial listing: Telnet, File Transfer Protocol (FTP), Gopher, and the Web. Think of them as different library systems, each with a different library card which may or may not be universal. All represent different parts of a single connection, and all of those connections are available in the library. What one uses will depend on the data required, as well as the appropriate marriage of computer and system access. Accessing the Web requires special software, as does the UseNet. Think of these different areas as strands of the general, Internet lattice, which itself is part of the center, whose sections (Internet, CompuServe, etc.) exist interdependently.

While the World Wide Web (WWW) is the most popular area of the Internet today, one where multimedia is possible and simple searches are facilitated, older parts of the system still deserve consideration by data divers who may require facts or documents housed in older, text-based sections. To ignore them would be like refusing to read anything written before 1995. Also, while the World Wide Web is becoming a commercial standard, many people with older computers, slower modems, and limited online access have neither the power nor the connections to access it. For them, these older systems remain the available state-of-the-art.

Telnet is a firm, thick, old-style strand on the Internet lattice. It allows users with a remote access account to send commands from their personal computers to the local host, which then sends them on to the destination computer. This happens so quickly that it may seem as if one was messaging directly to the distant node; but in fact the service provider's system is an amplifier and translator, taking any individual query and passing it on to another provider's system. Here is how it works. After connecting by telephone and modem to the provider, one types the command "Telnet" and then an address. This tells the computer the method of relation I wish to achieve (Telnet as opposed to, say, FTP) and the host computer I wish to achieve it with. So, for example, if I wish to check out library holdings at the U.S. Department of Commerce's Economic Bulletin Board, which has 20 separate shelves of economic and trade information, I would type telnet ebb.stat-usa.gov.

Once there, the other computer will ask my host for my "login" name at the prompt. My host computer, of course, immediately will mirror that request to me. At the ebb.stat. computer, all I have to type is "guest." Logins and passwords can be used to restrict commercial and private data sites. In the general collection, however, they are generally used as a simple means of keeping track of users. Since ebb.site is public data for general use, it is not restricted and so its password is easily obtained from published directories and open, online resources. So when asked for my login, I simply typed "guest" and my presence was accepted. I then messaged that I wanted to see the ebb. stat-usa.gov directory—the computer's library catalog. From there I searched from general heading to specific entry, looking for the data I required.

Telnet is a common method of accessing official bulletin boards, user groups, and some library resources. The U.S. government's many branches have made use of it for several years as a way of disseminating public information. Thus the U.S. Environmental Protection Agency has an information provider system that can be reached by Telnet (address: epaibm.rtpnc.epa.gov, no login required). Congress has another that tracks and describes pending legislation, beginning with the 93rd Congress (telnet locis.loc.gov then use the login password: Federal Legislation). Its directory is organized year by year, so for data on a bill passed in the 96th Congress, one would choose that year in the library's catalog hierarchy and then follow the menu down the data tree in search of the appropriate bill.

File Transfer Protocol (FTP) is a little different from Telnet. As its name suggests, it facilitates transferring files from a remote library to an individual's personal computer. FTP tells the computer what site to address, informs the computer of one's personal address, provides the appropriate password to enter the target library (Remember: Each part of the system is independent and can restrict its use to outsiders), and then directs it to the required resources. Many print directories of FTP resources include a "path" that takes users past the main catalog to the specific library shelf where the required data are stored. Like Telnet, FTP sites often require a password or login. That is the form, but because many are unrestricted—for public use—the password most often required is simply "anonymous." And so, unimaginatively, these nodes in the FTP section of the honeycomb are called *anonymous FTP sites*. To use an example from one of Crispen's Roadmap lessons, if I am interested in a file or resource at the sura.net computer site, getting to it would require that I type ftp ftp sura net. After that, I would have to enter a user name (login:) and a password, which at anonymous FTP sites is simply the user's address. The whole exchange would look like Example 6.1, with italics showing the entries I typed.

At the "command" request I can ask for the main catalog, which is the "directory" (dir) or the library shelf that holds the specific material I want. At sura.net, if I want its agricultural list (path: /pub/nic/agricultural.list), I would type:

Command: cd /pub/nic

Then, once there, I would be able to tell the computer what I wanted to retrieve with the simple command:

get agricultural.list.

Retrieving such files is easy, but reading them may be a challenge, depending on how they were written and the manner of their storage. Text files stored in "ASCII," which always carry the suffix .txt, are easy to read on a personal computer with any of the common word processing software. Others, however, can be either PostScript documents written in Adobe's page description language (with a suffix of .ps) or Microsoft Word documents, which are followed by .DOC. PostScript documents require a postscript-capable software reader, or at least a printer that reads the Adobe page format. Microsoft Word documents are binary files and may not be readable by all word processors. Fortunately, appropriate translators are stored in many areas of the online world and are usually freely available for downloading.

If this sounds somewhat confusing, well, it is. Is this system sensible and efficient? Not particularly, and certainly not yet. But since there is no Internet standard, people are free to use the procedures they prefer. It is the down side of the "anything goes," power-to-the-people mentality of the system at large. Still, the whole vast and competing software system is slowly moving toward standardization. Entropy rules,

Example 6.1

```
ftp ftp sura net

Connecting to ftp.sura.net 128.167.179, port 21 220 nic.sura.net
 FTP server (Version wu-2.4 (1)  Nov 14 18:26:38 EDT 1995
 read.
USER anonymous
>>>User Anonymous
225 Guest login ok, send your complete e-mail address as
 password.
Password: 71600.1123@compuserve.com
Guest login ok, access restrictions apply.
Command
```

and the early complexity of different readers, different standards, and different protocols is rapidly giving way to singular uniformity, a center/library cum bazaar–style Esperanto.

Why not? Despite these differences, the whole is still a message-based system that is dependent on a series of notes sent rapidly between the user and the receiver via a telephone-linked communications system. UseNet groups are message-based, as are FTP, Gopher, Telnet, and other parts of the whole. In fact, one can find and retrieve FTP resources with nothing more than electronic mail. It is a little slower, perhaps, but the logic is no different. To do this, one sends electronic mail to an FTP site, a type of dedicated mail depot, asking the message to be delivered to a service provider. The body of that message informs the provider what is needed and to whom it should be sent. Think of it as telling a local library you want a book from inter-library loan. Electronically, the whole works just like subscribing to a list. One mails the request to a node computer and, in the body of that message, informs its electronic "elves" where required material is generally stored (connect), where the material is to be found (what directory), and to whom it should be sent. Then, if everything goes correctly, the requested material shows up in one's mailbox within a few hours. The process takes longer to describe than to do. Example 6.2 is a search sent by FTP to ftpmail@ftp.uu.net, a FTP mail site in the United States. I sent it as a local telephone call (no charges) through the CompuServe/Internet gateway. The actual commands are in the right column, while a brief description of what each means is typed on the left side of the information box.

Dir? Chdir/pub/articles? These commands will be familiar to anyone who remembers the old, pre-Windows, pre-Macintosh days of online

Example 6.2

To the mail address: INTERNET:ftpmail@ftp.uu.net	
Description	*computer commands*
(Send all stuff to this address)	reply 71600.1123
(Get from this computer)	connect ftp.sura.net
(I can read this form)	ascii
(Go to the articles directory)	chdir/pub/articles
(This is what I want)	get fall92.issue
(That's it)	quit

computer command languages. It is the language of DOS, the Disk Operating System that early 1980-style computer users struggled with. DOS was a way of maneuvering through the whole to find a required file on the library shelf, send or retrieve a message, and read the accumulated UseNet wisdom. In it, the hierarchy of the data tree is stated from general to specific: directory/change directory/publications directory/articles section/fall, 1992, material. That is how all searching was done a few years ago. One way or another, one had to state the hierarchy, top-down, to retrieve specific material. Until recently, it was the only option everyone had.

Now, however, that naked and logical structure is being overlaid with more intuitive search methods, and with point-and-click software systems. These new user search systems make it easier for newer users to ignore the steps that they and their computers are really taking. But then, few long-distance telephone users consider the path search that automated system switches perform in a cross-country call to Aunt Bertha, Uncle Leo, or an errant daughter. Similarly, new Internet systems are enabling us all to ignore the steps we take and concentrate on the connection we want to achieve and the data we wish to acquire.

Greater ease of use with a point-and-click system of access is one reason for the enthusiasm that has greeted Internet's newest region, the World Wide Web (aka the "Web," WWW, etc.). It facilitates access to a variety of system files, discussion groups, and much, much more. In the last year, thousands of dedicated WWW sites have been added online, each capable of retrieving both traditional materials and data otherwise unavailable. Its expansion has been so rapid that, by some counts, a new Web site was added every 20 minutes in 1995. The Web can retrieve traditional, FTP, Gopher, and Telnet style text-based data. The general form for these addresses is:

protocol://server-name: port/path.

The form is the URL (Universal Resource Locator) and is used on machines equipped with WWW access programs for general use (for example, Mosaic). "Protocol" means the type of resource to be accessed (FTP, Telnet, Gopher, WWW, etc.). In this language, the two slashes (?//) that follow the type of protocol designated indicate a machine name or address. To reach the online Congressional location mentioned a few pages ago, for example, one would type:

telnet://telnet locis.loc.gov

The primary URL for the Web itself is http, the "hypertext transport protocol," that facilitates use of imbedded materials. It is called "hypertext" because any one page may include keys that, when activated, will link your computer to other data, reports, pictures, or sound bytes stored elsewhere on the system. Each primary address, the now famous "home page," may merely be a way station for documents from a variety of locations. So, for example, http://www.greenwood.com is the home page of this book's publisher, Greenwood Publishing Group, Inc. There one can find descriptions of their books by subject, a list of featured publications, and links to personal home pages created by authors, like me. Since geographic location is irrelevant online, one can easily imbed into a single document reference background documents or pages stored in England or Holland or Los Angeles, whatever the "real" address of the home page owner (Greenwood Publishing Group is in Westport, CT). Space collapses, and distance becomes, on a single page as well as in the greater system, a matter of seconds between computer connections.

To understand this idea of a page within a page,

http://www.surgery.pixi.com/body/

tells the computer to use the universal resource locator, http, to get to the wed (www) address "surgery" at the "pixi.com" computer site and then go to the library shelf named "body." Www.surgery/pixi.com/body/ was created by Honolulu plastic surgeons as both an "information resource" and an advertisement. Its directory, the *home page* in Web language, offers several options, including an image of a human body with different body parts highlighted by a box. Clicking on one of those boxes (breast, hip, nose, stomach, rear end, etc.) automatically brings forth a subdirectory for each body part. These include before and after pictures of changes plastic surgery could create (small breast to large breast, breast reduction, and breast reconstruction are subdirectories of breast) along with descriptions of each procedure. Another subdirectory gives the names and addresses of the page's participating doctors, so local residents might learn about the magicians who perform these cosmetic miracles.

Different? Sure. Very different? No. The environment that allows multimedia and hypertext is an extension of the text-only message system that has powered this evolution from the beginning. The use of the telephone system as a message facilitator, library-styled hierarchies of organization, and the medium of the written/typed message are still constant in the whole. Now, however, those written queries may return a song, a picture, a video clip, or a variety of texts, depending on what is requested. The process of access and retrieval is a simple and hierarchical tree, each level presenting choices, each choice affecting the next level's actions. The whole enforces a strict logic, a method of step-by-step thinking required by the many different parts of this anachronistic system whose many parts somehow combine into an accessible whole.

Within any one resource, there is a library catalog called a *directory* or *home page*. Each holds subdirectories that may include even more specific groups of materials, among which may be the single document, picture, or image that is required. This is what has not, and likely will not, change. The Web, FTP, and Gopher share this structure. So, too, do systems-at-large—Internet, CompuServe, Knight-Ridder Information, and the rest. One establishes an access system and an appropriate connection. Internet users then must identify the type of computer site to be visited, the directory to be examined, and the file required. A decision tree for users, then, is:

Chose access system
    gateway provider
    remote modem access
    direct access
Chose connection
    shell account
    PPP/SLIP connection
Identify type of library resource
    CompuServe
    Internet
    Knight-Ridder Information, etc.
Chose:
    Conference or Library
Identify File/Group
Read or retrieve

FINDING THINGS

Finding things on the Internet, and especially the World Wide Web, is a growth industry. Book stores and the book sections of computer stores are chock-a-block filled with not merely how-to directories (*The Dummies Guide to the Internet*), but also with directories of online resources. Some focus on materials and resources in specific geographic areas, *The Canadian Internet Handbook,* for example, while others are general, nonspecific print archives, like *The Internet Yellow Pages.*[3] A few minutes of browsing through one of these may save hours of frustrated, online searching. Now, these catalogs are being reformatted for CD-ROM, so they also can be searched offline by home computers with the appropriate drives.

Print magazines and newsletters (which usually have electronic versions) are another resource. In learning about the Web, for example, I subscribed to *Internet World,* which identified issue by issue hundreds of different Web sites of potential interest. I then faced a decision: do nothing but log onto potential useful sights all day, or cancel my subscription and find better ways of identifying personal resources. It is often more efficient to simply ask a more expert acquaintance what resources he or she prefers to use. For example, a colleage, CTV reporter Mark Schneider, recently asked me to provide him with a list of journalism resources on the Internet. It wasn't clear, from his message if he wanted resources on journalism or sources that might aide in reportage. Nor did I know what type of online access he had, or if he understood what search engines were. Knowing none of these things, I sent him a collection of sites I had been using myself (see Example 6.3).

Increasingly, user groups on all of the services have dilligently announced and sometimes cataloged Web sites. So another venue is simply to post a query in one or another conference. In the Compuserve Journalism Forum, for example, adepts have put together listings for those, like Mark Schneider, who are relative latecomers to the resource. The same is happening in every field and subject-oriented group.

Relying on the largess of friends who may be almost as ignorant as you are is not the most efficient strategy. Far better, and far more efficienct, is the use of an online serach engine designed to search for sites that will answer a stated search question. These automated librarians are what makes the Internet a real tool for data divers and not just a toy for surfers.

FTP users, for example, are probably familiar with "Archie," a searchable cataloging of more than 1200 "anonymous" FTP archives containing 2.5 million filenames. Archie is not a file retriever, but a file locator. It is used to search its sites for incidences of an individual word, and the name of the file title that carries it. Some remote modem access services (especially academic ones) have an Archie client on their local node, and using Archie from these sites is simply a matter of typing the name as a first command followed by the subject that one is looking for. The form is shown in Example 6.4.

This can be done by using Telnet to get to special online sites called "Archie servers," overburdened computers whose business is FTP files. A Canadian Archie server resides at McGill University—archie.cs.mcigill.ca—while in the United States there is archie.sura.net in Maryland and, among others, archie.ans.net in New York. Finally, one can use Archie the old-fashioned way, by mail. There are Archie sites in North America, Japan (archie@archie.wide.ad.jp), Switzerland (archie@archie.switch.ch), Australia (archie@archie.au), and, well, all over the world.

Example 6.3

To: Mark Schneider, INTERNET:MARKS@WIMSEY.COM.
Re: Koch references

You asked for it. Here is a small collection of journalism-related resources which might be of use to you and your work. Commands are in italic:

1. Society of Professional Journalists (SPJ):
      ftp://netcom5.netcom.com//pub/spj/html.spj.html
   This address links to John Maulowich's "Awesome List," Mark Leff's list of journalism-oriented BBS systems, Adam Gaffin's media email list, the SPJ chapter directory, Steve Outing's list of online newspapers, etc. For a one-stop journalism location, it's hard to beat. If you're not on the Web, just e-mail to the SPJ mailing list:
      Listserve@netcom.com   with
      subscribe SPJ-Online   on the message line.

2. An extremely hot place for breaking stories is the Poynter Institute of Media Studies' library and "hot news" sections. They're designed and fed by my friend Nora Paul, the Poynter's innovative chief librarian.
      http://www.nando.net/prof/poynter/home.hpml

3. There is also a "Clearinghouse for Subject-Oriented Internet Resource Guides" at the Univ. of Michigan. Gopher to
      gopher.una.hh.lib.umich.edu.
   and look for the following directories: Journalism-general info.; Journalism-listservs and usenet; News-regional non-daily posts; and J. Makulowich materials.

4. You also can use e-mail to get his lists from:
      Listserv@ULKYVM.LOUISVILLE.EDU
      [then send this message] *get Journalism Lists F=Mail.*

5. There is also the *CARR-L* List on computer-assisted reporting and research. At present it has 337 subscribers in 18 countries Send the message, "subscribe Computer Assisted reporting and Research, Mark Schneider," to
      listserv@ulkyvm.louisville.edu

Hope this helps. If you need more, let me know.

                                                      Tom

Example 6.4

```
Address: archie@aarchie.rutgers.edu
(And in the body of the message type)
find <search term>
set mail to <your address>
quit
```

In, say, 1990, Archie was state-of-the-art stuff. But then Gopher and Veronica became the "wunderkind" of online searchers. Gopher searches through various libraries for a single search phrase ("health" or "heart" or "cardiomyopathy") and brings the references it finds together for user review. It is not really a universal search engine, but one that roams through a major data collection and retrieves material which matches the terms that one has stated, the question addressed to the mega library.

Example 6.5

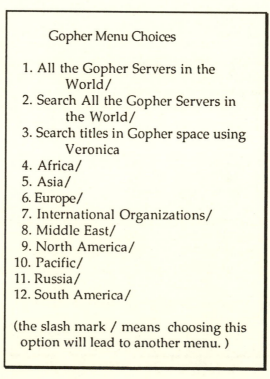

```
Gopher Menu Choices

1. All the Gopher Servers in the
     World/
2. Search All the Gopher Servers in
     the World/
3. Search titles in Gopher space using
     Veronica
4. Africa/
5. Asia/
6. Europe/
7. International Organizations/
8. Middle East/
9. North America/
10. Pacific/
11. Russia/
12. South America/

(the slash mark / means choosing this
 option will lead to another menu. )
```

Gopher is itself a network, a portion of the whole that allows users to access other computers with similar facilities, irrespective of their geographic location. Say, for example, that I tell my access provider to activate its gopher. I am offered a chance to use it to search a single collection (say, at sura.net) or to access other Gopher and information servers around the world. In the directory catalog for Gopher choices shown in Example 6.5, a slash (/) at the end of an entry simply lets the user know that toggling that choice will lead to another catalog or director with further choices. It says, "Don't ask me. I'm just a damn branch on this tree."

If I choose option 12, South American Gophers, for example, the next menu will offer the names of gophers in different South American countries that I can access. If I want to search the directories of International Organizations (the World Bank, UN, etc.), choosing option 7 will lead to categories of available resources, organization by organization. If I want international economic data, I might chose the World Bank Gopher files. For international data on the spread of AIDS, well, the World Health Organization is the place to go.

For directed searches, one calls on option 3, and queries "Veronica." Think of Gopher as a series of catalogs that can be searched one at a time or simultaneously. "Veronica," then, is the research assistant. Veronica takes key words, "medicine" or "soccer" or "Tom Koch," and searches through catalog listings of document titles to see if any have within their holdings the subject being sought online. It offers the possibility of searching for key words in document titles and general resource catalogs, or it can search only in directories. So if I was searching for "cardiomyopathy," an uncommon and very specific medical word, I would probably want to do a title search because it is unlikely that there will be catalog directories on the subject. But for a general query, "health," for example, a search of directories will be sufficient. In between is "heart," which would best be searched both in titles and directories.

In 1992 and 1993, Veronica was pretty much the state of the art. It cruised through hierarchies of varying library sites, identifying files for us all. It was masterful at guiding users through the wealth of interlocked but semi-independent libraries (read: gopher sites) around the world. But like most librarians, it was terrifically overworked. In fact, it still is. Searches often are aborted with the following harried reply:

*** Too many connections—Try again soon ***

In other words, I'm busy. I don't have time for you. Grab some coffee, eat lunch, take in a movie. Come back later. Other times, exasperated and overburdened, Veronica says simply:

*** Empty menu: no items selected or nothing available. ***

This means that the computers are so overloaded that they do not even have time to be polite. Anthropomorphizing, making the whole sound more human than it is? I am, I am, I'm guilty. But there is something human about these messages, about the curt "try again soon" and then the simple, "Forget it bud. Nothing available."

Beginning in 1994, WWW's power came to the fore. Not only is the material in the Web vast, its search facilities are light years ahead of anything else online. These are online programs, "addresses" whose computerized librarians will search across the Internet for material on subjects of interest to you. They have names like "Lycos," "Web-Crawler," "WWW Nomad," "Wizard," and "Yahoo." Most Internet software programs, as well as those available through services like CompuServe, come with several addresses programmed for immediate use. I use three of these with regularity. Yahoo and Wizard do a good job on general subject searches ("organ transplantation," "bicycling," "news or journalism," for example), while the WebCrawler and Lycos are better for pinpoint, narrow queries.

Lycos: http://lycos.cs.cmu.edu

Wizard: http://wizard.spry.com/

Web Crawler: http://webcrawler.cs.washington.edu/WebCrawler/ Home.html

Yahoo: www.yahoo.com/

Helpful as they are, however, successful searches still rely on searcher expertise. In a *CompuServe Magazine* article, for example, when writer Christopher Galvin insisted that the Web was not a good research site, a Scottsdale, Arizona, member disagreed. Galvin had commented that he could not find information on the mathematician Johannes Kepler and suggested that that signaled a lack in the system at large. Jim Richards replied in a letter to the editor that simply because Galvin could not find mention of the mathematician did not mean that it was not there. The problem, Richards said, was with the searcher, not the resource.

Using WebCrawler, Richards searched for data sites that would answer the challenge. His "search phrase," the words he typed into the WebCrawler, were: Johannes, Kepler, and Biography. This is a good, intensely narrow, directed search. He was rewarded "within seconds with a 'hit' on a link named Chronology of Mathematicians"[4] at the address:

http://alephO.Clarku.edu/~djoyce/mathhist/chronology.html.

Because it was on the World Wide Web, going to that Clark University educational address for a math history list allowed him to then access other data at other resources included in the Web page. These "hypertext links" included short and long biographies of the great mathematician, information on his "Laws," a photograph of Kepler, and a European map of the birthplaces of famous mathematicians.

Internet World writer Aaron Weiss tested several "search engines" in early 1995.[5] He asked the search program Lycos, his favorite, to find all documents or records pertaining to the photographer Fritjof Capra. It returned three references. Wow. Some librarian. Search programs like Lycos and WebCrawler may read house page abstracts as well as catalog titles. Lycos, for example, has two modes of searching: in the first, it focuses its attention on a "small" catalog of 237,000 entries; in the second, it examines a super catalog with more than 1.2 million searchable entries. The first is best for common searches, unless, of course, someone enjoys receiving 30 pages of reference material. The second is better for specialized searches for highly specific names, like Fritjof Capra, Phish, and cardiomyopathy.

Pretty impressive. Perhaps the best thing about these new tools is that they do not make the user walk step-by-step up and down the hierarchy of independent sections within the library/center; it does that for us. The computerized hierarchies (sura.net is in New York is in U.S. is in Gopher or FTP) and the paths required to find individual files are handled by the search system without much effort. At the Library of Congress, I can write a call slip for a book (Tom Koch, *The News as Myth*), include its locator (a Dewy Decimal number), and give this to the librarian, who then walks into the library's bowels, finds the book, and brings it back to me. If I tell her I want all of Tom Koch's books, well, she will tell me to list them one by one. I do not need to know precisely where any of them are in the library itself. It is the librarian's job to find the requested book or books within the whole, given the data I provide to him or her.

Like real-life librarians, each of these searchers—often called worms because of their ability to burrow through the mass of potential data— has peculiarities. Some are slow; some are speedy. Webcrawler enables searches for adjacent words (elder care) while others, like Lycos, do not. Some search programs look at the "descriptors" people load up to let directories know what data a home page holds, while others scan titles and the first twenty pages of page description. There are at present scores of different online searcher engines, each with its own individual strengths and weaknesses. Writing a home page these days is only half the battle. The other half is figuring out how to assure that search systems will recognize it and retrieve it in response to a query. That, some say, is a new art in itself.

I love these programs. They are amazing, awesome, stupendous. They are the future. Simple, easy to use, and encyclopedic. Online directories of addresses, like any directory, allow for similarly fast searches. If I wanted to know Clark University's online address, for example, I could go to the Internet directory of online addresses (http://www.internic.net.) and ask for Clarku or Clark University. Without Web access, I still could find this material by using FTP (ftp to ftp.internic.net) or Telnet (telnet to internic.net) for mail addresses. Similarly, if all I want is a Usenet group interested in, say, martial arts (or a specific art like Aikido), I use the Stanford Netnews Filter designed to search for Usenet groups and lists. On the Web, it is searched at http://sift.sanford.edu. Of course, it also can be searched by electronic mail. Simply send a message to

netnews@db.stanford.edu

and include "help" in the message body. Say what you want. Within a day, a list of pertinent groups will be returned by mail. This is "traditional" E-mail. Fill in the boxes, get the answer. Wonderful.

The Internet-at-large, this changing complex of services and semi-autonomous systems, is a curious place these days. Its User Groups may have startling, powerful discussions in some subjects areas and revoltingly silly trash in others. One can communicate with the best thinkers in a field, or listen as neo-nazis explain why everyone who is not a member of their group is worthy of execution. There are theoretical physicists on the cutting edge of cosmology, neurologists involved in unlocking the brain's working mechanisms, and philosophers seeking to make sense of both of these. There are also flat-earth fanatics, religious fundamentalists, witches, and would-be demagogues vying for time and the attention of others. The Internet has voluminous files on popular culture (from sites for the study of the Three Stooges to myriad resources for Star Trek fans), and powerful tools for research scientists interested in virtually every esoteric subject. Like other parts of the library/center/bazaar, it reflects both our shared, state of knowledge and our abysmal ignorance, mirroring prejudices and strengths alike.

It is not yet intuitive. From the days of ARPANet until the early 1990s, the Internet was dominated by bitchy, arcane computer languages that made the average user scream. Fortunately, that is changing as the World Wide Web sets the standard for ease of use and access. In the same way that the Macintosh computer's point-and-click mouse on a graphic interface changed the old, stodgy world of DOS-based commands, the Web is transforming the online world. It is still a message system, and it still navigates the hierarchies of knowledge on the latticed network of interconnected computers. However, it is a richer medium, a broader data roadway than its predecessors. That does not mean, however, that old-style text-based UseNet groups will disappear, or that documents now accessible through, say, Archie or FTP will be discontinued. Hypertext is good for some things, but not for everything. After all, not every document requires pictures and sound. Messages define the medium, methods of presentation, and distribution; it is not the other way around. And so, as the Web grows, text-based systems will be retained. And, of course, the library catalog type of logic of the whole—of the center/library/bazaar—will be retained.

The important thing, really, is how these resources can be used by people, and not where they are stored or the system used to access them. That, simply, is why the World Wide Web has been so popularly received. It joins, in one online location, called a home page, a number of disparate resources. Those materials can be text, pictures, sound, or video clips. The "page" becomes a location in and of itself, each page a gateway to other at least potentially pertinent data. For "surfers," perhaps, that is enough. But for those of us who seek data to make information that can resolve the issues of our lives, the medium is less important than the facts and opinions which are returned in these searches. In our general infatuation with the medium, the purpose of searching has been forgotten. A treasure hunt may be fun, but its purpose is real. It is not to reach a spot marked "x," but to retrieve the gold that is supposedly buried beneath. No gold, no prize. Similarly, on the Net and across the online world, what is important is not the medium, but the messages it can deliver. No matter how enjoyable the search, or how impressive the technology, if it does not present the data needed, it is as useful as a beautifully drawn treasure map whose "x" reveals nothing but sand, water, and fool's gold.

NOTES

1. The story of the origin of the interactive computer-based research and communications system has been told many times by different writers. See, for example, Patrick Crispen, Roadmap Course. (Filetype Lesson, Filename). October, 1994. (Litserv@UA1VM.UA.EDU Get Net Intro F-Mail). It is also told in most books purporting to teach Internet techniques.

2. Patric Crispen. "Levels of Internet Connectivity," Roadmap Lesson 03, University of Alabama at Tuscaloosa. October 31, 1994, 2.

3. Harley Hahn and Rick Stout, *The Internet Yellow Pages*. New York: McGraw-Hill, 1994.

4. Jim Richards. "The Internet." *CompuServe Magazine*, September, 1995, 4.

5. Aaron Weiss. "Hop, Skip, and Jump." *Internet World*, April, 1995, 41–44.

7

Mute Dialogues: Hope and Despair Online

Wonderful as they may be, these electronic resources are only as good as the answers they provide and only as efficient as the data they return. The essential question, therefore, is whether they provide access to public information, general opinion, specific data, and other resources that we as individuals need? Do they offer a "citizen news," one that couples the official word and the public voice? Put another way: Are messages available through this medium that are unavailable elsewhere? Increasingly, the answer is . . . yes. That is why so many people are turning away from traditional news and going online for help and data. It is also why mystery writers and moviemakers see in the online world a set of resources as compelling as the fictional subjects who use them.

These days, the final, fatal clue is no longer hidden in a twist of tobacco or a bit of shag carpet carelessly carried from the crime scene in the pants cuff of the murderer. But then, the self-confident, physically adept heroes who pursued such links between the murderer and his work—a pantheon of detectives stretching from Sherlock Holmes past Sam Spade and Philip Marlow to Robert B. Parker's Spenser—similarly are becoming passé. In their place, the gawky and socially inept computer genius is becoming the crucial agent to crime's solution and, in the process, a centerpiece of our fiction. In murder mystery stories like Patricia D. Cornwell's *Cruel and Unusual*, the crucial evidence is not found on the corpse left in the alley or even the one in the bedroom; it instead is hidden in the hexadecimal code of the state's computer system, a fact that is concealed to all but the maladjusted, teenage niece of the heroine, Dr. Kay Scarpetta.

The fictional medical examiner for Virginia wants Lucy, the visiting daughter of her divorced sister, to be a "normal" teenager, to "be considerate," and perhaps to "broaden" her horizons in socially acceptable ways. But the precocious adolescent finds computers preferable to people, and the hieroglyphics of a hex-dump more interesting than either the shifting codes of peer exchange or the more ordered but still often incomprehensible behavior of adults. With the aide of a kindred spirit, the teenage daughter of an FBI agent who is also involved in the investigation, Lucy surfs the structure of the state computer system until she finds the binary anomaly that points to a pattern of complicity, the code that breaks the puzzle of the case.

Patricia Cornwell did not invent the computer-literate but socially adept teenage character. From the novels of William Gibson through the media of TV, cinema, and novel, the kid and the keyboard have become as predictable a team as the spindly child and the wise martial arts instructor, or boys and girls in the thrall of first love. From the depths of their often illicit access to official documents, these investigators illuminate a crucial datum that will convict the suspect whose guilt everyone knows but nobody else can prove. Scanning and often altering supposedly inviolate official records from the solitude of a flickering terminal, these maladjusted but empowered electronic searchers create the context in which physically mature and socially secure but otherwise obtuse humans save the day. As a boon, the infant savants find their loneliness and angst diminished for a time, and their abilities and individuality recognized by those same adults who, at the beginning of a story, dismissed them as inconsequential and perhaps recalcitrant children.

It is not the least of ironies that online communication, long assumed to be the virtually exclusive preserve of lonely nerds and antisocial geeks, has become a refuge for those who seek in crises the solace of community and the support of their peers. Often at the urging of teachers, doctors, parents, employers, and friends, people of all ages and backgrounds are discovering online resources to be an antidote to the deficits of modernity. The reality of contemporary online communication bears only a faint resemblance to either the computerized searches of fiction or the promised land confidently described by experts—a landscape of multimedia presentations in a 500-channel universe of perpetual shopping, wrestling, and cinema. Instead, the online universe of conferences, newsgroups, and forums is filled with mute pleas and responses typed to the world in often execrably spelled and grammatically eccentric prose. Amazingly, the world answers.

Fumbling and uncertain though these forms of interactive, electronic communication may be, the future of the often promised and badly named electronic highway is being hacked out today, forum message by conference reply, on bulletin boards and information systems which themselves are rarely more than a decade old. Like the telephone, which in its early years was never perceived as a medium capable of carrying the common hopes, pathos, and mundane messages of ordinary people (it was to be a transmitter of official news and sanctioned arts), the potential of linked computers for human intercourse is being discovered by users who now are adapting online's power to their own needs in ways that commercial developers never anticipated. To them it is a medium to join with others, a place to seek information and advice, a means with which to slip by the restrictions of geography and the bounds of illnesses. Its attraction is first and foremost in its power to heal, one person to another. The use of computers to resolve emotional and ethical issues is one of the unanticipated boons of the democratization of bits and bauds, the kernels of characters transmitted over phone lines in binary code at specific speeds.

It does not matter if the exchange one uses is an Internet Usenet group, a CompuServe Forum, a conference on the Well, or a local bulletin board service set up by some city agency. What matters is whether the chosen venue provides an opportunity for appropriate discussion, for the exchange of necessary data, for a respondent who can speak to your immediate concerns. To understand the power of these services as they are being used today, consider the exchanges in Examples 7.1 and 7.2, in which preadolescent boys discuss the death or illness of their parents. Posted on a Toronto, Canada, bulletin board, its originator, 11-year-old Andrew first uploaded a message about the difficulties of being the child of a very ill parent. It was, he said, his intention to create an online support group for others facing similar situations.

This string of typed messages continued for months as both children and adults were drawn to its discussion. It was hosted and promoted by Ablelink (http://www.ablelink.org), a bulletin board (BBS) created and supervised by the non-profit organization, Ability Online. Both Ablelink and Ability Online are the creation of Dr. Arlette Lefebvre, aka "Dr. Froggie," a staff psychiatrist at Toronto's Hospital for Sick children and "sysop" (system operator) Brian Hillis. A retired fireman, Hillis' days are now spent solving the myriad problems the often quirky and sometimes difficult system computers seem to spawn daily. The identifying locators for each message—names, reference numbers,

Example 7.1

To: ALL   Refer#: NONE
From: ANDREW COBBER   Status: PUBLIC
Subj: DEATH IN THE FAMILY
Conf: KIDS TALK (27)   Read Type: TEXT SCAN

I was recently asked to write a short paragraph on coping with
a sick parent by Dr. Froggie. My father just recently passed
away. It would seem there is some kind of rule book on how one
should react or feel when a member of your family has passed
away or is terminally ill. People are always expecting me to
stop my life and grieve for my father but I can't. I'm a big
beleaver in letting life live on. I grieve in my own way on my
own time. While my father was dying (the last three years) I
had no one to talk to except for Dr. Froggie that could understand
how I was feeling. It would have been nice to have a club or
conferance where I could talk/write to others with the same
situation who would know how I was feeling but there isn't one.
My problem is over but there are many other teens out there
with the same kind of problem. Dr. Froggie and I are trying to
get a conference to help make it a little smother for those of you
with termanaly ill parents. Well I guess that is about it, so I
guess I should get going. So until next time, bye.

Andrew

---

and subject titles—have been altered to assure the privacy of system
users. Otherwise, the messages are presented as they were posted,
complete with the sometimes eccentric and occasionally poetic spelling
and grammar common to the prose of 7-, 8-, and 11-year-old children.
(See Example 7.3)

   On the Ability Online bulletin board there are about 250 different
conferences, each serving a different subject area or interest group.
Kids Talk (section 27) is a section set aside for children who wish to
discuss their problems, and adults who may wish to meet with them.
The system at large, and thus each section of it, is accessed by local
users through a single, coordinating telephone number (416-650-5411)
that automatically shunts callers to one of ten incoming lines; or, if

Example 7.2

```
To: ANDREW COBBER                    Refer #: 504
From: WARREN NIVITSKI                Status: PUBLIC
Subj: DEATH IN THE FAMILY
Conf: KIDS TALK (27)              Read Type: TEXT SCAN


  hi Andrew
i think it's a good idea you have but what about if you don't
know what is going to happen to your mom or dad because they
have a tumer that could get better or could get worse that's
tough too?

  Warren


            •              •              •


To: WARREN NIVITSKI                   Refer #: 513
From: ANDREW COBBER                   Status: PUBLIC
Subj: DEATH IN THE FAMILY
Conf: KIDS TALK (27)              Read Type: TEXT SCAN


  How are you doing? I heard about your mother. I'm trying to
get a program going for kids [with] an ill parent so that it will
be easier for them to cope. Well, I must get going now so it was
nice to hear from you and talk to you later.

  BYE-BYE
Andrew Cobber
```

they are all in use, it denies access with a busy signal. The system sysops, Mr. Hillis and Dr. Lefebvre, constantly are searching for new corporate sponsors who will pay for more lines and more equipment to serve their expanding clientele. In the interim, however, Andrew, Warren, and other young devotees often must make their forays into the communal solace of online communication at off-hours and odd times, when system use is less heavy.

Whenever they log on, however, suspended conversations await their return. Messages sit in the netherworld of computer storage, awaiting inspection by curious parties who then are free to reply. The

Example 7.3

> To: ANDREW COBBER   Refer#: 521
> From: WARREN NIVITSKI
> Subj: DEATH IN THE FAMILY   Status: PUBLIC
> Conf: KIDS TALK (27)   Read Type: TEXT SCAN
>
> hi Andrew.
>
> i got your message and your right it is tough when none of
> your friends have sickness in the famaly and they dont
> understand when your in a bad moude. bye for now.
>
> Warren

dialog grows almost organically, developing weight as more people find themselves drawn to the issues and feel compelled to participate by responding to a message string.

This is a far cry from the old stereotype of the online devotee, once described by Joseph Weizenbaum in *Computer Power and Human Reason*, as the "Bright young men of disheveled appearance, often with sunken glowing eyes, [who] can be seen sitting at computer consoles . . . until they nearly drop, twenty, thirty hours at a time." These are children simultaneously learning to write, to type and to express feelings; they are kids pecking away on a machine in Dr. LeFebvre's office, or on one provided for them by Ability Online. The program's administrators scrounge, borrow, and beg for old computers which it can distribute to needy members.

"Dr. Froggie," the online nickname used by Dr. Lefebvre, is a wry reference to the pejorative that once described French-Canadians to other Canadians. This nickname enforces her official position (she is, after all, *Dr.* Froggie) while simultaneously disarming her clients with a name as friendly as that of Jim Hanson's muppet character, Kermit. This frog, however, took an M.D. degree with a specialty in psychiatry and believes passionately in the power of online communication as both an analytic and a therapeutic tool.

Dr. Lefebvre had encouraged Andrew's original posting as part of her treatment of both him and of other children of ill and dying parents. There was, she said, simply nowhere else for them to turn; and in the community at large were sympathetic adults whose own experiences might assist her charges. Like a matchmaker in a European

Example 7.4

```
To: ANDREW COBBER                          Refer# 528
From: ALVIN NOGOLA                       Status: PUBLIC
Subj: DEATH IN THE FAMILY
Conf: KIDS TALK (27)            Read Type: TEXT SCAN


Andrew you are rite. my mom dide last nite but nobodee in my
 school nose what it is like. what did you do when you got mad ?

Alvin


            •            •            •


To: ALVIN NOGOLA                           Refer#: 532
From: ANDREW COBBER                      Status: PUBLIC
Subj: DEATH IN THE FAMILY
Conf: KIDS TALK (27)            Read Type: TEXT SCAN


 Sorry to hear about your mother. You asked me what I did when
I got mad. I would certainly not suggest for you to do this, but I used
to punch walls and broke my hand many times. Try to find some-
body you can talk to who'll understand or listen. You  need to get
this out of your system because it'll eat away inside if you do not.
 Take care,

Andrew
```

ghetto, she would urge one or another person to meet, to read a specific message, or to respond to another's queries or plea. A good match
creates a dialog that carries the emotions and insights of all participants
forward, as when Andrew equates his violence with a lack of dialog,
advising against this to another (see Examples 7.4 and 7.5). Soon after
Andrew's first posting, she encouraged me to join the discussion.
While it may seem strange that a specialist in elder care would join a
string dominated by the issues of children, I was quickly drawn to the
commonalities of bereavement and loss, to the isobars of emotion that
affect us all (see Example 7.6).

I had not thought of that experience, my first with death, in many
years. Alvin's message reminded me how often children are excluded
from the rites of grief that serve to comfort adults. It is not merely that

Example 7.5

To: Alvin Nogola   Refer#: 587
From: Tom Koch   Status: PUBLIC
Subj: DEATH IN THE FAMILY
Conf: KIDS TALK (27)   Read Type: TEXT SCAN

Alvin.

  Sorry to hear about your mom. Yes, nights are often the hardest. When my grandfather died, I had a bow-tie of his. I put it under my pillow at night. I also had his picture nearby. It helped a bit.

Tom

---

bereaved parents may ignore the emotional needs of silent children ("Actually, she/he's coping very well, better than me," says the parent), but that adults have resources we deny to the young. Those who have reached maturity may bury themselves in work, take refuge in alcohol, or choose what psychologist and geographer David Stea once called "geotherapy," travel away from the site of crisis to gain distance from its pulling power.

  But children seeking perspective from distance are called "run-

Example 7.6

To: ANDREW COBBER   Refer#: 538
From: ALVIN NOGOLA   Status: PUBLIC
Subj: DEATH IN THE FAMILY
Conf: KIDS TALK (27)   Read Type: TEXT SCAN

hi Andrew ,

  i already got some body to talk to about my mom dying. there is dr. froggie, and leslie at the daycare. but they are not there when i go to sleep at nite and thats when i miss her most.

  Alvin

---

aways." Those who take out their rage in schoolyard fights are called "problem kids." There is thus little wonder that a boy like Alvin, muted by the vastness of his grief, would go to school and say nothing. That Andrew would break his hand expending his fury and frustration against the hard surface of a wall is no surprise either. Violence often results from isolation, from a lack of people with whom to talk about an experience.

Adults often are trapped in the same loneliness and rage that affects these children. In my book, *A Place in Time: Care Givers for Their Elderly*, Margaret Nelson tells how, when she was caring for her ailing grandmother, she would kick holes in the wall behind the old woman's chair when frustration and isolation became unbearable. "My favorite thing was, I used to put my foot through the wall. I used to get so mad I would kick the wall . . . and sometimes I'd get my foot stuck in it. Literally, I had to take my aggravation out somewhere, and that was it." There was no one for her to talk to, no other way she could relieve the rage she felt. Plastering the wall became a part of weekly life, an additional irritant and an act of penance as well as simple necessity. Better, she said, to wreck the repairable wall than to attack the old woman she loved despite the problems they faced together.

"Get someone to talk to," Andrew says to Warren. Violence is not an answer. Find a way to make the fear go away, to allow the anger to settle. "Someone" means a person familiar with Warren's particular rage and fears, a like-minded soul who knows what it is to be a child who has lost a beloved parent without being able to talk to teachers and schoolmates about that fact and its ramifications (see Example 7.7). Too often, that person will not be found in the family, whose members are each absorbed in his or her own grief, or in the schoolyard, where priorities other than sympathy rule. But somewhere among the thousands who cruise the online world there will be those who have felt the same distress, who remember the rage and fear, and who can speak directly to it.

I had expected a polite but distanced response, the type kids often give to well-meaning but obtuse adults attempting to enter their world. But Andrew and I rapidly became pen pals, messaging one to another over a period of months. I learned about his family and home, about his battles with his sister, and the difficulties of his life and world. Occasionally, Dr. Lefebvre, who monitors the exchanges of her charges, would privately suggest a response to me. This dialog with Andrew was not private. Most of it was posted as "Public Messages," which everyone (including his sister) was free to read. Others entered our world as well. Warren, for example, quickly became a member of my, our, electronic world (see Example 7.8).

"It's constantly amazing to me," Dr. Lefebvre said over coffee one

Example 7.7

```
To: ANDREW COBBER                        Refer#: 504
From: TOM KOCH                          Status: PUBLIC
Subj: DEATH IN THE FAMILY
Conf: KIDS TALK (27)              Read Type: TEXT SCAN

Andrew

   Dr. Froggie suggested your letter to me. I'm a writer and work a
lot with adults facing illness or family deaths. Pretty great letter,
yours. How are you doing now? I understand grieving in one's own
time and one's own way. Although he died three years ago, I find
that I still think often of my father, who I cared for when he was
sick. In those first months after he died, I'd flash back to a time
or experience we shared. It was sweet, but tough. For me and others
I know, it took  months to begin to merge all the memories of our
times together. I suspect Dr. Froggie will have you--and me--
writing others going through what you've experienced. How old
am I? Old! 45 years old, in fact. But sometimes, I'm not sure that
matters.

Tom Koch
```

day, that "ninety percent of what comes out in therapy is bullshit. But
ninety percent of what these kids write is what we wait in therapy to
hear." Helping others help themselves is like blazing a path through
an old growth forest while looking for the perfect tree, she explained,
the one that will be set in the living room for the Christmas season.
Computers, she says, are "the great equalizer. When you talk through
a computer, everyone's equal." Appearance does not count online. Nor
does dress, title, age, or professional standing. Formal social strictures
are held in abeyance, freeing people to speak to one another without
reserve. Where else, she asks, would an 11-year-old boy confused by
the death of his parent find a temporary confident and soul mate in a
45-year-old bachelor who works with old people?

This is crucial both to LeFebvre's work and to the history of her and
Mr. Hillis' online system. A specialist in adolescents facing problems
of self-esteem, especially those resulting from obviously disfiguring illnesses, she searched in the 1980s for a means to bring her young

Example 7.8

To: TOM KOCH   Refer#: 586
From: WARREN NIVITSKI   Status: PUBLIC
Subj: DEATH IN THE FAMILY   Read Type: MAIL
Conf: KIDS TALK (27)

hello tom.

i read your letter. i know what it's like to have a sickness in the family too because my mom got a brain tumor 2 years ago. she is better now. but they could't take it all out because then she would be paralizied for life. It's scary.

Warren

---

charges out of their shells and into a community that typically would gawk at them on first meeting and stare at their physical deformities. The computer, she found, was a way for "these kids to just be people. They could 'meet' others online, and when it came time to see those others face to face, they weren't strangers. It gave everyone confidence, and the ability to see people as just people." To facilitate this type of exchange, there is a conference on Ability Online called "How to Answer," where kids with obvious disfigurements or differences can discuss what to say to others, schoolmates or adults, who ask rude, embarrassing, or simply ignorant questions about their condition.

The use of computers as therapeutic tools began in the 1980s at Boston's Children's Hospital. After a friend asked George Boggs for advice about how to boost the morale of his ailing, 11-year-old son, the GTE employee began to think about how computers might lessen the isolation of hospital-bound children. His friend's son was required to stay in a sterile environment for weeks following a bone marrow transplant. "It's a unique situation to have patients hospitalized for an average of thirty-five to forty-five days within several feet of each other, yet with no communication," pediatric oncologist Howard J. Weinstein, chief of the Bone Marrow Transplant Service, told Shirley Moskow in an interview for *American Medical News*.[1] "They're incredibly curious about who's in the next bed and what's happening. And they're concerned. If they sense that something is not going well next door, they worry, 'Is it going to happen to me?' "

Mr. Boggs first sent a memo outlining the boy's situation to fellow

GTE researchers, 60 of whom responded with offers of help. "I thought of it as a technological challenge, but it turned out to be a very different critter altogether," said research psychologist David A. Fay, an early volunteer. As the program progressed, he and others donated thousands of hours over several years in the design of what became the KidBits computer network. They then had to not only teach children how to use the donated computers, but also to train the hospital staff in the simple protocols of online correspondence. The system, which began with simple Dial-a-Joke programs, quickly expanded from a way to link children within the sterile ward to a system joining them all to the greater community of hospital patients. The next, logical step was to open the computer network to the greater community, linking the hospital and its environs by phone and modem. The result was a method that joined patients to the world of family, friends, and schoolmates. For parents of sick children, who were tied to the bedside of the sick child, it also provided a link to their world of acquaintances and out-of-reach friends.

There are isolations that are less obvious but no less limiting than placement on the sterile, quarantined ward of a modern hospital. They include the sometimes insurmountable geographies of place and time. Physical distance often separates once close members of a mobile society. Nor is there always leisure to seek advice from our communities of history, fragmented though they may be. The exigencies of crisis typically remove free time from a person's life at the moment when he or she most requires counsel and respite. Where else can adults turn, then, but to the computer?

In an Ablelink discussion with a man caring for his Alzheimer's afflicted mother and physically frail father (Example 7.9) I asked him about his day, and if he ever went to support group meetings. There was, he replied, no time for support groups, nor any free hours for visits with friends who might understand the pull between the duties of parental care, the demands of work, and his own need for relaxation or respite. Only late at night, while his parents were asleep, did he have time for himself. Computerized conferences are active 24 hours a day, and for many the early morning hours are the busiest. Late-night missals, messages written when sleep is impossible and the world is silent except for the desperate cries of all-night radio call-in shows, are a common feature of this mute universe. But then, as most nurses know, health crises most typically occur in the early morning hours. It is when we are all less certain and most vulnerable.

Several years ago, for example, Jay Allison, a Massachusetts-based radio announcer, periodically logged onto The Well in the early morning hours. Created by *The Whole Earth Catalogue* staff, The Well is a San Francisco–based conference famous for the friendliness of its members

Example 7.9

> To: TOM KOCH   Refer#: NONE
> From: PETER DONNER   Status: PUBLIC
> Subj: FAMILY MEMBERS
> Conf: ALZHEIMER'S (241)   Read Type: GENERAL
>
> It's just the three of us. I am the sole carer, with my father's
> help. My dad helps with the cooking and the shopping and my
> sister, who is married, helps out with Doctor [medical] appoint-
> ments and moral support. My sister helps when she can but she
> has a full time career.
> I work 12 hour shifts in an Oil Refinery and am away for up to
> 15 hours at a time. This is very hard on everyone. I come home to a
> real mess and being pretty tired after a 12 hour shift I let things
> slide until a day off.
> I do as much cleaning as I can, but the house is usually quite
> messy. We did try some cleaning help, but mother put the broom to
> them. She said, "No one comes into my house and does my job
> around here!" It seems that she still thinks that she is the woman
> of the house. She can't see to clean and her own hygiene suffers.
> We have a terrible time getting her to wash.
>
> Peter

and for their interpersonal concern. Jay Allison's messages, part reportage and part meditation, stretched across sleepless nights spent anx-
iously watching over his sleeping, seriously ill 2-year-old daughter.
While the very act of writing these messages to the world may have
been therapeutic, there is no doubt that Jay Allison found the supportive response of other Well members a crucial venue of support and
comfort. "They not only listened, they talked back. They helped." In
an article in *The New Age Journal*, Allison told writer Phil Catalfo, "I
found myself keeping a kind of online journal in the company of these
people I'd never laid eyes on. It seemed, kind of miraculous, really,
this communion late at night in front of the screen."

"In all of these cases, being able to reach out and communicate by
using a messaging or bulletin board type system lets me do something
I could not do before," wrote Bill Gates to John Seabrook in an online
interview that became a *New Yorker* article, "E-Mail from Bill." But
Gates, the chairman of Microsoft, was speaking hypothetically, looking

Example 7.10

To: TOM KOCH　　　　　　　　　　　　　Refer: #69
From: Bobbie Pinon　　　　　　　　　　Status: PUBLIC
Subj: Alz　　　　　　　　　　　　　　　　MESSAGE
Conf: Alzheimer's (241)　　　　　　　Read Type: MAIL

　　What do you think when an intelligent man, who worked for twelve hours a day without rest, now can't enjoy his last years on this planet? The only thing I can say in answer to my own questions is that God has worked this whole thing out. Perhaps he knew that I or others in my family couldn't have dealt with a sudden loss. Perhaps he's preparing us all for future trials.

　　Please keep me in your prayers and thoughts. Reply to my messages. I want to feel the closeness of others in this lonely apartment. I want to know that there's a purpose in this sometimes boring and uneventful job and life.

Bobbie

---

toward a future where personal and technical data would be equally available to every person. There is a feeling of "someday" in his evangelic vision, not a sense that future potentials are now in place and that today people of all ages find solace, support, and data through the electronic world he has helped to create.

"Kinship is healing," says Oliver Sacks in *Awakenings*, "we are physicians to each other." People of all ages find the very act of communicating liberating, satisfying, and essential. Sometimes, just the act of correspondence is enough. (See Example 7.10.) Bobbie, for example, does not seek advice. She needs the camaraderie of others who, like her, spend time with loved ones whose life is memory, whose only future is in the synapses of the remembered past. Bobbie seeks only to be reminded of the world beyond the confines of Alzheimer's, one in which future plans have at least an equal place to the unraveling skein of ordered response and orderly life. Others, however, are not so fortunate. They need not only community and solace, but advice, data on which to base decisions that will affect the rest of their lives and the lives of those they love.

At present, local systems like Toronto's Ability Online are joined together in a fragile series of "nets"—with names like Fidonet, Adanet, and Peacenet—creating larger systems linked through a series of dedi-

cated computers, called *servers*, which relay the questions and responses of any single community to other net members. Together,
these local boards create an international set of message systems that
are all accessible through a local telephone call. Thus MS patients in
Toronto who log onto Ability Online's MS conference (conference
number 245) with questions about new medication and research—or
simply to vent their frustration at the disease—will find themselves
communicating with people on local bulletin boards from Birmingham,
Alabama, to Fairbanks, Alaska.

Richard S's message (Example 7.11) on a CompuServe Information
Service (CIS) forum seemed, at first, unbelievable.[2] One is supposed to
ask family, priests, physicians, and lawyers about the life and death
decisions that euthanasia represents. Why resort to strangers one will
never meet in person, to faceless correspondents on a computer network? But, in a messaged conversation, Richard told me that for him
it was the logical place to obtain the data he needed. He asked questions in two online forums, one dealing with elder care and another
with religion. It was "absolutely essential, both personally and legally,"
he told me later, that he be able to state with conviction that he had
acted in a manner his mother would have chosen had she been able to
act for herself.

That is, after all, the wording of court-appointed powers of attorney,
instruments that give a loved one or trusted friend the legal power to
act for a comatose or cognitively dysfunctional person. Physicians, he
said, "gave me 'read-between-the-lines' advice and perspective, based
on their prognosis and my mother's condition. It was unsolicited, but
presented as part of their medical obligation . . . The hospital legal
department came close to harassing me, until I referred them to my
lawyer and refused to answer [their questions]." Family members are
often too close to the situation, too caught up in their own relationship
to the patient, and too involved in their own needs and memories. In
the vast membership of online, however, he could find a representative body of experience simultaneously distant enough to shed light on
his problem but personal enough to have a sense of empathy and
concern.

Within hours, people began responding to Richard's query. Almost
all answered with a reminiscence, a story detailing their own reactions
when faced in the past with a similar dilemma. One remembered how,
when a beloved mother had a ruptured aneurysm, the family had refused the advice of hospital surgeons who wanted to operate on her.
"Her heart stopped beating about 1 hour after admission to the hospital. Did I do the right thing? Yes. My mother's greatest fear was not of
dying . . . she was ready to do that . . . it was of living on machines
in a vegetable state, having others care for her." Fifteen years ago,

Example 7.11

From: Richard S. 85271,6716   To: All Topic: Some
Feedback, Please   Msg #6112
Section: Family Health   Forum: Goodhealth
Date: Wed, May 21, 1995

I would dearly love some feedback on this "pulling the plug" decision. If there are any of my mom's generation, it would help greatly to hear your perspective. She is 75, and a first generation American. Mom had her first stroke July 4th, 1988. I want to do the right thing, and many of these decisions are very tough.

My mother was scheduled to have a tube inserted in her belly so she could be fed a nutritional supplement. She was given a nose tube by which to be fed. Then she contracted pneumonia, and was shipped off to the hospital on the same Monday she was to be operated on. Two days later, I got that dreaded 2 AM phone call informing me she had suffered cardiac arrest. Three days later I learned she had lost four minutes worth of oxygen to her brain. She is 80 pounds, 50 below her weight in healthier days, and has been unconscious for six days now. On a respirator, the doctors feel that her heart beats only because she breathes artificially. So we come to "pulling the plug."

Do I have the right to decide if she dies? Was it interference with the natural process to resuscitate her, and so has she a right to die, which I must see fulfilled? Or is it interference with the natural process to take her life by turning *off* the machines that sustain it? I am life oriented, not death oriented. Even in the bleakest, loneliest and most hurt-filled and painful moments of my life, I wanted to live. I do not yet see death and its place in life. I feel as if I am messing with God's territory, and that is scary. Or has God's territory already been transgressed, and must it now be set right?

I have been so busy saying good-bye to Dad, that I don't know if I said good-bye to Mom. Dad is no longer dad, as the Alzheimer's daily robs what little pieces of his old being still remain. I have accepted that. Now he is settled into a responsible facility, and Mom dies in chunks. Have I acknowledged that?

If only God would come down and say, "It's OK, Richard." My own auto accident of two days ago, in which I survived a high speed rear-end collision while parked on the side of the highway, has made it more difficult, as I relish all the more the life I have been given through this woman whose life I must put to rest. In the back of my mind, I wonder if it is letting Mom die I am afraid of, or closing that chapter of my life ... forever.

another woman messaged, physicians had unilaterally stopped the clock on her mother, deciding without consultation that further care would be futile. Ever after, this respondent said, she has wondered whether she should have done more, should have spoken up. What is right, she and others concluded, is what comes from the agony of choice.

Months after his mother's death—she died naturally before he had to take any firm action—I asked Richard if the responses of his online correspondents had been important to him. "By and large, yes," he replied. "Some very much so. Some really projected 'hurting with me.' Many really cared, and although it happens to us all, they didn't minimize my feelings." Undoubtedly, there had been local news stories about "end-of-life" decisions. Or Richard could have gone to the local library and searched for books on bioethics. Or his lawyer may have researched legal precedents. All of these would have given him a view of the issues he faced, albeit one less personal than what he received. But those activities would have required hours if not days of research, time that he did not have. Online, through the agency of strangers, he found both case histories and intelligent advise that served his purpose well.

CompuServe is not a local volunteer service. It is arguably the largest international service of its kind in the world. In 1995, members paid $8.50 a month for basic service, including electronic mail, and an hourly surcharge for use of forums and specialized information libraries online. With more than 4 million subscribers worldwide, it has been the leader in creating an international network of user-driven forums and conferences, a company whose bottom line was built on turning the networked power of mainframe and personal computers over to nontechnical, everyday end users. The scale of its membership creates a worldwide base of member expertise. Traveling to Oaska, Japan? No problem! Log onto the Travel or Foreign Language Forums to Osaka members who are anxious to practice their English online.

Its history mirrors the growth of online resources generally. Begun in 1969 as Compu-Serve Network, Inc., an insurance company's in-house computer processing center, it went independent in 1975, one of a then expanding number of computerized service companies. Purchased by H&R Block, Inc., in 1980, CompuServe was an early leader in the business of online information for professionals when it decided to expand its services to individual users. It opened its computer banks to users with ideas for online conferences, called forums, creating a user-driven, subject-oriented service. "Early services were developed by 'cut and try,' " John Meir, vice president of Market Development and Services, told *Online Today*, the company magazine, on its tenth anniversary in 1989. "If you had a product idea and could put it together, we put it up on the Service. It was deemed successful if people used it."

From the start, CompuServe sought interested experts who would monitor and oversee client user groups. Thus its Human Sexuality Forum, run by psychologists Howard and Martha Lewis, combines the frankness and expertise of Doctor Ruth with the common sense familiarity of Ann Landers. An early leader in information for the AIDS community, queries to the forum are all answered carefully, whether "concerned" is the pseudonym of a 13-year-old boy concerned about the effects masturbation, or a transsexual whose specific concerns are, to the layperson, esoteric to the point of incomprehension. While many questions are simply answered by other members, the forum's health professionals also offer the best medical and psychological information their degrees and specialized training can provide. In recent years, HSX, as the forum is known, has also developed "closed sections," which are support areas for people with what are politely known as "special needs," that is, everything from men who have a strong preference for unusual underwear to HIV-positive individuals seeking communication about confronting life with AIDS.

This is not simply "feel good" pablum for the psychologically crippled. Both the conference center and the library together are increasingly the first venue approached by people faced with personal questions, dilemmas, and crises. These services similarly and seamlessly provide assistance to a reporter covering a plane crash, a child with a sick parent, and an adult facing a personal crisis. The reported data of writers, researchers, ethicists and theorists are in the library. But it is in the Conference Center that human experience is offered to balance that official body of data. Together, the Conference Center and Library are a combination whose power has been ignored by those critics who sneer at online resources.

They shouldn't sneer. More than 50 years ago, Alcoholics Anonymous was born out of the simple revelation that people coming together to share their pains and triumphs could achieve goals that few might gain alone. From those beginnings, a host of self-help and support groups has grown into a movement with more than 50,000 different venues in the U.S. alone. In addition to Alchoholics Anonymous there is Narcotics Anonymous, Weight Watchers, Stop Smoking groups, and cancer support groups.

They work. Cancer patients meeting for mutual support and information live on average more than a year longer than those who face their illnesses alone. This may be because support groups provide data on diet, stress reduction, and means to access better care. It may be, as some suggest, that human interraction is itself an immune booster, a positive factor for long-term health. I suspect that both are true, and that online or offline we all need a greater mixture of interpersonal observation and relevant data than traditional venues can provide.

Sometimes, what is needed is very simple—a sympathetic listener and a bit of information. Like the reporter whose need to know the scuttlebutt about Mitsubishi MU-2 airplanes was discussed in Chapter 2, often people simply require a datum or two. At other times when the dilemma is complex, facts will not be a suitable guide. Then, we turn to the experiences of others, to the reminiscence and the observations of our fellows. In both cases, the evolving online Center and Library offer users the potential of finding, in this complex of messaged responses, the tools they need to resolve the crises of their lives.

The world of early computer hackers, described by Joseph Weizenbaum as peopled by bright young men with "their rumpled clothes, their unwashed and unshaven faces, and their uncombed hair . . . oblivious to their bodies and to the world in which they move" is gone. In their place is a constituency whose members range from young Andrew Cobber and Warren Nivitski, kids trying to make sense of death and grief, to Bobbie Pinon and Peter Donner, who are learning to cope with the frailties of age. For all of them, online is a means to seek the data that will make life comprehensible, and perhaps, a bit more bearable. That many find a bit or byte of required data or shared counsel in this medium makes some people uneasy. It is, after all, a technology so new that many have yet to explore its current potential.

How can an isolated user find "community" in a medium where one sits alone in a room in front of a box? Where is the humanity in typing a message to post in an area where others may or may not read it? Critics argue that this is the cancer of modernity's fragmentation, not a cure or solution. "Our technologies have not yet eradicated that flame of a desire," writes Sven Birkerts in *The Gutenberg Elegies: The Fate of Reading in an Electronic Age,* "to be, at least figuratively, embraced, known and valued not abstractly but in presence. We seem to believe that our instruments can get us there, but they can't. Their great power is in the service of division and acceleration."

And yet, millions of people daily turn on their computers and log on to one of scores of commercial services or thousands of regional bulletin board systems that are linked, through one or another net, to the world. Online they join Alcoholics Anonymous, Narcotics Anonymous, and various less well known support and self-help groups, melding in association despite geographic isolation. They seek help, consolation, and information from the forums of CompuServe, the conferences of Ability Online, and the services of Prodigy, America Online, and the rest. Despite the dire warnings of erudite critics of modernity's electronic tools, these new technologies are attracting devotees at an unprecedented rate.

"Get a life," advises Cliff Stoll, the former apostle turned apostate of the Internet. In his 1995 book, *Silicon Snake Oil*, for example, he insists that a life spent online is no life at all. "Just say no," enjoins Sven Birkerts. Life is not in the electronic frontier. But they and others miss the point. Online resources are not a substitute for life, they are not an "alternate reality." They *are* an adjunct to our knowing in exactly the same way that the telephone, the library, and the mails have informed us and assured our communications. I spend hours online that once were spent doing library research; I answer electronic mail that, ten years ago, would have come to me courtesy of the federal postal service. I may "chat" online with a friend or colleage who, a few years ago, would have telephoned. The medium of our learning is irrelevant to the need we have to know. My research is the issue, not which library I visit in the search for data. It is the correspondence that is critical, not the service I use to deliver the message itself.

If nothing else, online computer resources are a boon to the cause of literacy, an impetus to the many forms of written communication. To use any of these electronic services, one must be able to write a comprehensible sentence, and to read the writing of another. To offer an opinion or confront another online member's position, eloquence in disputation is a virtue. The children who are growing up with CIS, Ability Online, and the Internet are developing written communication as part of their earliest socialization. Adults who for years wrote little more than annual birthday cards and Christmas letters now find themselves struggling with typing tutors, working on their online messages, writing and reading in a vast bazaar that joins the resources of the library with a literate party line whose participants stretch around the world.

Some insist that these marvels of the digital age are not and cannot be agents of community. Some agree with Sven Birkerts: their "great power is in the service of division." But the most vorciforous critics are rarely habitué of the forums and conferences whose power they dismiss. This is not surprising. Worthies of every age condemn the evolving media of public discourse and entertainment. Shakespeare's theater was an evil that pulled people away from worthy works, they said. Popular novels were corrupting the youth with licencious and daredevil tales. Radio carried "jungle music" that would result in mass pregnancies. And television, well, we know about that. Evil. Pure evil. But still, we who watch are informed, educated, and sometimes moved. The new is only a step forward from the old, but those who cannot walk forward always feel compelled to condemn it. And so it is, today, with online resources and the data they offer us all.

Since the days when love affairs first were carried out by hand-written letters, people have used words joined first in sentences and then in paragraphs to convey their feelings to others with whom they could not speak. And in those days, affairs not only of the heart but of the state were executed, quite admirably in fact, through the agency of written rather than oral communication. Why should it be any different here? The fact is one of distance between people, of isolation and separation. The act of writing is one of willful communication to overcome those barriers, and that in itself is a powerful force not for division, but for unity. Whether one's message is delivered by the hand of a court courier, slipped through a facsimile machine, placed in a home mail box, or sent to a digital address is secondary to the act of communication, and the data that is transmitted.

The telephone did not destroy literacy or render the international mail service obsolete. The cinema did not relegate the still camera to antiquity. Television news did not obliterate the world of printed magazines or newspapers. In the evolution that these new technologies represent, new potentials will develop as they always have, allowing the best of what has been to survive, but in a broader and more egalitarian way. Who cares, in the end, if the critical clue is in a strand of tobacco or a file on a computer service? The important thing is the detective's search, the villain's gile, and our touching belief that ill will be well in the end.

The often promised "information highway" of the future will be built along the network lines of the databahn that is in use today. It is a tenant of system theory that as old networks mature and become overfull, new ones spring up beside them, first taking the excess traffic the antiquated lines cannot handle and then carving out new territories for themselves. Footpaths lined the Mississippi River long before the steamboat dominated its water course. Later, trains paralleled the river's path, hauling freight at a cheaper rate than could their predecessors, the famous steam (and then diesel) river vessels. Boats have not disappeared from the Mississippi, however. Even though the automobile and airplane now dominate regional travel, trains have not ceased their travels along the river's banks. Similarly, the printing press did not cause storytelling to cease. Telephones did not end the world of literacy. Television left its predecessor's clientele, devotees of radio, largely in place. We add to the existing networks, we do not easily abandon what has served us well. And so it may be that the mute world of online communication, the silent world of the data searcher, will remain a potent resource long after the promised land of futurists comes into being.

By then, of course, Andrew will be an adult with children of his own, and I will be old, arthritic, and hard of hearing, tapping painfully on my computer's keys or whispering into its voice synthesizer, waiting for him to comfort me amidst the frailties of my own advancing, cantankerous age.

NOTES

1. Moscow, Shirley. "Making Hospitals User Friendly: Computers Help Children Fight Isolation, Ease Recovery in Volunteer Program." *American Medical News* 34:3 (January 21, 1991), 709.

2. For a longer analysis of this string, see Koch, Tom. "The Gulf Between: Surrogate Choices, Physician Instructions, and Informal Network Choices." *Cambridge Quarterly of Healthcare Ethics* 4:2 (1995), 185–192.

8

"Virtual" Realities: Sex and Love Online

There is no "virtual reality." From the perspective of daily experience, life is never "almost," or "nearly," real. Fantasies and imaginings are titillating experiences whether they are fueled by literature, the cinema, or an online forum. And yet, every day, someone writes another article about the glories of the new "virtual reality" as if experience came in degrees that could be measured against some external yardstick of the real. Crash a plane in a computerized flight program and the crash does nothing but end the sequence, perhaps with the message: "Try again, ace?" There is nothing "virtual" about such programs, their distance from experience is manifest and absolute. Crash a plane in the real world of passenger-carrying airplanes and there is only the sound of explosion, of crumpling metal and screaming people.

Reality is what happens to us as individuals and between us as a people. Fantasy is a means by which we work out the problems of our physical and emotional lives. These tools can be extremely powerful vehicles for understanding life's events. But that does not mean they approximate, equal or replace the lived reality that is our world. No matter how life-like or sophisticated a program may be, simulations are never more than shadowy approximations of the real. Even the most realistic movie or the most compelling book, early forms of "virtual reality," only inform but do not alter or replace the experience of mundane experience. Despite its popularity, the term "virtual reality" does not define but instead obscures what actually occurs when people interact electronically.

If "virtual reality" is an oxymoron, then the promise of a "virtual" community unfettered by geographic proximity is similarly incorrect. Communities exist over time as forums for ongoing interactions. They transcend a single interest or purpose. They are associations that stretch across the bandwidths of our lives. What one finds online is something very different. As the dialogs in the last chapter made clear, online associations are typically "pick-up" associations that are based on need or interest. Like the memberships of self-help and support groups that coalesce about a single problem, they are usually limited to a question, an issue, or a single interest and expand no further. Like all associations, online exchanges can be mundane or exceptional, feverish or lackadaisical, brief in duration or occurring over months. Whatever the realities of any single exchange, they are, for better or worse, a part of the user's reality.

An example of the interplay of online and immediate experience, one that balances the fantasy of distanced communication and the reality of immediate association, was presented in a long and mostly private exchange that began on CompuServe's Health and Fitness Forum. It started with a query sent to the forum by Fran, a woman whose in-laws objected to her children speaking "potty language," mentioning "doo-doo" and sometimes even "shit" in the grandparents' disapproving presence. To her this was normal, childish behavior. How, she asked, should she handle her in-law's recriminations? What did we suggest in this familial atmosphere in which her husband's parents were critical of both the children and her parenting of them? Because both she and her husband, a physician, were members of a strict Christian community in a small, Pacific Northwest town, Fran said that she did not want to speak to a professional counselor. She took the problem online, she said, because the potential for small-town gossip and community disapproval was more than she could face.

As this string started, I did not think that it would be a particularly interesting or long-lived exchange. After all, strict, old-fashioned in-laws that a spouse does not agree with but cannot challenge him- or herself is a familiar refrain, almost a cliché. And, of course, Ralph and Fran were religious people who believed in honoring their elders, even those whose judgmental, demanding, coldly disapproving attitude made them difficult to love or respect. And so, as the group's sysop, the section administrator, I replied by reminding Fran that grandparents often forget the realities of daily parenting, and that their values need not be hers.

I then asked what effect this conflict was having on Ralph and Fran's marriage. Her resentment and frustration were so apparent, I suspected that this—and not only the grandparents—might be an issue, too. Had she talked to her physician husband about his parents, and how their interference made her feel? Well, she said, their marriage had a number of problems, and among them this was actually a relatively minor issue. Switched from the public forum's message board to private E-mail, Fran then sent me several long and personal letters detailing her and Ralph's tale of cyberfantasy, titillation, and real infidelity. Edited both for brevity and to insure their anonymity, her story is presented here:

FRAN'S STORY CONSTRUCTED FROM ELECTRONIC MESSAGES

I have been through a lot in the past year and half. Our marriage has had some really big problems. I could have walked out, but decided to stay and work things out. I also decided not to reveal what has happened between us to anyone, and this made it very difficult to cope with things. Now it will be almost 2 years since this all happened, and I am feeling good about our relationship.

What happened initially is that Ralph had an affair, an infidelity that resulted from a friendship he formed while online in an adult conference. Although I did not and still do not like this particular conference, the one where he met the other person, once I discovered the infidelity, my husband made it possible for me to go into the forum and read all of his outgoing and incoming E-mail and conference messages so that I could see that he was sincere in wanting to save our marriage. If he had not done this, it would have been a much longer process of rebuilding the trust that had been destroyed. And it very nearly was destroyed.

I said it was an online relationship that turned into a real physical one, and to add a twist to the story, it was with a man, not a woman. This is what made it difficult for me to be able to talk about it to anyone. How do you tell someone that your mate thinks of himself as bisexual? He made friends with this guy online, and in the beginning of the friendship, there were no clues to me that it was anything but a normal friendship. I didn't know anything about this conference. All I knew was that he was spending a lot of time messaging on the computer. I didn't realize all of the other facets of this group, or the fact that it deals with more than marital relationships, etc. In fact, they tend to deal with everything else but monogamy and stable love.

Anyway, he started this online friendship in September, and by December I started wondering why he was so intense with it. When all of this first started, Ralph had his desk and computer situated so that when I entered the room, I could immediately look over his shoulder and read what was on the screen. As the weeks progressed, when I would walk into the room quietly, it would surprise him so that he would nearly jump out of his skin. I thought this was odd. And he was also spending an unrealistic amount of time online, sometimes until 3 or 4 A.M. each morning. Then, of course, he would have to go to work a very few hours later (he is a physician) and spend a grueling day there. He wasn't getting his sleep.

One time, he was online when I came in and read very quickly, before he blipped it off the screen (he was talking live with someone else), that he was exercising and building up his physique for this guy. I didn't really catch on to this, but I thought it was an odd thing to say. He then moved his desk around to the other direction, so that before I crossed the room he could blip it off the screen. He and this other guy also devised a code system so that either one would know when their women entered the room. They must have thought we were pretty stupid. All of these little things started adding up, though, and after a time I began to get suspicious.

He changed during this period. He was no longer caring towards me or our children. For example: Although he spent hours thinking about what to buy this man and his children for Christmas, he put off buying anything for us, his own family. He seemed unconcerned or angry whenever our children or I were hurt or sick; but when this man's son had an accident while he and my husband were messaging, Ralph jumped up all scared and excited and called long distance to see how he was. I confronted him as to why he was so caring over those children and not his own. He had no explanation at the time.

After Christmas that year he started planning a so-called "medical conference" trip to Vancouver, Canada. He was planning to go without us. That was odd, because he usually didn't like to travel alone. As it turned out, he paid this guy he talked to by computer $100 to find him a hotel room. And this was strange too, because a person can just call up the conference organizers to make reservations. That's how it is usually done. Then Ralph said that the medical conference was off, and it was just going to be a pleasure trip. So he did go to Vancouver, and when he called home to say "Hi," I immediately sensed what he had done, but I had no proof.

THAT is when I started doubting. My husband's brother is a homosexual, and I guess I never really associated him with what his brother was doing until I visited an old friend who asked me if I ever wondered if my husband thought he might be gay because his brother was. That was when I started going through his computer files.

I guess my intuition took over; after he got back from his trip, I got onto his computer. I didn't know much about computers then, but I sure do now! I fished around for a while, found information, put 2 and 2 together, and figured out what had happened. I called up erased memory loads and read through them. I figured this out at about 3 A.M. one morning, while he was asleep. (I was unable to sleep due to the stress of all of this.) When he got up, I confronted him with what I had learned, and he told me the truth about this man and their trip to Vancouver.

On top of that, I learned that seven years earlier he had done this before with a perfect stranger he encountered on a conference trip. Looking back on that time, I could see changes in his behavior that stemmed from that time period. He was cold and removed. I had fallen down the basement stairs and badly sprained an ankle. It may even have been broken, but he refused to take me to the ER for X-rays. He showed no concern.

Then when I got pregnant, his first reaction was fear, which turned to happiness weeks later. Now I know that at first he was afraid he might have had AIDS and passed it on to me and the baby, and his happiness was actually relief that that didn't happen. When he first confessed, the thing that scared me most was the chance of having caught AIDS from his infidelity at the "conference," and then his lack of concern for me. I was so relieved that he did not have AIDS, but so angry that he had been so foolish.

So all this was out in the open. The way we worked things out was that my husband and I discussed our relationship and went through our "therapy" by exchanging E-mail with each other. We were able to confront each other without letting the physical body put its arms up as an armor to the discussion. In other words, our guard was down and we could be honest with each other. There were times in the beginning when I thought that maybe I wasn't doing the right thing. I didn't go to a professional counselor because of this small town we live in. I was afraid most of the counselors would know my husband and that it would all eventually be leaked out to the community.

Although I did not and still do not like this particular conference he was messaging on, once I discovered the infidelity, my husband made it possible for me to come into the forum and read all of his outgoing and incoming e-mail and forum messages so that I could see that he was sincere in wanting to save our marriage. I could see what he was saying to his "friends," and what they were saying to him.

Yes, through this time he remained on the forum, and in touch with people there. That spring, for example, he insisted that we go to Las Vegas and meet in person a couple that he knew from online. Now, that was an experience! It really hurt that he found people like this worthy of his admiration, and that he was more interested in them than those who try to live an honest moral life. The guy was a bisexual, who was also really pretty good looking. The woman was an alcoholic drug abuser who chain smoked cigarettes. She popped uppers the whole time we were there, and she talked so nervously and fast that you couldn't get a word in edgewise. She wore hip boots and short-shorts and a lace bustier in the dead of winter, all under a thin jacket that she kept unzipped and open. I was so stunned by her appearance and behavior, and so scared that this was what Ralph wanted me to become, that I cried all the way back home.

She later told my husband that she thought I was too uptight and quiet, and that *I* may have some real psychological problems! I was too flabbergasted by what I saw that weekend to say much of anything. She later messaged to Ralph that she wanted me to be her best friend. I wrote back to her that I could not in all good conscience be her friend or even associate with her. She was furious and wrote very long e-mails about me to my husband, writing about how messed up I was. Eventually she quit harping about me and left it alone.

He has changed since that time. He is quieting down some. He tries to be honest with me in how he's feeling, and making sure I know about his thoughts. It isn't always easy to swallow, but I'm dealing with it. If I were judgmental and hard-nosed, it might drive a wedge between us. We've come far, but we are still and will always be working on our relationship.

His being on that forum has helped him to talk out his feelings about his temptations, but at times it also serves as enticement. He made friends on the forum with a young man who is dying of AIDS. I think it has been a good friendship for Ralph because he can see what is happening to him as the result of foolish behaviors. My husband was wanting to go to NYC to visit the boy both in hospital by himself. I asked Ralph, via e-mail, why he wanted to go, and whether he would be tempted to do anything. He wrote back via e-mail and said that, yes, he would be tempted. I told him that he must be pretty weak to be tempted to do something like that which could endanger his own life, as well as mine, for the sake of a few moments of thrilling sex. He agreed that it was foolish and in the end decided not to go.

Ralph continued being an active participant in that conference up until about a month ago. It did keep me from putting all my trust in him. I held something back for fear that he would again become entrapped in the same behavior. Finally, he has stopped, and although he still has a few friends that he corresponds with from that group I feel no threat from them.

There were a few that I told him I refused to meet or know in any way. For example those we met in Las Vegas. But generally, the people he still corresponds with are very nice people, although not ones I am personally interested in forming strong friendships with. These are people with whom he had what's called "cyber-sex." Sex online. You know. Because of my religious convictions, I feel that "cyber-sex" is a form of adultery. I guess you could call it "lite-adultery," like you would call something "lite"-beer or "lite"-wine. But, to me it is also a breach of trust.

Ralph says that he wants no one else now but me, and wants to us to be together for the rest of our lives. He says that he is a weaker person than me, and he just has to work harder at resisting the temptations. He says it's mid-age crisis. If so, I guess he'll pass through it. I told him that it's kind of like being married to a rebellious teenager. He laughed and said he thought I was right. I did tell him, though, that if he decides to go off and do something like this again that there will be no second chance: do not even come home. I told him I couldn't go through it again.

I think his behavior in the past two years stemmed from how his parents have related to him. They were extremely strict, dictatorial types. She was always a clinging mother, he was a cold father. Ralph and his brother were never allowed to make any mistakes. It just wasn't permitted! Now, Ralph says he would like to disown them and go on. But I feel like that is giving up too soon. I don't feel it's right to give up on his parents. After all, they are in their early 60s, will be getting feeble, and will need to be taken care of. It would not be morally right to "dump" them. Plus, I see them making great strides in taking responsibility for their own actions and lives. They are seeing that maybe they have behaved in ways that were influenced by their own dysfunctional upbringings.

Yes, our love is stronger now, and our commitment and care for each other has grown. I can see such a change in my husband's behavior towards me. He has been consistent in this, too. There's not been any waning or coming and going of his love and concern. I think if he was not completely serious, I would have seen some inconsistencies. I think that for myself, I need to work on showing my care for him more. We are much more verbal about what we want from each other. We're not perfect. We have to work at it. A good relationship has to be worked on—it doesn't just happen.

None of this was virtual, neither the fantasies of "cybersex"—a messaged seduction—nor the reality of Ralph's sexual activities. It was all very real to both Fran and her husband. Much of it was excruciatingly painful to both participants, and some of it—the period spent waiting for the HIV test results—was absolutely terrifying. Messaging in the early morning hours, when there was less chance of detection, took as much energy and concentration as "sneaking around" to out-of-the-way hotels and restaurants always does. The ruse of the medical conference was, like all subterfuge, eventually transparent. The early infatuation, while confined to computerized messages and electronic chats, had a real effect on Fran and Ralph's relationship, and on his relationship with their children. A result of Ralph's growing involvement with the man he eventually met in Vancouver was a marked decrease in attention to the people he lived with every day, his wife and children. Christmas became for Ralph an opportunity to shower the "other" man and his children with gifts, demonstrating an affection and largess that Ralph could no longer show his family. The relationship was real, and so were its effects.

There is a long, long history of long-distance love, of infatuation and association at a distance. It dates back to the Middle Ages, when an affair might be begun with letters sent between respondents, handwritten notes that carried compliments and declarations of affection.

Our ancestors were smarter than we are. They knew that because it was messaged, the emotions were no less real. In those days, they did not distinguish between affairs of the heart and the physical experience that sometimes consummated these literate and literary exchanges. Love-at-a-distance was still love, and they knew that was what was truly important. Much of Fran's narrative is about a real relationship that was carried out clandestinely and at a distance, one that was, by definition, less physical than emotional and spiritual. But that does not make it less real to the children whose father seemed uninterested in them, or to the wife who only knew that her husband's mind and heart were somehow and for some reason absent. That the vehicle of this estrangement was the computer and not the post—or a scented missal hand-delivered by a trusted servant—is of less interest, perhaps, than the fact that this old form of distanced love and declaration has stood so long a test of time.

One difference between the old-style lettered love and Ralph's affair is that from the start his was more than a secret association between two people. It began and was pursued in the context of generally supportive subscribers to a specific online conference whose members generally advocated full exploration of sexuality without regard to marital bonds or other traditional restrictions. Another difference is that the messages, those electronically saved by Ralph and eventually discovered by Fran, were balanced by "real-time" chats. On most services, two or more people can meet in restricted sessions to discuss things, one typing words which will appear on another's screen. It is called "chat mode" on CompuServe and "IRC" on the Internet, and perhaps by other names on other services and bulletin boards. These are like the party lines of the early days of telephone service—shared access for people in a single area. But here, the communal service is restricted not by geography—all of those home phones served by a single trunk line—but by a subject area of interest to the participants.

All of this is very different from the 1–900 "sex-chat" telephone numbers advertised on late-night television. Those fee-for-service fantasy lines in which men can talk to "Mary-Jane" or "Betty-Sue" are studiously anonymous. They are fantasy releases with no opportunity for client and performer to meet. Here, however, the correspondents were people who shared intimate details of their respective lives, dreams, fantasies, and hopes. Ralph became concerned with the family and daily events in the life of his Vancouver friend, and others in this conference, in a way that one can never enter the life of the faceless telephone professionals on, "Call: 1-900-FANTASY (427-8279). Now!"

Fran calls all of this "lite-adultery," sin in thought if not necessarily in physical form. And, to the extent that Ralph's infatuation affected her and their children's lives, it was a real alienation of affection. Of course, she is a religious person who believes in the old hierarchy of transgressions, including those of the heart and mind, as real and palpable violations. But then, even so obvious an icon of rectitude as former president Jimmy Carter has admitted to sins of the heart, infractions of thought but not necessarily of deed. But Ralph's meeting in Vancouver was not fantasy. The online interaction, that affected his relations with his family was only a prelude to Ralph's Vancouver meeting, where he had sex with another man.

If Ralph's fantasies offended Fran, who believes in marital fidelity and strict heterosexuality, the changes in his behavior to her and their children were a greater concern. What concerned her most, however, was Ralph's active homosexuality, both with the man met online and years earlier with a stranger. This was, she believed, a real, physical threat to both her marriage and her health. Unprotected sex with a bisexual partner who presumably has had other physical encounters does raise, in the age of AIDS, the real possibility of sexually transmitted diseases. That Vancouver was not Ralph's first homosexual encounter complicated the whole incident. It revealed a side of her husband that Fran had never perceived, one that had been secretly active for years. I suspect—although this was not raised with Fran—that Ralph had other heterosexual encounters which were not revealed in this message string. His experience seven years before was sufficiently shattering. As Ralph admitted, worry about the possibility of a sexually transmitted disease had initially kept him from being particularly joyous about her first pregnancy. That AIDS or another disease might have been transmitted to her husband, and then to her and their unborn child, was a reality he had faced alone.

What is perhaps most interesting about Ralph and Fran's story is the manner in which they used electronic mail and messaging to heal the breach in their marriage caused by both his online role playing and his physical, extramarital acts. Because face-to-face discussions would have lead only, on her part, to violent recrimination—and defensive behavior by him—they decided to use the medium of his infatuation to rebuild their life together. Online, each could message frankly, saying his or her mind, and then read the other's response. In the same way, perhaps, that Fran was able to inform me of events she had been unable to share with others, she and Ralph were able to work out their crises together. The very combination of anonymity (I've never seen Fran nor Ralph, nor have I ever sat at a table with them, and yet I'm privy to this extremely personal story) and very personal revelation can be incredibly potent. Indeed, before telling me of these events, Fran showed Ralph the earlier messages we had exchanged on the "potty language" problem as evidence of my understanding and nonjudgmental nature. He then agreed that she could tell me their tale.

It seems clear to me that by opening his files to his wife, and inviting her to meet the people in his conference, Ralph was fighting a rear guard action. Certainly, the Las Vegas meeting was an attempt to introduce her to the world he had secretly inhabited. I suspect that he hoped she might like the people he liked, and perhaps become interested in the type of liaisons to which he was still attracted. But while she found the online conversations less than compelling, they also did not prepare her for the reality of her physical meeting with her husband's online friends. Not only did Fran not like the couple he introduced her to, she formed a powerful antipathy for a woman whose demeanor and habits she found distasteful. She did not want that person as a "best friend," or as any friend at all. That she was rejecting not merely a friendship but a courtship was a thought that never entered her mind.

What really terrified her, she says, is that Ralph might want her to be like that woman. If this is what he finds attractive in a woman, she asked herself, is it what he wants me to become? The disembodied fantasy of online associations was given a physical presence, and the idea that she might have to approximate it to appeal to her husband was, for Fran, almost more than she could bear. This is a common experience transposed, I think, to a slightly uncommon situation. Many married couples have had the experience of hearing paeans about a spouse's former great love, the man or woman they once almost married. Usually, those people are described as beautiful, brilliant, kind, and understanding. They are held up to us as standards against which we are to be judged, as opportunities passed by, perhaps regretfully, for the mundane realities we share today.

What a shock when we finally meet those objects of past affection and current sentimental esteem! They are inevitably less beautiful and less brilliant than a partner's description would have lead us to believe. "After I finally met this woman my husband talked about for years, I cried all the way home," a woman whose husband I've know for years once said to me about meeting her husband's great teenage love. "This quiet, mousy woman was what he had held up as an ideal to me for so many years! I was so mad at myself! I'd beat myself up for years because I wasn't like her, or at least, like the woman he had talked about."

And so Fran found that her husband's fantasy was one she could or would not share. But why the shock? After all, this was a person they had known in online messages, notes, and chats. The answer, I think, is that the difference between the online fantasy and mundane reality is necessarily vast. "Cybersex" is titillation. Physical intercourse is real. Fantasies and theories disappear, the "virtual" becomes real. At their Las Vegas meeting, all of Fran's concerns—and, I suspect, Ralph's hopes—where given a physical presence. And perhaps Ralph, seeing his wife in his milieu, understood finally that she would never be a part of the world he visited occasionally. That either he could maintain his life as a small-town physician, or his membership in the demi-monde of bisexuality he had always been attracted to.

Some would argue that as the online system evolves, the "virtuosity" of such encounters will grow. Voice activation will replace keyboard input, and visual representations of our physical selves will replace the currently mundane typed word we use in online encounters. In 150 years, there even may be the type of physical "virtuosity" promised by fiction's creators. The famous "holodeck" of "Star Trek: The Next Generation" may become a reality. "Virtuosity" may become a physical sensation. Who knows? Even then, computerized encounters will have power precisely and only to the degree they allow us a field of action, a means of experience which to the user is very, very real. It is not virtual but *simulated* experience. A reality born in technology but felt, in each individual, as excruciatingly real.

For the present, however, it is at least in part the practiced anonymity of the typed word that powers the medium. The attractions of this medium include the ability to write a message to an unseen person, and to speak without the interference of body language or vocal eloquence getting in the way. In the end, it was this exclusion of all of the many gestures and emphatic if nonverbal signals that we use in face-to-face communication that allowed Fran and Ralph to use the written message as a medium first for revelation and then reconciliation. And it was, I suspect, the faceless anonymity of our encounter that led Fran to confide in me.

There are many stories in the online world of infatuations that lead to real meetings, and sometimes to romance. The popular media loves stories of online flirtations that became real-life associations, and promotes them whenever possible. But then, in our grandparent's day, "mail-order brides" were common, and long-distance, lettered affairs were not unusual. Assignations at a distance have always needed the message, and the means of its transmission has always been a matter of logistics. Can one trust the manservant to get the letter to the lady-in-waiting? Will the postal service deliver my letter in time? None of this is wholly changed by the new electronic medium. Perhaps Grandma and Grandpa healed their tiffs by leaving letters for one another on the morning table. I wouldn't doubt it. Their generation was as prone to problems, affairs, and extramarital inclinations as our own is today. And for them, as for us, there was nothing virtual about the feelings, needs, and conflicts that they wished to express and needed to work through if life was to be a permanent association and not a matter of transient titillations and ephemeral events.

What the new technologies do is bring these age-old interests, inclinations, and concerns into both the vastness of the conference center and to the library at its core. In past years, a small-town physician in the Pacific Northwest who was a church-going pillar of the community had little opportunity to safely indulge in bisexual affairs. The world he lived and worked in was just too small, and too judgmental to accept such things. Medical conferences or out-of-town conventions might provide the chance encounter, like the one Ralph had some years before. That would be all one could hope for, however, if one wanted to maintain a "position" in society without fear of discovery. In a small town it would be hard indeed to find a group willing to discuss and fantasize, to role play and explore bisexual and multiple partners.

Among the millions of online participants in the conference center, however, it is easy to find a like-minded group with whom to correspond and chat. It was, for Ralph, a benefit of the scale of these services that he could find a small coterie that encouraged those desires both his wife and their community reflexively censored. But that did not alter the reality of the world in which he lived, day by day, or the choices he had to make. Nor, of course, did it affect the dangers of unprotected sex. Those are realities, and the "virtual reality" of "virtual communities" does not alter those hard facts.

Similarly, the vast stores of the online library carry extraordinary archives of sexually explicit materials that were formerly only available in brown paper envelopes discretely delivered in the mail, or in tawdry book stores that proper people were not supposed to visit. A friend of mine, the head of a large educational institution, has a huge hard drive that feeds his office computer. Whenever I'm shown into his office he waits until his secretary leaves and then asks if I wish to see his "latest." We then spend a few minutes reviewing the latest pornography he has downloaded from one or another online source since my last visit. To him it is one of the miracles of the machine that he can indulge his passion for anatomically graphic illustrations without having to visit dingy, back-alley bookstores or subscribe to overpriced and poorly printed magazines. Where's the harm, he asks?

Not surprisingly, there are conferences and groups online that seek to meld our almost universal interest in sexuality with the best possible information available in the library. Online services dealing with sexual issues have been the object of official concern of late, and also of political censorship. Unfortunately, their potential for education and for help has been generally overlooked. The best service of this kind that I have found is CompuServe's Human Sexuality Forum (GO HSX). It is run by Howard and Martha Lewis, psychologists dedicated to assuring a venue where questions about sex and sexuality can be answered without fear of censure or misinformation. Begun in the 1980s, it was an early leader in providing online support and information for HIV-positive individuals. In those days, when knowledge about the illness was hard to find and prejudice against AIDS victims rampant, HSX was a model of how to bring data and self-help support to a widely dispersed community that had few other places to turn.

More generally, its message board allows questions to be asked and answered by clinically trained personnel. HSX has 44 "editors," clinicians from the fields of medicine, psychology (including Dr. Joyce Brothers), and social work, any of whom may respond to a person's query. There are messages of every imaginable level of interest, knowledge, and variety here. It is a place where 13-year-old adolescent boys may ask if masturbation means that their hands will grow hairy, and where older males can seek data on penile implants. It is endlessly fascinating for voyeurs, like me, of sheltered background and upbringing.

Example 8.1 is a short sample of subjects recently listed on the Hu-

Example 8.1

TO ERIN, 15: It's normal for women to experience some bloating and cramping a day or two before they begin their periods. Your breast tenderness is also normal. For more, GO HSXKEY and enter MENSTRUATION.

TO PAT, 35: You'll find others who are interested in sharing experiences and observations about swinging in the support group called "Intimate Partners." To join, GO HSX200 and follow directions.

TO ALEX, 46: Yes, the anti-depressant your wife is on could be causing her lack of interest in sex. She should let her doctor know about this side effect. GO HSXKEY and enter DEPRESSION, MEDICATIONS, for more.

TO BETH, 17: No, you cannot become pregnant from swallowing semen. But several sexually transmitted diseases can be passed this way. For additional information, GO HSXKEY and enter FELLATIO, VENEREAL DISEASE GENERAL.

TO DAVID, 40: Yes, there are other diseases besides AIDS that are sexually transmitted and involve diarrhea with a watery stool—Giardiasis, for example. For more, GO HSXKEY and enter GIARDIASIS.

man Sexuality Forum's "what's new" information board. These brief listings are changed, week by week, in the general, open section of the forum. There are, in addition, special message areas—with questions and responses—for adults involved in special areas, from men who enjoy wearing rubber pants to men and women involved in bondage or other atypical behaviors. Admission to those areas of the online centre is restricted by the sysops to members who are consenting adults. In Example 8.1 each message (to Erin, to Pat, etc.) signals a longer question and a full response from one or another HSX expert detailed to answer the person's questions. Those full-section strings, stored in the conference itself, may also include responses from forum members.

Besides its general directory system, which leads members from the main board to subdirectories that describe specific areas of subject interest (bisexual, fantasy, male pleasure, illnesses, etc.), the whole is designed for "key word" searches. HSXKEY is a section index that allows members to use any one word (depression, venereal disease, fantasy, Giardiasis, etc.) as a search phrase that will lead to data strings stored in the forum's library section. This reference section in the conference center, the sexuality section, is an accumulation of facts that give people the data they need to weigh another's advise, or to further research an issue with which they may be unfamiliar.

This means that people seeking answers to specific questions can go directly to literature bearing on their concern, or they can use the search system to turn up more data on a response that does not fully answer their needs. Just as in old-style libraries one might go again and again to the card catalog while looking evermore deeply into a single topic, so, too, the key words allow one to explore multiple references when extended data are required.

As an example of how questions are handled with both good data and suggestions for further key word searches, Example 8.2 is a typical entry from the Human Sexuality Forum. The section it was located in what might have been labeled, on the Internet: alt.sex.male.fantasy.hsx, a section on fantasy for males in the sexuality section of a conference called HSX. A person's question, one that he (or she) might be reluctant to explore at the local library, is answered with a general reference by an authority in the area. References are available, as is more general data on both the general subject of "fantasy" and in individual sections of the forum, the experience of those who participate in them online.

When giving public lecture demonstrations on the subject of online data in the early 1990s, I would describe HSX as a model of information storage and retrieval. The quality of its presentation, its use of HSXKEY, and its nonjudgmental responses to potentially value-loaded questions were things that I admired. But after a 1991 lecture demon-

Example 8.2

DO STRAIGHT MEN HAVE GAY FANTASIES?

:: QUESTION: I'm a 35-year-old happily married man. I've never had sex with another man. But for about the last 10 years I've had some sexual fantasies about other men, although I would never really want to act them out.
 I hadn't told anyone about this. But I got up my courage at a men's support group I recently joined, and shared this with the other men.
To my surprise, four of the seven other men —all married or involved with women—said they also sometimes had gay fantasies. One said he watched "a fair amount of gay porn." Is it common for straight men to have gay fantasies?

::::::::::::::::::::::::::::::::::

:: ANSWER: Apparently so. "One research project investigating men's sexual fantasies reported that fantasies about homosexual activities are among the most common fantasies revealed by heterosexual males," says June M. Reinisch, Ph.D., former director of The Kinsey Institute and author of *The Kinsey Institute New Report on Sex.*
 She goes on to say that most people who have such fantasies have no intention of acting on them. "They simply use them to induce or intensify sexual pleasure."

For more, GO HSXKEY and enter FANTASY

stration to the annual meeting of the Freelance Editors Association of Canada (FEAC), I regretfully abandoned that part of my talk. For the editors, I had prepared an hour-long introduction to online resources of importance to editors. In addition, I attempted to describe the general structure of the electronic library and its potential uses for text editors. When I saw interest flagging, I used the Human Sexuality Forum as an example of the structure and its application to a complex subject area. Immediately, those beginning to nap woke with a start as neighbors nudged them, one by one. I described enthusiastically the use of key words as an example of how complex topics could be easily searched. "Why," I said, "the whole is arranged alphabetically, with

'M' for mammary, 'B' for breast, and . . . well, you, pick the letter. The subjects range from the simple—an adolescent's question about masturbation—to queries of such mind-boggling complexity that I have trouble understanding the question, let alone the answer." Everybody laughed, and then I moved on with the rest of the mundane material I had been hired to present.

After the lecture ended, I offered to research any question or problem audience members might bring me during the 30-minute rest break that followed my presentation. If the question was factual, I challenged; and if I could not find the answer, I would pay the editor $10. This was sheer showmanship, of course. My willingness to use online resources to research problems was, in those days, a drawing point for my public presentations. Offering to pay the questioner if I failed was bravado, pure and simple. I assumed that most would have questions about the texts they were working on, and there was no question in my mind that most would be easy to reference.

The conference organizers therefore had placed a Macintosh computer, hooked to a modem, in a janitor's closet off the main hall. The little room was like a confessional, small and intimate, with the screen as the confessor. During the break, and well into the next lecturer's talk on "The Future of Print Publishing in Canada," editors filed into my small closet, one by one, sat next to the computer and phrased their queries. One asked about financial returns of the fur trade in eighteenth century Quebec, for example. Another needed references on the extent of Japanese whaling in the nineteenth century. Those were the types of queries that I had expected, the type of research that I am used to.

They were, however, the exception. Most entered the room, closed the door, and sat in silence for a moment. " 'B,' please," the first said. "Show me 'L,' " said the next. Of 18 queries, 14 were directed to an exploration of the HSX library and its key word index system. All read the responses avidly, and regretted bitterly the lack of a printer with which to capture the response. As a researcher, of course, I was sworn to secrecy and promised never to reveal to anyone what they had in fact asked about "B," "L," or "M" in private. The second speaker on that day was somewhat annoyed, I later found out. His carefully prepared talk was punctuated by the comings and goings of different editors who visited my closet and then returned to the lecture hall with introspective looks on their faces, unable to give the future of Canadian publishing in an increasingly electronic age their full and undivided attention.

9

The Widow's Syndrome and Other Online Tales of Money

- Hey, wanna' make some money? There's this small company where you're guaranteed to triple your investment . . .

- Listen, this firm is taking off in the biotech'/robotics field and it's a sure thing. For a mere $15,000. . . .

- Wow, if the *Wealthy Barber* is right, I just have to invest a few hundred a month, every month, and by the time I'm forty I'll be able to retire, with a condominium on Maui and a Ferrari. Cool!

As every conman knows, greed and avarice are powerful drives. Almost as powerful as sex and love. The idea of making a fast dollar, of being in on the beginning of the next IBM, Apple, or Polaroid-style stock winner is, for many, simply irresistible. Cold-call specialists run through the lists, letting perspective "clients" know about great bond values, amazing stock opportunities, and superior mutual funds that are almost guaranteed to make us all wealthy and powerful. The operative word, alas, is usually "almost."

These guys are slick. Ask them why, if the deal is so good, they are offering it to a complete stranger—or not just buying for themselves—and the cold callers will say that they are getting others to join in so we can all be wealthy together. Ask them for a Standard and Poors sheet on the golden opportunity, for a bond rating, or a comparison of yields with other SIC group listings and, somehow, their enthusiasm dries right up. "Sure, sure. I'll send it," one said to me recently. "But let me warn you that time is money, and if you wait too long, well, this one will pass you by."

We are a money-driven people. Like the Ferengi on TV's "Star Trek" series, our culture is based on acquisition and profit. And so it is not surprising, perhaps, that the online universe is replete with hundreds, perhaps thousands, of financial conferences, forums, and analytic tools that are designed to allow anyone with even minimal intelligence to hook into good advice and a ream of easily understood data that will help them make financial choices. Unfortunately, these are data sources, not iron-clad information caches. Thus none will turn the financial idiot into an immediate investment sage. Nothing does that, online or offline, alas.

Whatever the available resources, they do not replace the competent investment counselor who works with a client over time to help him or her match resources to needs. They do, however, allow people to learn, and provide tools so that even an ignoramus can probably figure out when the risk greatly outweighs potential gain for a person with little capital. Most people, even the new investor, can use these tools to learn to distinguish between cautious addition to the long-term nest and a real flyer that may, in the end, be worth no more than a sea map noting the location of Davey Jone's locker. It is not surprising that these online business tools are useful. After all, they are the same ones that are typically used by most full-time financial analysts, portfolio managers, and the very well healed, venture capitalist. Fortunately, however, they are downscaled and simplified for the neophyte.

In the pit, where stockbrokers hang out, it is called the "widow's syndrome," and the unscrupulous among them may think of it as a guaranteed down payment on the next BMW or a nice little yacht. Women who have never written a check, managed money, or been informed of their familial resources find, after the deaths of their husbands, that they have anywhere from $100,000 to several million dollars to manage. Their husbands provided for them, and now, suddenly, they have this wealth to manage for themselves.

But how? The brokers talk about price-earning ratios, beta quotients, growth versus security, and income as opposed to growth. Then there is . . . risk. And all of these factors must be considered both for the portfolio at large and for each stock, fund, or bond within it. Grief is bad. Poverty is worse. Combining grief with the prospect of poverty is a recipe for investment disaster. For those without the wealth to hire an "investment counselor" who takes over the control of one's savings, there is no better place to learn about money than through the online conference center library.

I learned this in the 1980s when I was caring for my father, an astute businessman who because of illness could no longer write a check, let alone manage his considerable savings. He kept telling me how poor he was, but when I was given his "power of attorney," a paper that allowed me to act for him in financial matters, I found out that he was very well off indeed. While he had extraordinary health-related expenses, he also had over $600,000 in stocks and bonds. I was legally in charge of that money, and responsible for its use. And in the world of finances, I was an idiot.

At that time, my oldest brother sent me a clipping from the *Wall Street Journal* which said that mismanagement of money by caregivers for the elderly often resulted in lawsuits against the "attorney of fact" by other family members. I was, in short, put on notice. Any actions I took on my father's behalf would have to be ones I could defend in court. As I was first a geographer and then a journalist, this was not my area of expertise. I was, as another brother helpfully pointed out, the "hippie son," the one who never cared about material things.

How ignominious. An adult male, 35 years of age, and I was caught in the widow's syndrome.

At that time my father was about 75 and his stockbroker perhaps eight years older. Bert was a pleasant man who, like my father, believed that holding a stock for 30 years virtually guaranteed success. That was not a perspective, however, that inspired my confidence. An accountant who helped my father with his taxes, a man in his mid-70s, said I should trust his and Bert's advice while learning about both the market in general as well as the 30+ stocks in my father's portfolio. To do that, he advised that I read the *Wall Street Journal* every day, *Business Week* and *Barron's Magazine* every week, and of course the local newspaper's daily business page. Over time, I would become familiar with money management, these men said. And, of course, in the interim they would be glad to help me with any decisions I might need to make.

I tried to read *Barron's* and the *Wall Street Journal,* but I soon found that all of these publications had lots of data but little pertinent information. One week there might be an article on PPG earnings, and the next week there would be a few inches on a proposed rate hike for Long Island Lighting; occasionally there would be a feature article about the costs of elder care. None of it really helped me understand, however, what stocks to hold and what stocks to sell to support an old man with major medical expenses. But that is the problem with newspapers. Lots of data, but turning each day's reports into something definitive and useful would have taken months or years of clipping stories and reading general articles.

I needed knowledge quickly. There was no time to spend a year or two leisurely reading about the business of investments. Because parental care was a full-time job, I did not have an extra two hours a day to peruse business periodicals. A college friend who then was working as an investment counselor made a better suggestion: get online. Use an electronic information service to get brief descriptions of my father's stocks, check their performance over a several-year period, and find out what each yielded. Get some data, he said. Fit the parts to the whole. And then, he said, save each record that you have read onto a floppy disk in case someone questions your data or judgment.

In those days, the Dow Jones News Service was *the* source of online business news. But even in the mid-1980s, when the Internet was reserved primarily for academics and the occasional hacker, more popular services like CompuServe were adding easy-to-use business resources to their online world. And so I used CIS for basic research and the Dow Jones for more detailed data. On CompuServe, I accessed Standard and Poors, one of the standard data evaluation services, where I was familiarized with the individual companies whose stock my father held.

Best of all, the system was designed for ignorant novices like me, folks with both a need to know and a little background in finance. GO: S&P brought me to a set of directories, each of which helped me to get closer to the data I needed. Each time I typed a message giving a direction, the computer responded with another screen that brought me through the hierarchy of directories (all data are stored hierarchically!) to what I needed. Example 9.1 is the first directory in the S&P data-

Example 9.1

> "S&P Online" Copyright(c) 1995
> McGraw-Hill Inc.
> All Rights Reserved
>
> 1 S&P Recommended Master List
> 2 Investment Ideas
> 3 Individual Company Profiles
> 4 "S&P 500" Index & Directory
> 5 Understanding "S&P Online"
> 6 S&P Terms and Definitions
> 7 S&P Disclaimer
>
> !3

base. Although all of this occurred in 1986, I have recreated those searches to assure that the examples include current data and directories.

The first item in the main directory, Standard and Poor's recommended list, is a collection of stocks the S&P analysts' recommended. "Investment Ideas" describes more general investment programs and sector strategies. It would have been useful if I was building a portfolio rather than attempting to evaluate the one my father had built. The third entry, "Individual Company Profiles," was obviously the one best suited to my needs. Option 5, "Understanding 'S&P Online'," helped with definitions of some of the indices included in the Standard and Poors reports, and with an overview of the system itself. Option 6, "Terms and Definitions," explained the arcane language of analysis, from the difference between alpha and beta indicators to price/earning ratios. It was something to which I referred frequently in those days. Choosing option 3, however, lead immediately to another directory, one that gave me a chance to begin researching individual stocks in my father's portfolio (see Example 9.2).

All stocks are known by a company's name or initials (IBM, PPG, RGE, BB, etc.), numeric strings (the Cusip number), and as parts of a broader industry that is tracked as a whole. So, for example, IBM can be searched as part of the computer industry, and Rochester Gas and Electric Company as an element in the utilities industry index. "Recently Changed Profiles" lists stocks whose evaluation or recommendation have changed in the last month.

One of the companies my father held was called "PPG Industries." I did not have the foggiest idea what it was or what it did. I did not know its symbol or Cusip. So I chose option 2, "Access by Company

Example 9.2

```
INDIVIDUAL CO. PROFILES

1 Access by Stock Symbol
  or Cusip
2 Access by Company Name
3 Access by Industry Code
4 Recently Changed Profiles
5 List of Industry Codes

!2
```

Name," which gave the stock symbol and other data, along with yet another directory (see Example 9.3) describing the data available on PPG Industries. One could check earnings, stock prices, get a short paragraph on what the company's basic business was, and review figures that describe how well it has done in recent years.

This is what I needed: background data that included earnings, dividends, a balance sheet, and an idea of the company's core business. I didn't know what "Business Line Table" was (Example 9.3), but I decided that since the cost was the same whether I accessed only one part of the report or all nine items, I might as well type in "ALL." That returned what I needed—a short and clear profile of a company. I immediately received, for example (Example 9.3), both the company stock symbol and an industry code that could be used to compare company performance with that of its sector. (For example, Key Bank as a part of the banking industry.) This series of examples show the type of data returned in these reports, with a brief description of their utility. For this demonstration, I entered the Standard and Poors online area in 1995 and asked for a company profile by Stock Symbol (Example 9.2), and then all available data listed in Example 9.3.

The background data (Example 9.4) offered a brief profile of the com-

Example 9.3

```
Enter company name:
! PPG Industries

PPG Industries    06-Dec-95
Industry: 2400  Symbol: PPG

1 Background
2 Outlook
3 Business Line Table
4 Earnings Per Share
5 Dividends Per Share
6 Market Action
7 Balance Sheet
8 History Part 1
9 History Part 2

Enter choice(s) or ALL
! ALL
```

Example 9.4

```
                Screen 1. Background

 PPG Industries   06-Jan-95   Industry: 2400  Symbol: PPG
 Makes glass, fiberglass, chemicals, coatings, resins... '93 EPS
 down 8% on slightly lower sales... 9 months '94 EPS up 50% on
 7% sales gain... 12/5/94  said co. "not uncomfortable" with
 analysts' EPS estimates of $2.60 for  '94, $3.10 to $4.00 (with
 average of $3.30) for '95... ESOP has 14%.
```

pany and its general performance, including EPS (the "terms" Option said that means "earnings per share").

So that's who these guys are, I said. The symbol is PPG and the industry code, which allows one to look at the industry at large, is #2400. What is really important, however, is the general overview of the company's performance. Earnings per share (EPS) were down in 1993, but up in the first nine months of 1994. The company is "not uncomfortable" with what analysts think PPG will earn. To me, that doesn't sound like a ringing and enthusiastic endorsement. Of course, these are estimates, and I'll take them with a grain of salt. The next item on the menu, the "Business Line Table," gave a general breakdown of sales and profits for the company's main division. It wasn't of use to me, and since it didn't bear on the problem—which stocks needed to be sold to pay for my father's care—I eliminated it from future searchers. The fourth screen (Example 9.4), however, "Earnings per Share" was very important. It was data I required and understood.

Example 9.5

```
            4. Earnings per share

       --------- EARNINGS PER SHARE ----------
 9 Mo Sep        1.71
 ..Prev. Yr.     1.14
 Last 12 Mos     1.96
 P/E            16.07
 5-Yr. Growth %  Neg
```

The company's 5-year growth as a percentage of earnings per share was negative, and its earnings in the first 9 months, while better than the previous year's, were lower than they had been over the previous 12 months. The price earnings ratio was not cheap, but neither was it extremely high. The next screen, "Dividends per Share," (Example 9.6) told me that this stock was not a huge income earner. Its yield, in a period of high inflation, was well below what a bond fund, savings account, or certificate of deposit was paying in those years.

About the only thing I knew about stocks at that time was that one was supposed to "buy low, sell high." So the market actions report (Example 9.7) on the year's trading range let me know where the stock sat at that particular moment. While an S&P ranking of A − is not bad, it also means that PPG is not a barn-burning, sure-thing, through-the-roof type of issue. The "Beta" is another measure of quality and performance that I've since read about but never really understood. It is shown in Example 9.8 for those who may be more knowledgeable than I was, or am, in these matters.

"History Part 1" was a list of the company's stock prices, high and low, over the previous several years, its price earnings ratio—important if one is considering the stock's value to a portfolio—and the amount of dividends it had paid each year. "History Part 2" dealt with the "book value" of the company, the shifting relationship between revenue and income. They have been combined here into one chart in Example 9.8.

The "High–Low" range told me that, over time, the stock was certainly appreciating in value. From 1991 to 1994 the stock's price had increased by 60 to 70 percent (divide 29.68 by 42.12; or 20.75/33.75). That is pretty good, even for a growth stock whose growing value is supposed to compensate for its lower yield. And, over this period, its dividend had increased significantly as well, from $.86 to $1.12. From

Example 9.6

```
        5. Dividends per share

PPG Industries    Last Updated  13-Jan-95
--------- DIVIDENDS PER SHARE ---------
Rate              1.16
Yield             2.95%
Last Div. Q       .290
Ex-Date           11/04
Pay Date          12/12/94
```

Example 9.7

```
6. Market Action

PPG Industries                Last Updated 13-Jan-95
Industry: 2400                         Symbol: PPG
    ------------ MARKET ACTION ------------
                1995 Range
High  39.87                    Low  37.12
Average Volume                 37,1525
Beta                           1.0
Institutional Holdings         51%
Primary Exchange               NYSE
S&P Rank                       A-
```

1990 to 1993, however, both revenue and income had decreased, and the EPS—earnings per share—was also down. So it seemed like the rapid appreciation in the stock might be slowing. In 1994 the company had a 2 for 1 stock split in which investors received two shares from the company for every one they had held earlier. Folks in the Investor's Forum, a stock-based conference on CIS, explained to me that this was good in the long run because it meant that they thought the stock would go up, and a lower price would attract more investors. But in the short run it "diluted" the value of each individual share.

Now I had an idea of how this stock fit into my father's portfolio,

Example 9.8

```
              8 & 9. History Part 1&2
         PPG Industries   Last Updated 13-Jan-95
                ( 2-for-1,'94.)

    -------- CALENDAR YEAR HISTORY --------
```

Yr	High	Low	PE Range		Div	EPS	Revenue	Income	Share
94	42.12	33.75	....	....	1.12				
93	38.12	9.68	27.4	21.4	1.04	1.39	5753.9	295.0	11.57
92	34.18	25.00	22.7	16.6	.94	1.50	5813.9	319.4	12.72
91	29.68	20.75	31.3	21.8	.86	.95	5672.6	201.4	12.50
90	-	-	-	-		2.21	6021.4	474.8	12.00

and how I felt about it as a vehicle for his care. The stock had grown significantly in recent years, but that growth seemed to be slowing. Its yield was modest. My college friend told me how to calculate the capital gain based on the stock's price, and my father's accountant showed me how to balance stock gains against the costs of home care and medical expenses. Clearly, this was a stock that I might consider selling to assist in his maintenance. A good company, but not one whose immediate, short-term potential argued that it be held against immediate necessities.

After downloading a stock's information, I wrote a brief summary of each stock, including its earnings, current situation, and its place in the portfolio (a utility, a growth stock, a short-term and thus more speculative purchase). Some stocks were not going to generate the revenue he needed. Others, while offering high income yields, were decreasing in value because of one or another problem. This was especially true of a few utilities whose applications for rate hikes had been denied. These companies I checked against Standard and Poors' "Recently Changed Profiles." When the picture still was not clear, I used the Dow Jones News Service to check for further information.

Finally, I took seriously the advice of someone I met on an investors forum who suggested that I track expenses and income carefully. So I created a spreadsheet that listed all of my father's expenses, and those I thought we could expect in the future. This gave me a picture of how much money would be needed, and allowed me to balance needs against income from his holdings, and the general yields of those stocks. I figured out how much I needed to increase earnings to pay for expenses. Armed with that information, I explained to my college friend the research I had completed, and we then discussed what I thought it meant in terms of my father's holdings. He made some suggestions on improving my presentation.

Then I visited both my father's broker and his accountant, showing them what I had learned. They were impressed. Both of these advisors disagreed with some of my conclusions, albeit each did so for different reasons. The accountant was most interested in tax ramifications, and the broker in my suggestion that certain stocks he believed in should be let go.

But they listened to me, and I to them. Much to every one's surprise, the "hippie son" was no longer an ignoramus who could not handle money. I was in the game, and had created a paper trail which could show that not only was I acting for my father, but I was doing that intelligently and responsibly.

In 1986 it cost me approximately sixty dollars to gather this much data on the thirty or so stocks, bonds, and mutual funds my father held. I did perhaps five searches an evening for one week. By that time, I had a pretty complete picture of his holdings, the relative growth rates of these companies, and their near term potential. It was hard work, but I gained a basic understanding of both his holdings and the language of finance. I no longer had to listen only to the advice of my father's broker, or even that of my college friend. Still, it was not easy. I worked with a primitive spreadsheet program and had to manually enter an individual stock's symbol if I wished to check its price online. Calculating gains and process required me to create a formula in a special section of the spreadsheet, and then manually enter the correct data in each cell.

These days there are more sophisticated tools available to those who wish to learn about money online. New investor-oriented software automates the process of record keeping, price checks, capital gain calculations, and even the data search itself. A decade ago, complex portfolio management programs cost hundreds of dollars apiece. Today, easy to use programs like MicroQuest's *Inside Track* cost less than one hundred dollars. Enter the stock's name, its purchase price, and its symbol if known. Presto, the software will then go online to check stock price, multiply that quote by the number of shares owned, and calculate current value, profit or loss. Linked to data services and stock quote prices through either CompuServe (GO MicroQuest) or the Internet (http://www.microquest.com), the point-and-click software will automatically search through a series of news services to see what has been recently written about a stock or company the investor wants to track.

Do they guarantee success? No. Do the accumulated online resources available to average people offer basic data that will help them make intelligent decisions? Yes. In this, they are a bullwark against the unscrupulous who prey on the ignorant. Last week, for instance, a pleasant man called to offer me a great opportunity. Ontario Provincial Bonds were paying 9 percent, he said, and he would be glad to help me buy some. Jeez, a 9 percent yield, that is like money in the bank, he said. Lots of money. As it happens, I had recently done a search on bond rates for an elderly friend. I knew that yields were relatively high, and likely to go higher in Canada. I also knew that Ontario's economy was not rosy, and that its bond rating had been downgraded earlier in the year. Even more important, I had downloaded data to construct a graph charting the relative values of both Canadian and U.S. dollars. At the time of this call, the Canadian dollar had dropped to about $.71, but many expected it to go as low as $.65. And as the dollar dropped, the "yield" of the Ontario Provincial Bonds, compared to their U.S. counterparts, dropped as well. I pointed this fact out to my unseen benefactor, thanked him for his suggestion, and declined the offer.

When someone calls and offers me a swell opportunity on a hot new stock, I ask for its Cuisp number and an S&P sheet. If they say, sorry, they just ran out, I then ask if they know its price–earnings ratio, its dividend history, and its Beta coefficient. Gee, they say, I just ran out. "No problem," I answer. "I'll database it tonight. Call again tomorrow." They never call again. When a broker I know makes a recommendation on a stock I have never heard of, I check online for some background before we discuss it. Good brokers appreciate well-informed clients. They encourage educated investing. Unscrupulous ones do not.

The vast world of online financial information is not just for those who have money. It can be as valuable for those who are starting to build equity as it is for those, like me, charged with preserving an established portfolio. Last summer, for example, a 19-year-old neighbor stopped by to chat. Months earlier, Randall dropped out of college after getting a job working for an insurance company. He had put aside a little money, and after reading a book or two on finance had decided to invest it. His school-teacher parents are friends of mine, and over the years he and I have discussed various things when he wanted another, sympathetic adult's reaction.

"I read *The Wealthy Barber*, and the book says if I just put money aside every month in a mutual fund, by the time I'm 40 years old I'll be able to buy a Ferrari," Randall told me. He wanted my thoughts on this idea. I asked what funds he was going to invest in, and he replied that, "*The Wealthy Barber* says it doesn't matter. All I have to do is put money in a mutual fund, reinvest the dividends, and I'll be rich."

Well, perhaps. But all mutual funds are not equal. Some are brilliantly managed, I suggested, and some are not. Even following *The Wealthy Barber*'s advice, I continued, he had a lot of decisions to make. Did he want to invest in a Canadian, U.S., international, or sector fund focusing on one geographic region? I asked. Whatever the geography, was he interested in stock or bond funds? If stocks, should they be growth-oriented, dividend-oriented, or aim at a balance between future worth and financial return? Would he put all of his money into one fund or spread it around between two or more, just to be on the safe side? Randall found all of these questions aggravating. Apparently, *The Wealthy Barber* had taken the broad view, not one filled with such details.

"Let's get some help," I suggested. I explained to him about online forums, and logged a description of his general goals and outlook as a message in CompuServe's Investor's Forum (FIND MONEY or GO INVEST). I solicited comments from members who might want to spare a moment to give a young investor some suggestions. I explained that Randall wanted to begin investing with a lump sum of $2000, and then invest $1000 a month in mutual funds for the next 20 years. Were mutual funds better than stocks, and where should he go to find the best investment vehicle, I asked.

One person responded encouragingly. "Sounds like a great plan," he said. "I ran the calculation with the numbers you supplied and found that such a program of investing would yield $645,127 at the end of 20 years, if compounded annually and without accounting for taxes." Another reminded us that many mutual funds have commissions "higher than 5%, which means, in theory, that you need that fund to earn about 7.5% in six months (if you were to sell at six months) to beat a passbook savings account." His advice: "Pick one or maybe two funds, sink the money in, and sit back 20 years or so; then get the Ferrari."

Perhaps the most helpful comment, however, came from a correspondent who was both encouraging and concrete. He helped us answer the question of "asset allocation," without making personal recommendations on any one stock or bond fund. I always feel better when someone makes suggestions altruistically and generally, explaining where to look for information rather than offering data they have collected on their own. Wendall's note is shown in Example 9.9.

The next question was: What should he buy? Randall had talked to several brokers, each of whom then loaded him down with glossy brochures for different funds, each one promising riches to investors who chose them as their vehicle of investment. I told Randall that they all could be investigated online, but suggested that we first consider our online friends' suggestions. We should look for a fund paying at least 6.5 percent (long-term holding meant that we needed less than passbook returns), investing in large companies paying regular dividends, and perhaps look for another that was an international fund. Together, Randall and I found three mutual funds that allowed minimum first purchases of $1000 with "no-load," or no up-front fees. I suggested that one of the two picks emphasize Canadian stocks, which tend to be resource-based. But I also searched for an "international" fund that would diversify his holdings among growth stocks in the larger, industrialized world. We stayed away from "sector funds" that advanced one geographic region (Latin America, Chile, Japan, Europe) in favor of a broadly based fund. I showed him reports on two funds to demonstrate how, while many of these offered great potential, their prices fluctuated widely over time. Finally, I suggested that he might want to think about an investment in a fund specializing in something like technology or biotechnology stocks. These are riskier, but if well managed they may have higher rates of return. "This is something you should look at in the future," I said, "when you're making more money. Let's start with these two, first."

Example 9.9

Subj: Help a kid invest   Section: Mutual Funds
From: Peter R. Donald II. (27251,7122)   Msg. # 398625
To: Tom Koch, 71600,1123   Date: Oct.11, 1995

Tom,

If your young friend has the discipline to actually do what he wants to, invest $1000 a month for 20 years, then I would say that he has a bright future ahead of him. For the purpose of discussion I'll assume that he does.

Historically, stocks have an average annual return of 9% while long term bonds about 5%. If these averages hold over the next 20 years that 4% difference will have a huge effect. And while stocks are more volatile on a year-by-year basis, over a 20 year period the risks are not that great, and making regular investments reduces the risk even further. Therefore, I would recommend he use an <u>asset allocation</u> that is heavy on stocks. I would also choose 3 or 4 mutual funds each investing in different types of stock. A possible mix would be a fund that (a) invests in large companies that pay regular dividends, (b) a fund of small fast growing companies, (c) maybe a natural resource fund to protect against inflation, and finally (d) an international fund. Then if he wants further diversification he could add a bond fund.

I still use this system today to manage my own monies.

PRD.

Finding funds that met his criteria was pretty easy. There are online resources very much like Standard and Poors that are designed for mutual fund analysis. Rather than using their directories to find a specific company, however, different directories allow a user to input parameters (type of fund, yield, load or no-load, etc.), and it automatically narrows down the potential funds that meet a user's criteria. Not surprisingly, they also can be used to analyze an offering in terms of risk, past performance, costs (Do they charge when you purchase the fund, when it is sold), is it a "no-load" fund?, etc. As my old college friend said, "How do people think we find these things? We have the same type of tools on our desks."

On CompuServe, the system I used was called Coscreen (GO:

COSCREEN). Virtually every commercial online venue has this type of resource available. They can be found through the online directory, "FIND" on CompuServe or "Invest" using the World Wide Web's Web-Crawler search tool. However one accesses these services, the best combination is hard "data" shelves in the library and advice on what to look for—and where—from user forums or conferences.

Randall, by the way, has decided to go back to school. He found the whole process so interesting he has changed from a science program to business and business management. He still wants the Ferrari, and with a business degree, some online data, and a bit of financial discipline, he says, he might even get that sports car before he's 40 years of age. In the interim, he is investing. But when he becomes a student again, Randall says he will have to decrease his monthly investments. In fact, I suspect he already has done so. He has a new girlfriend, and they like to go on little trips together, and to nice restaurants and clubs. No online advice can help one balance the fun of being 20 years old against the promise of a sports car when one's 30 or 40 years old. It is not the type of choice anyone can factor into a spreadsheet, no matter how good the data it contains.

Business-oriented news writers have been slow to understand the use of online data for their stories and columns. But then, most business reporters spend their lives reporting corporate statements, official investigations, and the daily ups and downs of markets, at least as they are described by professionals. This is changing, however. New tools always find new users, people who find ways of making them work. In 1987, for example, the Akron, Ohio, daily newspaper, the *Beacon Journal*, won a Pulitzer prize for its 1986 reportage of the take-over of the city's major employer, The Goodyear Tire and Rubber Company.

When general wire stories announced in 1986 that the company was among the most actively traded stocks, it was widely perceived as being a takeover target. Those were the years of high-powered mergers, after all; corporate cannibals reigned. To trace the rumors, analyze potential buyers, and discover the facts, *Journal* reporters used several widely available, computerized resources to fashion their stories. These included specialized resources like *Disclosure*, a record of federally mandated corporate filings to the Securities and Exchange Commission; insider trading files, which listed large trades by company officials; and the libraries of other newspapers, where they could be accessed by computer.

"If a rumor came up on deadline," one editor said, "several of us could access a lot of information on Vu/Text." Vu/Text was an independent data company that digitized newspaper libraries, and then sold those newspaper files to the online world for a modest fee. It has since been bundled into Dialog Information Services (renamed Knight Ridder Information Services in 1995), which offers news files for general reader use through a variety of online venues. A Goodyear suitor which proclaimed it "never broke up an acquisition," would find reporters looking at the files of newspapers in towns where previous acquisitions had occurred. Another which described itself as an "exemplary corporate citizen" that did not fire the workers at companies it bought might be faced, the next day, with a *Beacon Journal* story about all of the firings workers at its subsidiaries had endured, and the lack of corporate participation in the urban affairs of cities where it had plants.

Step by step, *Beacon Journal* reporters were able to piece together individual datum on the financial affairs of suitors (could they afford Goodyear?), their history as takeover barons (did they break up companies, or did they improve them?), and those suitors' relationships with the cities in which their plants existed. It was a sterling piece of work, an example of how news can be transformed by online resources, and how easy it is for amateurs who are not financiers to access financial data on any corporation.

The next year, 1987, saw the stock market crash, a mini-meltdown caused, in retrospect, by a real liquidity crisis. It is hard to recapture the anxiety of that brief period in October when many believed that a full and desperate, 1929-style crash was inevitable. At that time, popular online resources were in their infancy. They were new and exotic tools to most small investors. But those who used online resources— and the first brokerage houses that allowed clients to buy and sell stocks online—were amply rewarded. For two to three days, the markets were in such panic that investors literally could not reach their brokers. The volume of telephone calls was just too heavy. People who wanted to sell, buy, or simply be reassured found that the personable people who were their advisors were simply out of reach.

Online user volume increased tenfold at both the Dow Jones News Service and CompuServe Information Services. Those seeking stock quotes, news analysis, or financial statistics electronically faced no wait. People with online accounts could buy and sell at any time, and with minimal delay. The crisis of 1987 was a wake-up call to many in the financial business. But perhaps as important, it was a watershed event in the world of small investors who perceived, many for the first time, the power of the conference center and its library.

Afterwards, officials at CompuServe and the Dow Jones announced that as a result of the volume of online callers who used their services in October, both were adding new computers to assure that, in the event of a future meltdown, they, at least, would not be caught with overloaded phone lines and plugged telephone circuits. Since 1987, use of these resources has doubled each year. And in 1995, that rate of increase shows no signs of stopping.

By the mid-1990s, the primacy of traditional information sources for business and finance was being challenged by these newer, alternative means of data gathering. Through the conference center's many doors, online users could attend any of a number of conferences, forums, and discussion groups whose often extremely knowledgeable members were willing and eager to discuss investment strategies, tactics, and the merits of specific issues. At the click of a mouse, all had access to evermore extensive realms of data.

Growing membership in the online community had already lead a series of prestigious business publications to shift a portion of their resources from print publication to online dissemination. Thus, by 1995, the news resources of the *Wall Street Journal* (Dow Jones News Service), *US News and World Report*, CNN, and *MONEY Magazine*, to name a few, were available online on CompuServe. With their competitors, they also set up resources elsewhere in the center, either with another commercial data vendor (AOL, etc.) or through the Internet. In each case, these "news groups" offered users access to the organization's news library, discussion sections, and the opportunity for comments, story suggestions, and criticisms with business staff members.

For more than a decade, "discount" brokerage houses like Quick & Reilly have been opening online accounts for computerized customers. No waiting. No lines. No delays. Since trading occurs in major markets through computers, having customers buy and sell orders entered at the brokerage house this way makes sense. And because electronic houses require less personnel—automatic purchase and sell orders cut down on paperwork and paper handlers—they can charge less for their services. And so, first slowly and now more and more rapidly, online brokerages are becoming a constant in the financial world.

At the same time, primary data servers like Reuters Canada are offering their news resources online as well as in traditional venues. In the late 1980s, only a few specialized services—the Dow Jones News Service, for example—offered the type of hourly market and financial data that news writers use in crafting their stories or the hard figures that analysts employ in deciding whether or not to recommend a stock or bond issue. The average person did not receive the news services in his or her home. He or she had to read the papers, and the writers who had chosen this or that story from the wires. Increasingly, however, primary financial reportage and data—from bond rates and international currency valuations to SEC files—are available electronically to everyone online. The trend continues on the World Wide

Web, of course. For stock and mutual fund data for example, http://www.marketedge.com is a new one-stop data center available to all no matter which door they use to access the lender library.

In all this we may see the emerging shape of the future. If current patterns continue, electronic venues for business data will continue to expand from their current position as an interesting but experimental means of financial research and trading to the dominant medium for user research and analysis. In this shift, electronic forums and user groups will become evermore critical areas of dissemination and analysis for members who are eager to discuss and analyze corporate returns, product announcements, industry trends, and the management changes in any one company.

Similarly, the nature of business news itself will change. Traditional print publications will disappear as electronic versions will dominate. Why should I buy the *Globe and Mail* if I can get stock prices and company data more quickly and more efficiently online? Business reporters will increasingly take the raw data available to everyone and use the data in innovative ways. They will have to do this because their traditional niche, reporting on press conferences and officials statements, will have been subsumed by the library/conference center's data retrieval systems.

A recent example of the type of information that will be considered "news" in the new electronic center was offered by Bud Jorgensen, a business writer at the *Financial Post* in Canada. At the time of his story, in late 1994 and early 1995, the country again was discussing the possibility of an independent Quebec. In this debate, a central issue was the financial viability of separation of that province from the nation as a whole. Secessionists insisted that Quebec would prosper as an independent nation, while nationalists insisted that separation would result in a serious decline in the standard of living for the province's inhabitants. Day by day, different politicians made their cases in the newspaper. Every opinion reported was assumed by its writer to be equally correct. Nobody described a context or methodology that might allow the average person to judge the issue independently.

Jorgensen decided to find a simple indicator that might be described as the economic potential of an independent Quebec, one that would compare its leaders' statements (Quebec will do better as a separate entity) to those of Federalists who insisted that Quebec would be an economic disaster on its own. To do this, Jorgensen decided to determine the value of the "Quebec dollar." Could it be possible to describe the real value of the Quebec economy irrespective of its ties to Canada? In fact, he saw that it would be relatively easy to describe both provincial and regional dollars, compared to the real rates of the federal dollar, in a way that took into account each province's or region's population. With data available online, and a simple spreadsheet program, anyone could do his analysis and test his conclusions.

Using Reuters News Wire, a commonly available business service, he downloaded ten-year national bond rates as well as those for each individual province. Since all areas borrow monies, as does the country at large, these data are readily available. Bond rates vary between provinces and the country-at-large, reflecting the cost of borrowing money for and thus the value of each economy. So, he reasoned, the difference between national and provincial or regional rates (those of the Atlantic provinces, for example) would give a good indication of the value and buying power of a regional dollar compared to Canada's. He loaded the bond data and provincial population statistics into a simple spreadsheet, compared it with national data, and then tracked his "provincial dollar" bin for several months.

Quebec's separatist leaders were wrong. Separation, he showed, would result in an immediately weakened provincial currency, and thus in diminished economic power in that province. Over a period of several months, the Quebec provincial dollar's value hovered between 58¢ and 63¢ during a period in which the Canadian dollar sold on international markets for between 74¢ and 70¢. At this time, other province dollars, most notably those of Ontario and British Columbia, were valued at between 69¢ and 74¢. Thus their economies were stronger than Quebec's and in some ways supported it, just as their leaders had often claimed. Quebec was, in effect, being supported by others, and that was support which could be expected to erode in the face of separation.

Jorgensen's story was published in February, 1995, under the title "The Buck Stops Here for Quebec."[1] It created a minor stir among economists, he later told me. In its preparing he had talked to experts who insisted that a simple, everyman's analysis using general data and a simple spreadsheet could not return accurate data. But when he presented his material, most agreed with his findings. "After one of these people finished telling me that it couldn't be done, he asked what I had come up with," Bud told me. "I told him that the Ontario dollar was around 74¢ to 75¢, and the Quebec dollar was around 58¢ to 60¢ at that time. There was a long pause, and he said 'well, that's about what I'd say.' "

Even the generally savvy investor is unlikely to be knowledgeable enough about bonds, or sufficiently well grounded in national economics, to be able or interested in doing this type of analysis. They may use Reuters Wire to see the price of a bond, the dollar, or to check for news on companies they own. But applying that data to create aggregate information is a skill that stands out. Newspapers will fold and television business reports will decline in popularity as these new systems come online. But news writers like Jorgensen will continue to work in the evolving media. It will be their task to take available data and analyze it in other ways that require more time, expertise, and insight. "News" will be double-tracked: primary data available to all and analytic presentations of that data offered by business writers. Thus one may expect the quality of data presented through the news medium of the future to increase. At the least, then, one can expect the future to continue current changes, probably at an accelerated pace. Investors will seek general background and discussion from their contemporaries whose user groups and conferences may have excellent if small library resources of their own. General business data increasingly will be found by users online, using simple clipping files to collect data and search filters to automatically retrieve pertinent stories or facts.

Business news organizations, for their part, will become hosts to these groups, or at least contributors of the data they use. Secondarily, news writing will shift from general translation (he said, she said) and unreflective reportage (" 'The Newton is the future of personal computing,' Apple President John Scully said today at a press conference where the new, pocket size personal computer was finally unveiled after months of anticipation") to ever more critical attempts to present financial and product-specific data in a context that is defensible, usable, and testable. News professionals, in other words, will have to provide what individual users cannot easily garner on their own online, alone or in groups.

NOTE

1. Bud Jorgensen. "The Buck Stops Here for Quebec." *Financial Post:* February 4–6, 1995, A3.

10

Quality: Fact and Opinion

Remember the "War of the Worlds," Orson Wells' great radio play? It convinced the nation that aliens had landed and were taking over New Jersey. Superbly produced and brilliantly voiced, the "War of the Worlds" was believed because it was radio, and in those days public news on radio was trusted as the truth. When television first became an ubiquitous part of national life, people believed in it absolutely simply because the medium itself seemed so powerful. It portrayed a reality that could be seen, after all. And we all had been taught, in the fashion of good skeptics, to "trust our eyes." That television portrayed falsities, inaccuracies, and untruths as easily as any medium was a lesson that took years to learn.

New media are always trusted at first. They have such promise, such a scent of truth. It takes time to learn skepticism in the face of each turn of technology's wheel. In the halcyon days of radio, the world trusted comforting voices, like CBC broadcaster Lorne Green's in Canada, assured that words scripted on the page and read into a microphone were gospel. A generation ago, TV anchor Walter Cronkite was the standard by which public realities were measured. What he said the nation, and perhaps the world, accepted. Since then, however, we have learned to be skeptical of the data presented on television and to consider the source of its news pieces, even when there are pictures to accompany the anchor's words. What do they know, anyway? We do not trust Dan Rather, at least not in the same way or to the same degree that we trusted his predecessor, "Uncle Walt." It is not that we distrust Dan Rather the man; it is instead a healthy and growing skepticism about television in general, and specifically the medium of television journalism. We have learned to question its perspective and to wonder about its exclusions. Just as experience taught that radio could tell fictions and that newspapers might report half-truths, it has also taught that a minicam's "Live at Five" pictures can describe a reality that is partial, incomplete, and skewed.

The issue is not an inherent flaw in the medium, but the use we make of the medium itself. The nature of the signal does not determine the quality of the message that it carries. The medium defines a system of encoding and a means of transmission, but it cannot guarantee the veracity of data distributed to the world. Radio signals carrying the "War of the Worlds" allowed a complex interplay of modulated voice and composed sound elements (the "crash" of a collapsing building, the "zap" of an alien ray gun), special effects that, while fictional, gave an approximation of reality. The TV signal that beamed "Bonanza" to the nation and the world, where it has been in syndication for almost two generations, added a complex overlay of visual images to the richly audible array that radio had presented exclusively. But neither media guaranteed that the data in its stories (news or dramatic) were real. That was and is a determination we all must make, time after time, whenever we use external resources to seek the context of a fact or opinion presented in one or another venue.

This is a hard lesson that is relearned each time a new method of data dissemination appears. For years actors have complained about television viewers who cannot distinguish between the actor and his character. Dramatic doctors—from Ben Casey to members of the "ER" cast—are assumed to be able to handle medical emergencies. Hollywood cops like "Miami Vice's" Don Johnson are looked to for help when danger looms in a viewer's life. Dan Blocker, who played the character Hoss on "Bonanza," was sometimes accosted by ardent fans who wished him to give a message to his fictional father, Ben Cartwright, when he returned to the Ponderosa. It all seems so real, and its presentation so immediate, that the limits of fantasy sometimes can be lost in the barrage of images, words, and text that are the way we know our world.

Discrimination and selection are characteristics of our species. But because we *want* to believe, we are seduced, generation by generation, by the advancing technologies that we serially embrace without reservation, at least for a time. It is no different with the newest medium of the conference center/library. Advocates and devotees want to believe that all answers are available, that with a click of the mouse and the tone of a modem, nothing but reality will be returned. Alas, this is the Holy Grail of our shared knowledge, and it remains as elusive as ever. Because it is online does not mean that it is true. An opinion is no more valid when it is offered online, a fact is no more substantial when it is logged into an electronic file. However it is presented, the questions are always the same: Whose idea is this? How is it presented? Is it opinion or "fact"? And if the latter, how substantial and important a fact might it be? What has been left out to make the case?

Reuters News editors learned this the hard way. In 1994 they read a story on the PR Newswire, an electronic venue for the dissemination of public relations releases, about a report on the causes of multiple sclerosis. PR Newswire is a general service presenting "news" reports issued by corporations for public consumption. Purporting to be the advance of an article in a prestigious scientific journal, *Nature,* the two-page, single-spaced release described a California researcher's new explanation of the chemistry causing multiple sclerosis. The PR News wire release promised that, as a result of this work, new drugs that could control the illness were only a few years down the road.

Not surprisingly, the story was carried by scores of newspapers and broadcast stations. After all, it reported a major medical advance that might positively affect the lives of 500,000 U.S. patients with multiple sclerosis. And the publication, *Nature,* is a premier publication. What could be better? The next day a *Wall Street Journal* reporter called the researcher named in the release to discuss the findings and the new drugs that would soon result from his research, and perhaps to find out how it felt to be the man who had busted the back of a terrible disease.

The researcher was shocked when he learned what had been written about his work. While interesting and suggestive, he said, his research was not a breakthrough of the first magnitude. He had not seen the news stories, or the release they were based on, and certainly had not approved their optimistic exaggeration. His work reported in the article was based on a small sample of the bodies of MS patients after the subjects had died. It was therefore not conclusive. He said it would take years of testing, research, and work to confirm his findings and then, if everything checked out, years more to develop effective medication. And so news organizations around North America published corrections the next day, saying that their original pieces had been in error. The PR Newswire release had been written by representatives of a development company allied with the researcher's university, one whose purpose would be to develop and market drugs based on advanced research of this nature.

Because it is written in the newspaper does not mean that it is true. Because a statement, promise, report, or conclusion is posted electronically does not guarantee its veracity. Users of this medium, like those of every medium, have to be discerning. What the online evolution has not changed is the necessity to weigh sources and evaluate statements against some external yardstick. Hearty skepticism is still the perspective required by data seekers, irrespective of the medium.

Online data are no better than their source. Sources may be outdated, incorrectly entered, or just plain wrong. People may claim knowledge they do not have, state opinion as fact, or twist a simple datum into an unrecognizable and nearly unrelated assertion. The first question must always be, "who says?" The second is necessarily, "where did they say it?" If the fact or opinion is in a *Journal of the American Medical Association* article describing a "series of rigorous double-blind studies that showed a high correlation between . . . ," well, that is substantive. But if the data come from *The Farmer's Journal of Traditional Medicine* or *The Hippie-Dippie Holistic Journal of Health*, their quality may be less than secure.

Similarly, a correspondent insisting that he is a medical researcher in Boston, Massachusetts, may in fact be a shoe salesman in Keokuk, Iowa. Reporters are told to always check their sources, to confirm the identity of the person who calls with supposedly definitive news. We do this, too, when telephone salespeople ask for our credit card numbers after offering us a deal that is too good to be true. The habits of skepticism learned in other medium are not to be abandoned because this one is new. And, fortunately, there are a number of ways to check an individual's identity online, even when he or she is using a pseudonym. How one finds out "who is doing the talking" depends on where one happens to be in the center/library. Commercial services like CIS, for example, have online member directories, and their moderated forums are supervised by administrators who can insist on appropriate levels of disclosure. Users of the Health and Fitness Forum interested in sysop, Tom Koch can check that section's directory where sysops and their backgrounds are recorded.

Some things are easy to confirm. If someone claims to have published 12 books, *Books in Print* is available online as a fact-checker. Claims of those who insist that they write for newspapers—the *Sacramento Bee* or a magazine like the *New Yorker*—are making claims that can be verified quickly. Use an older technology and call their editors. Go online into the library and check for their by-lines (one can use "author" as a field for searching) in the collection. Even those whose only claim to public fame is their presence online leave traces that can be searched, examined, and verified.

Scattered throughout the conference center are public address databases that can also quickly identify online correspondents. On CompuServe, for example, they are called.Phone*File (personal addresses) and Biz*File, for business names and addresses. These are the electronic version of telephone directories for the nation. It makes sense, when you think about it. Individual entries for each directory are stored electronically before being printed for each community. These are simply databases that are updated, year by year, when new editions are issued. Combining them electronically and making them accessible to a single search is another way for companies to sell that accumulated data. For the user this means not only simple searches for individuals, "Koch, Tom," for example, but also topical searches based on subject or category ("bicycle stores in Colorado") or nationally ("delicatessens in the U.S.").

So if a CIS correspondent says online he is a Michigan veterinarian working at the Humane Society in Ann Arbor, one can look up the address of that Society location, or check under "Veterinarians" to see if someone with his or her name (H. Schlemmer) is listed in the yellow (or white) pages as in Example 10.1. The file contains information on the "SIC code" for veterinarians (useful for those doing market research) and the date of the first advertisement carried in the directory. Older entries suggest established businesses, which to some is a mark of veracity. Is this proof? No; it is suggestive. Those who must know if their correspondent, H. Schlemmer, works at the clinic can telephone the Ann Arbor number ("Hey, did I talk to you about Bull Terriers online the other night?").

I use this type of resource all the time. For example, I was recently asked by an online correspondent for information on bicycle rental sites on the island of Maui, Hawaii. Mike found me "on the Web" because my bicycle touring guide to Hawaii, *Six Islands on Two Wheels*, is listed on the Hawaii Bicycle League's home page. He and his wife were contemplating a cycling holiday and wanted advice on renting bicycles and cycling on that island. The book's appendix carries a list of bicycle rental stores, but it is now out of date because the book was

Example 10.1

BIZ*FILE Sample Entry

HUMANE SOCIETY OF HURON VALLEY
3100 CHERRY HILL RD
ANN ARBOR MI 48105
Telephone: 313/662-5585

Yellow Page Category: VETERINARIANS
SIC: 0742-01
Ad Size: Display ad   First year in this category: 1985

---

published in 1990. To update it, for my own files as well as for Mike's use, I used another version of the complete, electronic U.S. yellow pages developed by Nynex telephone company: http://www.niyp.com. Searching for bicycle and rental and Maui yielded a list of stores advertising rentals in the bicycle section of island yellow pages. With an e-mail copy of that list and a copy of the book (which he ordered online), Mike's holiday research was complete.

The common electronic mail carrier, the Internet, provides several tools that allow the suspicious user to seek data on a message sender or a real world place. "Finger," for example, is the traditional way to match a person's online address (pcrispe1@ualix.ua.edu) with basic data on that person. Most important, perhaps, it gives a "real name" behind the online handle, and that is always a first step in getting facts about a person who has sent a message electronically. "Finger" is a command that can be accessed directly through many nodes or via electronic mail. To do this, message to

infobot@informania.com

and in the command line use this formula:

finger ⟨user@address⟩

To finger Patrick Crispen, for example, one would type

finger pcrispe1@ua1ix.ua.edu

(see Example 10.2) and, in a few hours, basic data are returned by electronic mail, including Pcrispe1's real name (Patrick Crispen) and his tenure online. The name of the computer node pcrispe1 logs on from ua1ix.ua.edu, describes the type of connection he has (educa-

Example 10.2

```
        Finger pcrispe1@ua1ix.ua.edu

   ua1ix.ua.edu
   Login name: pcrispe1@ua1ix.ua.edu
   In real life: Patrick Crispen
   Directory: /u/as/econ/pcrispe1                     Shell: /bin/sh
   On since Nov 09 06:27:38 on ttyp0 at ua1ix from ua1vm.ua.edu ...
```

tional, government, commercial, foreign, etc.) and a geographic location (the educational institution ua.edu, University of Alabama). Knowing how long a person has been online may also help in assessing the quality of data provided. Is this some "newbie," or a veteran who has been around for a while? If the latter, well, at least one knows he or she has experience, should that person be advising on technical issues.

A similar tool, "Whois," provides names, electronic and postal mail addresses, and sometimes phone numbers for people listed in it, which are more data than "finger" provides; and having a telephone number can be a handy way to track another person's data. But like the "finger," it takes an online pseudonym or complex address and translates it into common data that can be examined. It also opens the field to other medium, like the telephone. Upon receiving a number (604-723-8556) one can simply call and ask, "Hey, is the guy who won the Noble Prize in 1967 there?" If the phone is answered, "Jo's Bar and Grill," don't ask. You know. If, however, the phone is answered by a cool voice announcing, "Good morning, this is the department of philosophy, Harvard University," well, chances are good that you have received a message from a star.

To try to locate someone with this tool, telnet to internic.net (no login or password required) and then simply type:

whois ⟨name⟩

So, for example, I can type—Whois jfesler@infomania.com—and get some basic data. This is especially useful when, in the middle of an IRC chat on the Internet, someone makes grandiose claims. Like folks in bars and coffee houses, online devotees get caught up in the debate, and sometimes are less than judicious in their statements and claims. You may type

/who ⟨chan⟩

to see the electronic mail addresses of those on an IRC channel at any time. If, however, you want to know more about a single person ("that fellow with the nickname 'Gandolf,' I want to ask him a question privately when others aren't around,") simply type

/whois gandolf

and the computer will kick back the person's E-mail address. And if you want to know about a person who was online but has departed before he or she could be fingered, well, the command then would be

/whowas gandolf

In the language of my youth, that is truly, awesomely, cool.

As the Center matures, search tools are becoming more sophisticated. Increasingly, user directories do not depend on telephone listings but on electronic membership itself. For example, CompuServe's more than four million members are all listed in that service's searchable directory database. On the Internet, search programs are becoming commonplace. Several now offer "white pages" searching based on personal, online addresses. Http://www.four11.com/, for example, has more than two million user names and electronic addresses at present. And another search system attempts to combine "white and yellow worldwide Internet" listings at http://www.aldea.com/whitepages/white.html. These are newer, more sophisticated fingers that bring location data of the online community closer to the individual user.

Basic searches are what private investigators have always done. It has the reputation of slow, tedious library work through directories and corporate records. This, too, is automating. CD Infotek's Computrace, has developed a file that automates this type of basic data search through three separate files. The Living Individual File has 140 million entries that include name, city, state, and zip code. It's Deceased Persons File lists the names of people whose survivors have filed with the U.S. government Social Security Administration death payments since 1928. Finally, it includes a mere 15 million records of active and inactive corporate or limited partnerships filed with individual secretaries of states in the United States. It is all public data, and thus theoretically available to any citizen. What the Center/Library has done is bring that data together and make it ever more available to the individual, untrained user.

Not everyone is thrilled with the ability of these and other tools to unearth personal addresses, telephone numbers, and bits of computerized personal information. These are, after all, the basic tools of hackers, a first step in obtaining the basic data required by those who may wish to violate system security and break into the computer accounts and files of others. In 1994, for example, The *Chronicle of Higher Education* reported that many college and university computer system directors were restricting the data users could glean with these tools.[1] It may also be that system administrators at different locations were irritated at the inventive but to them frivolous use made of these tools by some young programmers.

Digitally stored records—from university records to employment histories and federal filings—have created what journalism professor, J. T. Johnson calls the "parallel personality," the traces of one's institutional interactions with others. These were always there, and long have been accessible to official researchers with the time, expertise, and man-power to backtrack an individual history. Now, however, the tools of those trackers have leaked into the digital world, and more people than ever have a chance to peruse supposedly restricted, personal data. But it is no more or less "wrong" to sneak into the registrar's office and alter a grade on file than it is to do so electronically. The new medium has not changed the rules of the game, although it has allowed more people to play it.

Not all such intrusions are illegal, immoral, or in violation of moral and legal codes. In fact, most are not. Among the more famous nontra-ditional but harmless uses of the "finger" occurred at Carnegie-Mellon University in Pittsburgh. Science students found themselves too often traipsing down the stairs to the soda machine at night only to find that it was empty. What they needed, they decided, was a remote system that would allow them to know the number and temperature of sodas in the machine before they left their office to make the trek to the only cola machine in the area. So they hooked the coke machine to the In-ternet and used a text editor to write a file that informed all callers how many sodas were still in the machine, whether those sodas were cold, and which dispenser trays were empty. At least as late as 1995, the machine's status was accessible to a "finger" command from any com-puter in the world.

For those wishing to confirm the machine's continued service for themselves, the address is: finger coke@cs.cmu.edu. I did (see Exam-ple 10.3), and I am pleased to report that as recently as April 4, 1995, the university coke machine was well stocked with cold refreshments. Again, although this may be the Internet and university programmers, the basic tool being used—question and answer—is still the lowly elec-tronic message. Whether a user flings this query across the collected world of the conference center/library—using search programs like WebCrawler or Lycos—or electronic mails it to a specific addressee, the medium is still the personal mail message sent from computer a to computer b (or c or d).

Almost everybody and everything creates a data trail. Even soda dis-pensers. If someone is online, there is an address on file in one or another electronic directory that leads to the online correspondent, even when he or she uses a pseudonym. If someone online has a tele-phone—and to be online they must—then a phone directory some-where probably has their listing. Knowing the person's real name and the location of their computer server (cmu.edu is Carnegie Mellon Uni-versity, which is in Pittsburgh, PA), means that one can go to a phone book and search for their geographic address. Online or print directo-ries provide location data and sometimes telephone numbers to go with those names. From these, further research is a snap. Books are

Example 10.3

```
[cs.cmu.edu]

[ Forwarding coke as "coke@l.gp.cs.cmu.edu" ]

[L.GP.CS.CMU.EDU]
Login: coke              Name: Drink Coke
Directory: /usr/coke        Shell: /usr/local/bin/tcsh
Last login Wed Oct 12 14:27 (EDT) on ttyp1 from
  PTERO.SOAR.CS.CMU.EDU
Mail came on Tue Apr  4 10:44, last read on Tue Apr  4 10:44
Plan: Thu Sep 29 17:33:39 1995
M&M validity: 0      Coke validity: 0  (e.g. da interface is down,
sorry!)
Exact change required for coke machine.

M & M          Buttons
/-----\          C: CCCCCCCCCCCC.............
|       |        C: CCCCC......   D: CCCCC......
|  **   |        C: CCCCC......   D: CCCCC......
|*****|          C: CCCCC......   D: CCCCC......
|*****|               C: CCCCC......
\-----/               S: CCCCC......
   |         Key:
   |         0 = warm; 9 = 90% cold; C = cold; . = empty
   |         Leftmost soda/pop will be dispensed next
---^---

 [in short: the drinks are cold. The machine is full.]
```

reviewed in journals, articles are criticized or lauded in other citations. News reports are carried in papers and broadcast scripts stored online. Corporate records and legal decisions all can be found somewhere in the conference center/library cum bazaar.

A decade ago these were called "paper trails," the accumulation of writings by and about any person, project, or proposal. That "paper" has been digitized does not change the fact that we are a record-keeping people, writing fools who cannot stop leaving traces of past work, ideas, and performance. Each report, each entry, is merely a datum, a thing whose information content is minimal. But add them up, and one has a composite portrait whose accuracy quotient is the sum of the whole.

Knowing a person's name does not assure the quality of his or her opinion, however. Even if the person is famous and established, he or she still can be wrong. Several years ago, for example, I became interested in the work of Daniel Callahan, director of the prestigious Hastings Centre Bioethics Institute. He had been hired as a keynote speaker at the annual meeting of the Canadian Association on Gerontology, CAG, an organization to which I belonged at that time. Because of his fame, and in his field Callahan was very well known, they thought his presence would be a coup.

But I had read one of his books, *Setting Limits: Medical Goals in an Aging Society*,[2] which argued against vigorous and full care for the elderly. He seemed to me ageist, one of those folks who wanted to take away from our clients on the discriminatory basis of age. "Why," I said politely, "this is like inviting Goebbels to the bar mitzvah!" I decided to research Callahan and his work before the conference. I did a basic electronic search across a range of references which, I hoped, would allow me to critique his work.

The electronic resources I used to search for "Daniel Callahan" (and Hastings Centre) were low-level, easy-to-find, general-access resources, ones that print-based librarians know well. (See Example 10.4.) This, of course, is the beauty of the conference center's library. It allows more efficient searching of materials in the center's library, even if the resources used seem little different from those in the traditional print library. Here, it's all before you, all on the same shelf.

I discovered that Callahan wasn't a gerontologist or directly involved in elder care. His training was in philosophy, and his practical experience in patient care was clearly minimal. While most of his work was highly regarded, a number of reviewers were extremely critical of his argument for restricting care for the elderly. Where those articles appeared in full-text libraries I read them online. Several were noted in bibliographic files, and to get those articles I had to visit the library. I quickly became an expert on the criticisms his restrictive policies had attracted.

I had a list of questions and citations ready when he rose to speak to the Canadian gerontologists. But despite all of this preparation, and the knowledge I had gained about him, in the end I was unprepared for the man himself. Daniel Callahan might have been wrong headed, ageist, and flawed in his perceptions of the place of the elderly in our society. But he was also a smart, savvy, intelligent, articulate, and erudite man who listened carefully to questions and criticisms. Much to my surprise, I found that I liked and admired him. No article or search could have prepared me for the challenge his real-time, real-body pres-

Example 10.4

Search Sources: Daniel Callahan

- Who's Who (Basic background. I hoped to learn he was five times divorced and a murderer, but discovered he was a mundane and hard working family man with an exemplary legal and professional record.)
- Books in Print (What had he written, and in what areas)
- Book Reviews (general precise of those works)
- Magazine Indexes (what articles had he written for general or academic consumption).
- Magazine Reviews (I searched Callahan and (age or aging or setting(w) limits) and review, seeking good critiques of his work).
- Newspaper Searches (*New York Times* and *Washington Post*), mostly to see how much he has been quoted, and in what contexts.

---

ence presented. Since that meeting, he and I have corresponded from time to time. It would be nice to think that he appreciated the questioning of a person obviously versed in his work. And I have noted, in subsequent meetings, that he has modified his position on elder care.

Because it is online does not mean that it is complete, or even true. There were lots of things about Callahan's life and work that were not uncovered in my search. *Who's Who* told me his general status, but not intimate details of his personal history. The review articles critiquing his writing were helpful, but they were, of course, no more or less than informed opinion. Reviewers who liked Callahan's *Setting Limits*, and there were several, talked about him "showing" or "proving" something, while others described differences of opinions as "failings" and "limits." Given my personal opposition to his arguments, my readings focused on the latter, not the former. But then, this was a subjective trail, a hunt for opinions and ideas not hard facts. Some paper trails are solid and firm, requiring a hard source for a single hard datum ("How many Muslims live in Bosnia?" "What is the chemical abbreviation for arsenic?"). Others, however, are as flimsy as a spider web caught in the rain and the wind ("Is Boston cream pie a better dessert than key lime pie?").

A general yardstick for weighing opinions retrieved online is to forget that the material was found through the conference center/library. If it was received elsewhere, would it be credited? Opinions online are no better or worse than those vehemently argued in the coffee shop or the neighborhood pub. It is source that needs to be understood, and discounted, in any search. Review articles in the *Journal of the American Medicine* are generally more authoritative than those published in, say, *Anarchist Weekly*. In our society, legal decisions have greater weight than the exhortations of lobbying groups. It does not matter, in searching for corporate data, whether the 10K form is read online or at the Securities and Exchange Commission office. The important thing is what that filing says.

What electronic resources assure is ever faster delivery of data, better and better search mechanisms for those seeking it, greater access to those distanced by physical geography, and ever wider circles of informed acquaintances who may share one's interest in the subject at hand. Consider, for example, the electronic availability of U.S. Supreme Court decisions. It used to take months for a Supreme Court opinion to make its way into the nation's law libraries. All of our knowledge of crucial judgments came from news reporters who were rarely lawyers. It was their job to summarize sometimes highly technical judgments they themselves rarely understood. But with Project Hermes, a system disseminating Supreme Court rulings electronically, all of that changed. Now, the high court's decisions are available online to everyone within hours of their announcement. They can be retrieved from a number of digital sources, including via FTP (address: ftp.cwru.edu and path: /hermes/ascii), or by telnetting directly to: info.umd.edu. I learned about this in the conference center, of course, when asking about a recent Supreme Court decision in a controversial case. And, of course, both the center and its library provided a wealth of other materials—for example, law journal collections—that offered depth and understanding to the court's split decision. As important, the Center offered legal conferences whose members were more than willing to discuss and debate that court decision, explaining its intricacies to me. Internet fans need only use Lycos or Yahoo and search for "law" to see how much is now available to us all. Using Yahoo, for example, I recently found Cornell University Law School's "home page site" (http://www.law.cornell.edu/), a quite wonderful place to start this type of research.

Facts are only as good as the people who prepare them. Opinion is only as valuable as the facts that support them. The Supreme Court may rule unanimously and be overturned by a more enlightened or reactionary court years down the road. Because everyone says something does not mean that it is true. Sometimes, working the center's library provides a counterintuitive perspective which denies the opinions of even the most knowledgeable of conference groups.

Several years ago, for example, reporters at *US News and World Report* decided to test the widely held assumption that recent immigrants were "living off" more established Americans, draining the welfare coffers and generously living like parasites. Polls conducted during the 1992 U.S. presidential campaign suggested that the sentiment was pervasive. But nobody had questioned whether the widespread anti-immigrant prejudice reflected a reality that could be demonstrated. So *US News* downloaded census data on recent U.S. immigrants, including the degree to which members of various ethnic communities received public assistance or financial support. Crunching through more than 1 million census files on immigrants in the United States, the *US News and World Report* team found that prejudice against immigrants was just prejudice. Newer Americans were, as a group, more self-sufficient and less likely to drain public resources than were second-, third-, and fourth-generation citizens.[3] Public sentiment may be focused, just as the voices of the conference center may be unanimous. But on the databahn, facts from the center's library can distinguish between hope and reality, prejudice and certainty. The potential for such distinctions is a positive force for us all.

Unfortunately, even those who should know better often forget to do this type of research. When the foreground is compelling and obvious, why look to the background data? This has lead to a number of embarrassing demonstrations of the importance of combining center and library resources. Call it "proof by omission." In 1994, for example, Joe Queenan discussed two then recent cases in a *Barron's Weekly* article titled "Executive Search: A PC Could Have Saved Scully an Apple-Red Face."[4] Its long lead sentence gave the sorry facts of the tale:

> Last October John Scully, formerly chairman of Apple Computer, made a complete fool of himself by accepting the chairman's job at Spectrum Information Technologies, a small wireless-technology company on Long Island that had no profits, a less-than-sterling reputation, and what's more, was currently under SEC [Security and Exchange Commission] investigation for running up the price of its stock last May by issuing a misleading statement about a new licensing agreement with American Telephone and Telegraph.

What was embarrassing was not that Mr. Scully took the job offered by Spectrum president Peter Caserta, but that he did so apparently unaware of the company's many problems, including the SEC investigation. The father of popular computing, the one-time champion of the people's resource, John Scully probably expected the press conference following the announcement of his appointment to be a quiet, civil, and respectful affair. Instead, he faced a barrage of pointed questions about the status of the company he described as "a little gem that fell into my lap." At one point in this conference, he told a *New York Times* reporter, "It sounds like you know more about it [the company and its problems] than I do at this point." Ouch. They did. Anyone with a modem and access to the center/library would.

Several months later, John Scully quit his post at Spectrum. He unnecessarily lost a great deal of prestige in his brief tenure at the "little gem." Had he logged onto some investor forums and asked people what they knew about Spectrum, it is likely that members interested in high-tech companies would have warned him away from any association with the company. Had he checked digital newspaper files almost anywhere in the conference center's library, he would have found articles chronicling Spectrum's problems. A teenager could have shown him how to do this. Even if he had, of course, he still might have taken the job. But in that event he would have done so with full awareness of what he faced, and thus would have avoided being caught unawares in a reputation-destroying and embarrassing position.

Senior managers are often the last, however, to pick up on the tools and technology they sell and promote. They have people to advise them and to do their research for them. It is the desperate and disenfranchised, the independent entrepreneur or scrambling freelancer who rushes to grasp new media as a lever to raise their posture and position. As Queenan concluded: "The fact that John Scully, chairman of the visionary, iconoclastic, upstart Apple Computer did not have the smarts to run one of these database searches to spare himself immense personal humiliation shows how much work still remains to be done before the personal computer truly becomes integrated in the daily lives of senior American managers."

Information is the end point of fact and opinion developed over time. The essential meaning of the databahn, the electronic pathways of library and conference, is simple: It allows us all to formulate positions based on the best and most powerful data available at any time. Until the advent of these digital systems, what was available to us was restricted by distance, and the time it took to access primary resources. It would take too long to sift through the whole of the 1990 census, manipulating the data to define the relation between immigrants, income, and social service. To search medical, popular, and philosophic journals for a record of articles on and by Daniel Callahan would have taken weeks, not minutes, using any other system. To find a phalanx of people knowledgeable in a single subject area, and willing to talk to a layperson, was until recently nearly impossible. Public information thus has always been the best data which officials might provide through news reporters who then transmitted the official viewpoint to us all.

But the gatekeeper's lock on official data is disappearing. The ability of a minister, senator, academic, physician, judge, or president to state a fact not only with certainty, but also with the assurance that nobody will presume to contradict it, is diminished to the extent that everyone has access to primary data and alternate interpretations of that data. Finally, there is the potential for a "Citizen News," a venue of truly public data, in which we all can participate. There is, however, no magic wand. Because it is online does not mean that it is true. Digitized reports and electronic conversations are not necessarily more insightful or more truthful than printed data and polite discussion in the tea room. Then as now, and whatever the medium, the question is how we choose to use the resources available to us. We can accept the statements of officials, or we can question them. We can shout and protest on the basis of personal prejudice, or seek towards information bit by datum by fact. That is something which has not changed. Information is always the end point of a search, never a medium in and of itself. The information highway is modernity's El Dorado, a dream of ease and wealth without effort that, while nice to contemplate, remains a fantasy, pure and simple.

NOTES

1. *The Chronicle of Higher Education.* July 13, 1994, A15. Quoted in Patrick Crispen, Roadmap 25, "Address Searches and Finger." December 6, 1994.

2. Daniel Callahan. *Setting Limits: Medical Goals in an Aging Society.* New York: Simon and Schuster, 1987.

3. That material is stored in the *US News and World Report* library under "immigrants" and "census." Check it out.

4. Joe Queenan. "Executive Search." *Barron's Weekly.* 1994.

11

Speculations: Past and Future

"Should I be on the Net," Barb asked, "or in the Internet? What's the difference? And is there somewhere else I should put my business on-line?" She is a direct-mail marketing whiz whose clients include charities raising money for research into specific diseases. She is one of those responsible for the plethora of direct-mail requests we all receive for financial assistance, and for raising public awareness for non-profit associations representing, for example, people with kidney disease. Something out there in the online world is pertinent to her business, she knows. How can she bend those online resources to her needs, she asked, while keeping her overhead costs at a manageable level?

"What do you want?" I asked. If all she needed was an electronic mail address to put on her business card—and since E-mail is a status symbol as well as a facilitator, that's all many people want—then a local account at the Ability Online Bulletin Board (or the Toronto Freenet) would serve her well. But if she wanted to keep abreast of new reports on medical research in the areas in which her groups are involved, I said, then she might want to collect news stories on CompuServe, Dow Jones, or another service with automatic clipping files. If she needs the medical texts, the work of researchers, however, then a Knight Ridder Information–style news file would be better. Finally, I advised, if she planned to create a site where people online can go for information on the groups she represents, then the World

Wide Web is going to be a necessity for her clients in the next year or two.

Peter Wolfe, on the other hand, is a psychologist who knew exactly what he wanted. "What I need is the ability to exchange electronic mail with colleagues, a discussion group where I can review issues with other psychologists, and access to *Psychological Abstracts* for my research." I advised him to join CompuServe, which carries *Psychological Abstracts*, a review of the journals in his field. The American Psychological Association has a closed user group for its members on the Internet, but that was not a priority for him. If it were, he could access it through CIS's Center door. Finally, mail exchange with everybody is as easy via CompuServe as another service. But he was seduced by the many stories of Internet's perfect riches, and decided to pay $60 a month for a corporate account through a local access vendor. A few months later, I asked if he was happy with his choice. Peter said, in true psychologist fashion, "Well, yes and no."

"It's fascinating, and I'm glad to see what all the talk is about. But for me it's not very useful," he explained over coffee. "I do have an electronic address, but *Psychological Abstracts* is not available through the Internet. And all of the user groups except one allow anyone to join. In trying to analyze clinical and theoretical issues, it is not very helpful to have patients involved in the discussion. I mean, their perspectives are interesting, but they have their own issues, and those are not germane to my research." I smiled, a nonverbal, "I told you so." Peter now has two accounts, his general Internet corporate account as well as one on CompuServe, which allows him to access the technical data he needs from that center's library shelves, material that is not easily available through his Internet door.

Advising people on which conference center/library door leads most directly to resources answering their specific needs is an interesting business, a side-line enterprise. As the conference center matures into a system with a single access point for the whole, I'll rapidly become redundant. But at present, some people still need a guide who can help them map the evolving online terrain, directing them to different center doors and the resources they facilitate. Barb needs the Internet, and probably a World Wide Web home page with links to those of her diverse client list. They will pay for its development, of course, but she needs to know where to go for help with page design. A service account with Web access will give her electronic mail capabilities, access to user groups involved in public relations and direct-mail marketing, and a general array of background materials. If she needs to create clipping files from Canadian news sources for her clients, then she may also require a second account elsewhere. At present, what she really needs to know is what can be done, and where to find the services that do those tasks. Peter's needs, on the other hand, were not answered by the Internet-at-large or its Web component, glitzy though it may be. He needs high-power research assistance in the center library (*Psychological Abstracts,* Medline, etc.), and the shelves he requires are not easily or universally available through the Internet's center door, yet.

Now my general advice to people is to define the types of services that they want, and then find the least expensive way to acquire them. Electronic mail? A bulletin board like Ability Online provides it—and interesting conferences, too—at no cost to the member. It is a community service. Insomniacs in Toronto wishing to spend a few early morning hours browsing online resources might try the Toronto Freenet. During the day and early evening, however, its lines are in such demand that few people can get aboard without long and frustrating delays. Business people can check stock prices, user group discussions, and basic business data on almost any commercial service. Simple stock reports are cheaper on CompuServe, however, than on the Dow Jones Information Service. Those needing access to current SEC documents will find them on most of these services, too, but those with a basic Internet account will find them least expensively in the center section called "town hall.org." Historical data, however, is not there. For that one must go elsewhere.

As a consultant, my job is to find for others the least complex combination of center access sites at the best price. I also offer a session or two of training, familiarizing tutorials in the center, and can program software on client computers to include a list of "bookmarks" that lead to relevant online sites. This is lucrative hand-holding, and it rarely takes more than a few sessions before clients understand that I am not really needed, that they can do it on their own. Even those using KRI, which is a relatively complex library resource, quickly discover that company representatives are more than happy to answer telephoned questions at no cost at all. I, on the other hand, charge by the hour.

The electronic library and its digital conference center remain, at present, under construction. How can a new or fairly inexperienced user choose between the completing venues—AOL, CIS, DJNS, KRI, Internet, Prodigy, and the rest—when each insists that it is the best place to gain entry into this electronic world? Each has its advantages. Nobody can belong to all of them. How does anyone decide between the many choices available today in the fractured world of this databahn?

The answer is simple. Shop around. These days, new computers come loaded with free software from a variety of venues, all offering a trial membership on several different online systems. CompuServe, AOL, and the rest provide step-by-step sign-up instructions when you buy a major-brand computer or modem. Microsoft Windows and IBM OS/2 have Internet gateways configured within the operating system. New users can spend months trying and then rejecting different doors to the conference center/library, each one accessed on a 30- or 60-day free trial membership. Once one has tried two or three, the match between available resources and personal need should be very clear.

CompuServe has served me well, for example. Its library connections have carried me through the research necessary for six books. Its forums have informed me and sometimes amused me. Its mail gateway assures that I can continue to communicate with friends linked through other venues. It's Internet links have carried me seamlessly through Telnet, FTP, UseNet and of course the Web. Similarly, I sometimes require the advanced technical library resource of KRI, and on occasion the Dow Jones Service's resources. After all, data is my business. What I use is typically billed out to clients, or written off as a deductible expense.

But in my travels around the conference center, I watch carefully for bargains. Costs for any particular resource range from the general cost of Internet service, currently averaging around $20 a month for a single password, to $160 an hour for access to a high-priced medical database. If I know that something is free in one venue and costly in another, I opt for the cheapest venue. For example: Reuters News Service costs $90 an hour on KRI, while Reuters Canada—a wire devoted to Canadian news—costs $15 an hour on CompuServe. So if my primary concern is Canadian news with an accent on business, I log onto CompuServe and not onto KRI. Similarly, if a client needs a current 10K filing from a competitor, I can retrieve it from CIS, KRI, DJNS, or the Internet. These are federally required annual statements that are filed with the Securities and Exchange Commission, and each contains a wealth of data. Some online sites have the complete submission, including footnotes; others do not. On the first three systems I am charged for the data, but not on the Internet via anonymous FTP at ftp://town.hall.org/edgar. Were I researching past business data, however, that site would not serve. Unlike DJIS and KRI, its data are not historical.

And so, in choosing a door to the conference center, one first must ask, "What will I need? What do I want?" and then, "Where is it least expensive?" Most people insist that they want Internet access. Many, in fact, want nothing more. It offers electronic mail, conference groups, and library resources. In Toronto, monthly access for individual users at present begins at a cost of perhaps $20 a month, depending on the type of service required. Peter Wolfe paid more because he had special needs—security and instant access—based on the confidential nature of his business. For those who wish to see the conference center from the perspective of the Web, the Net, and "surfers," the Internet is a wonderful place to begin. To me, it makes little difference whether one signs up through the Windows Microsoft network, IBM's access door, or a private vendor. If Bill Gates wants to give you a free trial visit via Windows '95, accept his largess. And if IBM offers the same and you happen to buy one of their computers, well, the cost of the come-on is figured into the price of the machine.

This is comparison shopping, pure and simple. Decide what you need, what you want, and what you can afford. Then look for the best price.

Many, like me, are devotees of commercial online systems like AOL and CompuServe. Increasingly, these services offer access to both the Internet and their own conference sites. Bicyclists, for example, may choose AOL because that is where the folks from Rodale Press' *Bicycling Magazine* hang out. Others who need a wider range of technical library data on an occasional basis—and who do not want to purchase a service like KRI—find the CompuServe libraries compelling and its Internet gateway intuitive.

Whatever service one starts with, newer users are advised first to search for a conference or forum that mirrors their general areas of interest (sailing, medicine, skiing, journalism, business, politics, religion, etc.). Ask in the conference about library resources. Find out if the conferences are moderated or not. See if the group's library has files that are of interest. If not, move on. Conferences are resources that inform users about the library, and the library's directories list available conferences. Both work together. If they don't, then the service does not answer your needs. And because the whole is changing so rapidly, everyone needs to evaluate old choices as new resources become available online.

It is 1996, and the evolution is continuing. We have come a long, long way in the 12 years since Apple Computer introduced its small-screened, easy-to-use computer-in-a-box, the Macintosh. Modem-equipped personal computers are rapidly becoming standard home equipment, like the telephones whose lines they share. Video feeds off the TV cable now can be watched in a window on the computer screen of the newest machines. The future is here.

We know with surprising certainty the general shape of this evolution's near future. We can predict with some precision the next steps in the computerization of data. The conference center /library cum bazaar is first and foremost a network, a system of conveyance, and thus it necessarily will obey the rules of growth common to all such systems. Railroads, road systems, telephone networks, the mails: all systems of communication and transmission follow similar patterns of growth and development, irrespective of the cargo they carry or the

precise nature of the medium itself.[1] This evolving system is no different. That is the story of the network's growth to date. It is also the
blueprint for its future.

What we know, simply, is this. Systems first are created when distant and disconnected nodes or points are slowly connected, tenuously
linked to create a first fragile and then strong network in which communication between any two points is a single good connection that
links nodes A and B to each other, and to the world. At first, connection is minimal. If one line goes, the whole breaks down. Slowly, however, as use increases, multiple connections develop across the system. This was the idea behind the original Rand Corporation plan for
ARPANet, remember? Link a few sites by multiple ties so that destruc-
tion of one node or connection does not destroy the greater whole. It
is system theory, the observed principles of network growth. And it is
a very powerful, quite mathematical region of our shared knowledge
base.

Think for a moment of trains. At first there were a few lines, each
connecting several large cities: Boston, New York, and Washington,
DC, for example. Then, those links branched out to other places, back-
waters along the frontier. Places like Albany, for example, and eventually even Buffalo. As the whole grew in size, new links developed as
cities developed along the line and additional track was laid to bring
Hartford, New Haven, Pittsburgh, and other places into the mix. It is
like the child's game of connect-the-dots, with each dot representing a
city, or household. But in the real-life version, the number of nodes
expands in any single area (density) and across the system at large
(area).

As the train system matured, multiple paths between any two points
were developed. And in this maturation, standardization necessarily
came to rule. A system requires interchange, and for the railroads this
meant a single gage for all tracks. It meant cars that could be coupled
behind any engine owned by any carrier on the network: the Burl-
ington Northern or the Southern Pacific. So not only were track and
car design standardized, but the engines that drove the trains across
the tracks had to be standardized as well. Within this process, the companies that developed the rail became not unique controllers of their
individual domains, but common carriers in the system at large. A developing system not only standardizes the medium of transportation,
but insists as well on making otherwise independent and idiosyncratic
companies into interchangeable parts of the whole.

Finally, the mature system is defined not only by consistency and
standardization, but by redundancy. Different companies offer similar
services along a network so developed that multiple paths join all individual members of the whole. Thus, if any one company goes out of

business—or if any single line of track is destroyed—travel is not halted and the network at large survives.

Remember, too, that new technologies do not destroy their predecessors. Established networks do not disappear quickly when a newer and more efficient means of transportation appears. The railroads still carry coal, grain, cattle, and other bulky goods. Cars are too small and the cost of flying such materials is prohibitive, except perhaps if one is sending emergency relief to a disaster region. Similarly, the telephone did not eliminate the need for the mail system. The introduction of private cars did not remove the need for public transportation. In fact, new technologies typically parallel the lines their predecessors have developed, mirroring their growth and needs. The railroad did not explode into a new world. Its routes paralleled older horse and foot paths, from the Natchez Trez to the Erie Canal. Highways first paralleled and then linked older rail sites, slowly taking on the burden of carrying travelers and goods.

Newer systems begin by taking up a part of the load that older, mature networks previously handled. Over time, of course, as they become more efficient, they carry an increasing percentage of the load. Think, for a moment, of how railroads took over some of the work of the waterways, and then how trucks took on the load of railroads. The telegraph's speed allowed it to transmit faster than the old mails ever could. And then the telephone superseded both for personal, nonurgent materials. At each step in the development of technology, service begins where an older service is most burdened, and then gradually the upstart technology carves out new, independent territory for itself.

This happens because maturing technology always develops increasingly vast and progressively less-expensive carrier capacities. Early trucks were no threat to trains. Their inefficient engines could not compete on the old roads that restricted their rate of safe travel to perhaps 30 miles an hour. Today, of course, it is a different story. Old trucks would collapse if they had to carry the loads that 16-wheelers routinely run these days. Old tarmac would crumble if it had to carry a single year's volume of modern traffic. Similarly, a 1920 telephone system would jam in a minute if it was faced with today's normal calling volume. Technology always works to improve a system's capacity. At the beginning of this century, longer and more frequent trains ran simultaneously on more and more tracks as engines became stronger and routing became a more exact process. The rails were ascendant, a fully mature lattice network that was paradoxically ripe for the challenge of the private automobile and delivery truck.

While this may be the story of the railroad, it is also the history of all technology that utilizes networks for the delivery of goods or services across a region or the world. Think, for a moment, of the telephone. Local systems expanded to regional networks, which in their turn joined other regional companies until a national system was in place. At first, the ties between its most distant parts was tenuous and liable to breakdowns when a storm destroyed a major intercontinental line. Now, however, redundancy is complete; the developed system has expanded into a worldwide network with a honeycombed structure that links callers from Beijing to Paris to Tokyo and back. In the same way, online resources have piggybacked on the existing telephone network, approximating its vast capacity for its digital interchange. Its growing network, however, has been along the network of libraries, universities, and official resource caches, not grain terminals, cattle yards, coal fields, and natural resource centers. Like the train, it carries goods between two points. But the goods it carries are data, not produce. Still, the idea is the same.

The history of other common carriers—roads and rail, mail and telephone—is being played out, again, in the development of online electronic communication. What started as an esoteric military network, tenuous and fragile, has become an international communication system which I have called the conference center. Growth has been incredibly rapid, and the public system has enlarged with amazing speed. In the early 1980s, a few independent companies—the Dow Jones, CompuServe, LEXIS-NEXIS, for example—put out tenuous lines to the world. These first commercial experiments offered general users the resources previously reserved for the privileged few. Each had its own protocol, its own language and method of signal carriage. This one used 8 bits and no stops; that one used 7 bits and one stop. Membership in one organization promised no connection to another.

By the early 1990s, the system was connected, and standardization began. A single mail service using the Internet address system (716600@compuserve.com; ridgley@unix.uh.edu; Aikido@aol.com, etc.) passed from the separate venue into the public system, allowing connectivity between people entering the conference center through any of its doors. The cost of use decreased as increasing pathways opened, and this has resulted in more and more nodes online, more and more resources, and evermore individual users. Now we see a growing redundancy appearing as different and competing services offer similar materials, often at different prices. User choice has increased, forcing prices down again and allowing even more users access to the whole. This is not a new story, but an old one.

The rapid growth of the center/library cum bazaar has led some traditionalists to worry that its continuance will mean the death of cherished and "crucial" parts of our traditionally literate culture. These obituaries for the tried and true are premature. Just as the acceptance of the automobile did not mean the death of the railroads, the center does not portend the end of writing, the death of libraries, the termination of the mail system, or the demise of literature. The reverse, if anything, is true.

Because it is a message-based system, the center demands writing skills of its users. Millions of people who rarely write traditional letters and have never thought of publishing a story or report now are communicating by electronic mail and "uploading" text files describing their experiences, recommendations, thoughts, and feelings. For the foreseeable future, writing will continue to be a critical skill for people accessing the conference center and library cum bazaar. Similarly, and to me quite important, publishing will not be destroyed by the availability of the center's library. More and more material may be made available, in part or whole, through the electronic center. New tracking systems currently are being developed which will grant writers who publish electronically royalties based on the fact of online access. This is a new market for the work of people like me, a new opportunity whose potential will more than compensate for the decline in other areas of traditional print sales.

Nobody gives up control of their privileges easily. The history of popular publishing is one of successive bans and prohibitions, rearguard actions against the popularization of data and opinion by one or another medium. The idea of public scrutiny of official proclamations has always terrified those in positions of power. When Samuel Johnson was writing for *Cave's Magazine*, journalists were not allowed to enter Parliament when it was in session and publishers were barred from distributing accounts of Parliamentary debate. Now reporters are invited and encouraged to attend Parliamentary sessions. But "public interest" in our age still generally takes second chair to "national security," however it might be defined. The means of restriction and arm twisting have become a bit more sophisticated in the last 200 years, but the struggle for control has not been eliminated or even fundamentally changed.

Why be surprised? Worthies of every age reflexively fear the new. In Shakespeare's day, live theater was decried as an opiate driving people from Godly pursuits. In the eighteenth century, teachers and religious leaders feared the influence of "popular" literature, "penny dreadfuls" they were called, on the young population. They should read the "classics"—and, of course, the Bible—children were told, not tales of adventure in the Wild West. Easier to hold back the tide. The world of print had gone over to the masses, and the effects were feared by all those whose lives had been spent as guardians of previously restricted knowledge. More recently, rock and roll music was to be the ruination of my generation. Radio stations banned Elvis Presley in his early years. B. B. King was not accepted as a great musician-singer. And, of course, television has been the whipping boy of those who wish to decry, again, a new technology and its popular appeal. Is it any surprise, with this history, that the electronic center now is being condemned for its egalitarianism?

For a generation the assumption has been that the medium is the message, and that message promises to presage some doom. In the longer view of history, such fears always have proven groundless because, I believe, the equation must be reversed. It is the message we should be analyzing, not its means of transmission. If a new system offers more universal access to data, better forums for debate, and new means of exploration, then it is good. Popularization is inevitable. And if officials do not like it, well, their loss is the greater public's gain. Better and more complete access to ideas, opinions, and data inevitably serves us all.

In the short run, the maturing Center/Library cum bazaar will become more available and offer more and more types of data. Video and sound will be added to text. Speeds will increase as new methods of storage and delivery are added to the whole. As capacity is added, usage will grow. Already many banks are offering their customers online access to personal accounts. Realtors are uploading home listings to World Wide Web sites; and medical diagnostics are going online. Just as the telephone and television have become necessities of modern life, computers will be wholly integrated into the new millennium's civilized culture. In 1994, U.S. House speaker Newt Ginrich was laughed at for suggesting that children from impoverished backgrounds be given a computer to assist in their education. Within a generation, it is unlikely that any child or any home will be without at least one data access terminal. After all, today we provide telephone and television access to families on social assistance because these are crucial modern necessities. Why assume the computer—which is also a library, a bank access machine, a news dissemination system, and a meeting place—will not be treated in a similar fashion?

What this will mean for society-at-large is anyone's guess. Some are convinced it will be the ruination of our culture. Literacy will die, and the classics will languish. Pfui! Shakespeare's work has survived adaptation from the stage to book publication, radio performance, and television and movie presentation. His insight and his language promise a message that is clearly heard irrespective of the medium of its presentation. Bach is more popular now than in the days when he was alive because his genius can be enjoyed by anyone with a radio, a television, a phonograph or a CD player. Whatever the medium, the best survives. We may be ignorant, but we are not idiots. People know how to pick and choose. My own suspicion is that the evolution of the Center/Library cum bazaar will have less social impact than most people assume. At the time of its introduction, the systems that spawned it were so much a part of our world that a single conduit based on mail, telephone, and library service will optimize the best of what was, not utterly destroy it.

Perhaps the most thoughtful description to date of how the future of public information will unfold in a mature conference center was presented by science and science fantasy writer David Brin in his book, *Earth*.[2] Set in the twenty-first century, the story line involves black holes, quantum singularities, and a dire threat to our world. But woven into the book's structure is a series of electronic news releases, discussion group conferences, and online research projects, each carried out at a different level of access. Brin suggests that individual users will have different levels of access, depending on needs, money, and social position. All will have access to some parts of the center and its library, but some will have more than others.

In his vision, "news" will be a complex mixture of video footage, processed reports, conference group interpretations, and background research. Everyone will have access, although the level of data one can use will be defined by user status and ability to pay, perhaps. Using his examples, I have fabricated a user's page from the information menu of the future in Example 11.1. The news story includes a reporter's script (retrievable as text, audio file, or in audiovisual format), and the option to capture some or all of a press conference and its corollary events. In addition, each section of the report carries a marker allowing viewers to click on that mark to receive more detailed information on any single aspect of the story. These may include requesting raw footage, user group discussion materials or position papers, economic analysis, commentary, and so on. Finally, the whole includes not only a byline (Tom Koch in Toronto), but data on the reporter, including his believability quotient as defined by both general and specialized user groups.

Brin's vision is a dramatic device advancing a fictional plot whose real purpose is the discussion of certain concepts in modern physics. Still, there is much to recommend it. The use of toggles keying to other, background data is the "hypertext" system of the Internet's World Wide Web. The inclusion of position papers or active discussion strings by conference/user group members as background material is already happening, just as video clips are becoming increasingly available online to people with the most modern software and machines. What has not changed in his future is the constant struggle for control of public data, the insistence by some that they want knowledge which others are unwilling to provide. In Brin's future, people hunt for data that officials wish to hide, using search programs to uncover disparate facts that together will describe a situation nobody wants to admit pub-

Example 11.1

World Net News: Channel 265/General Interest/Level 9+
AN=C.R.S./Koch 70453.'95   Time: 46 sec.

"This is Tom Koch reporting from the Genetic Testing Labora-
tories of Toronto, Canada, North America, where the first artificial cyborg to be grown to maturity has been grown to adolescence."
[Image: adolescent cyborg with close-up of humanoid head's enhanced visual aids, panning to electronic panel implant on cyborg's
right wrist].
   Σ for raw footage.
"Unlike earlier attempts to create a purely artificial life form,
GTL's current model combines enhanced, neural pathways with a
unit-controllable enzymatic pump giving its cyborg personal
control of body chemistry unavailable to normal sentients."
   ΣΣ for description of the pump.
   ΣΣ for cyborg-controllable enzymes and their functions.

"Named 'Asimov' after the 20th Century science and science
fiction writer whose "I Robot" broke new ground in the consideration of artificial life forms, the cyborg's programming uses sophisticated algorithms designed to emulate and improve upon
human self-regulatory organic feedback systems."
   *Σ for the text of "I Robot."   ΣΣ for a review of Asimov's "three
   laws of robotics."   ΣΣ Σ links to cybernetics and philosophy.*

"Human-first pressure groups in North America demonstrated in
front of the GTL, scuffling with AI advocates carrying signs asking
"What's so great about US?" GTL officials insist this technology
will have a number of commercial ramifications. "We're creating
evolution's next step," said GTL president H. Schlemmer.
   Σ for image of protesters shouting and scuffling.
   Σ for complete GTL pres. Schlemmer speech.
   *Σ Groups menu: IN user groups 1675 (Humans First.org); position
   paper A-13B; AI Advance (AI.AU.EDU) discussion 1/5/7/
   March 13; for analysis of GTL see DJIS channel 240/biotech/
   Level 11 report CT/Jorge 716543.'95; for commercial ramifi-
   cations see biz.group.int (commerce/bioetch) current 13.*

"For CNN/Reuters/Shin Hwa, This is Tom Koch in Toronto.

   *Σ Reporter bio' CT/Koch/CRS-345. Credibility Ratings: AAaa-1
   North American Viewer's Union; ABaA-3, European Viewer's
   Union; Aaab-4, Popular Science User's Group.*

[adapted from D. Brin. *Earth*]

licly. This, at least, rings true. Wonderful as these tools are and promise to be, the tension between public and private, the struggle to learn more than is generally offered, is a constant that will not change with the new technologies or the new millennium. It is us. And in all of this, we are the constant.

The technology enabling this vision is available today. Some of it is very new, an expensive novelty awaiting a future market; some of it is already in use. One reason to believe that Brin's vision will be the future is the old commercial dictum: Capacity creates commerce. Use expands as systems grow. Because it can piggyback on telephone lines and utilize cable facilities to distribute data stored in underutilized and very expensive digital storage facilities, the capacity for use is already vast. It is unreasonable to believe that online use will not grow, and that the databahn will not become the primary disseminator for a multimedia montage of public data and information. The system is in place, the infrastructure is available, and the advantages in terms of data to be retrieved inexpensively are compelling.

Some worry that these changes will create two classes, those with access to the center/library cum bazaar and those without. Let us go slow, they argue, until we know that this will not become a medium for the privileged alone. Supporters of capitalist enterprise in all other venues, in this area alone the critics are cautious. What they forget, of course, is that we already live in a multitiered society of information haves and have-nots. Among the have-nots are the 20 percent or so of U.S. citizens, for example, who are functionally illiterate. The homeless who are literate are still denied access to the mails because they have no domicile that can be listed as a return address. And without a fixed address, they are also denied library cards. Also currently without full access are the multitudes who are excluded from using specialized and supposedly public library collections because they do not belong to a privileged association, whether it is a university, a profession (law libraries are sometimes restricted), or some other group. Others are excluded today because they cannot afford to pay the required fee for a government document or a private report.

Online storage and retrieval is not the creator of these ills. Nor is it the necessary corrective for every social deficit. But it may well be that, like the print library that preceded it, the electronic center and its library will be a force in the egalitarian move towards data for all. Among those who believe this to be true, not surprisingly, are experts in the cash-strapped world of the public library system. Their mission, after all, is not to assure that the average citizen has "books," but that the greater public has access to the accumulated store of all public data. Knowing the expense of print cataloging, the difficulties of collection maintenance, and the needs of clients and users, librarians have been anxious to find better and more cost-effective ways to increase public offerings efficiently. For some, the answer has been to create online venues, collaborations, electronic collections, and digital distribution systems. Most have been challenged by the evolution of this technology, not threatened by its potential.

This trend began in the 1980s when a few large academic libraries developed extensive online capabilities. Ohio State University, for example, was a leader in not only putting its catalog online, but in creating a mini-network linking its 13 member libraries (commerce, engineering, law, medicine, science, etc.) with those of other sites in the state. All were digitally connected so that a student or faculty member could log on from his or her personal computer, search across the accumulated digital catalog for a book or text, and have it delivered to a campus mail address. In addition, each library was responsible for one digital collection of material stored online (medical databases, legal databases, newspaper databases, etc.). The branch libraries brought these early and specialized digital collections within the grasp of all system users. Because the electronic catalog and electronic collection was the sum total of all participating library resources, the collection of each member in this digital consortium grew, in effect, through this process. For the user, it was a double boon. Not only were there more resources at hand, but they all could be searched more efficiently. "All for one and one for all," as one librarian explained it to me.

In the 1980s, this was an advanced and radical idea. But by the mid-1990s, it was an increasingly common practice at the level of the public library, too. Think of local libraries as small towns on the highway, secondary linkages in the developing system. In 1995, for example, Ontario's North York public library system was spending $56.25 per capita on online resources. A member of the Metropolitan Toronto library system, the suburban library of North York was also a member of a consortium that included the libraries of the University of Toronto, Trent University in Peterborough, the Ottawa Public Library System, and the University of Alberta. Magazines and journals available digitally were purchased by the consortium and shared among its member systems. Book purchases were coordinated between the whole regional system, allowing for economies of scale. Users at any point in this geographically distanced system had access to the whole collection (from Ontario to Alberta), wherever the linkages had been forged. The whole results, as Toronto reporter Trish Crawford explained, in an integrated system that provides North York residents with the opportunity to borrow "interdepartmentally" from any place in the group, even when the book or document they seek is lodged elsewhere.[3]

This was possible because, as we have seen, a single article digitally stored can be mirrored to many users simultaneously. And, for more traditional collections, interchange between network members was facilitated by the maturing system's standardization. All members of the consortium used the same computer software, for example. That meant that their messaging systems were compatible, library to library. By the mid-1990s, vendors offering digitized publications had proliferated, and so participating libraries had an evergreater opportunity for electronic publications from which to choose. Finally, the system was made possible because in the center/library cum bazaar, physical distance is irrelevant. In the world of online data and transmission, Alberta is as close to North York as the University of Toronto. Over time, one may assume that this small Canadian network will grow to include more and more public libraries. Indeed, it is almost inevitable that regional libraries everywhere will become evermore interdependent parts of the expanding electronic library section within the center/library cum bazaar at large.

Such changes typically occur first in large urban centers like Toronto before they come to small prairie communities, like Medicine Hat, Alberta, or northern communities like Inuvik, NWT. But then, systems of communication and carriage always develop first in industrialized and densely populated regions, and then extend slowly to underdeveloped areas. Systems grow in sections, with high concentrations always occurring in the most economically advanced regions where there is more capital, and where the old system's capacity is already stretched to the limit. Train travel began in the United States among its oldest eastern cities, with only tenuous entrails extended over time into the then "wild" western regions. But as the system grew, its importance grew with it until its completion was a national priority. How else would Kansas cattle get to Chicago packing plants, and from there to New York dinner tables? Use increases to meet capacity; systems create their own demands.

What this means for the future of the conference center/library cum bazaar is fairly obvious. Current trends will continue, perhaps at an accelerating pace. The system is developing, not developed. Voice-recognition technology and multimedia capability currently are available and soon will be cost effective. System traffic will increase as more connections join various nodes online. Standardization will continue, which means the choice of an online vendor (CIS, AOL, Internet, etc.) will increasingly be a matter of billing convenience and not one defining a user's level of access to the system at large.

In this process the "Internet," as it is currently defined, will disappear as an independent entity. It will survive as a name, perhaps, and as a series of linked protocols available across a complex, interwoven network of commercial, official, public, and academic nodes. But in its current incarnation, the descendent of ARPANet, is not designed to carry the interplay of public and private nodes now vying for digital dominion. The network's cost, to date, has been borne for the most part by the military, academic institutions, and the government. It has been funded by tax revenues, although for most of its history that financial support has been hidden from public view. But the whole is too public now, and while economies of scale (and regulation) will assure that the evolving system is affordable, its total cost will be shifted to the consumer. It is likely, I think, that the developed network will be treated as a public utility whose cost necessarily will be carried by capitalism's interesting mixture of private subscription and corporate control. Just as each letter we send today requires a federal postage stamp, and every telephone call is billed by a carrier to its customer, so too will online access follow the pattern of its predecessors.

In these its early years, people have willingly provided goods and services online at no cost. The pleasure has been in exploring the medium itself, in the realization of a new mode of communication and data retrieval. The Soviet Union had its *Samazat*, the underground publishing business using old mimeograph machines. Westerners have had the nascent Net. But people will not continue to provide their services for free, and that means that the center/library's costs increasingly will be shifted to the public at large.

This is already happening, as most users know. Mead Data General's Internet services are available only to billable users, to those who will pay the fee. Online newsmagazines and news organizations receive public relations benefits from being online, but the most successful also earn revenues from user subscription charges. Private vendors with proprietary software are making the network available to all, but that access comes at the price of a monthly bill calculated on the basis of the degree of service a user requires.

The battle between public and private control of data will continue, as will a parallel fight between public and private control of the system at large. No balance has been found between public service and private avarice. The first shots in this war were fired during the years of U.S. President Ronald Regan, who sought to sell public data to private distributors who were then free to charge market prices for its dissemination. We can expect increasing competition between primary suppliers of data and online access to the greater system, as well as struggles over regulations that will attempt to balance the public's right with the desire by companies for a "reasonable" profit. Every generation fights this battle on its own terms. Our great-grandparents saw it in terms of the rails, and our grandparents perceived it in the war between competing telephone servers. Then it was a question of toll versus free highways, and free broadcast airways or a British-style system of television subscription. Our children will fight this again in the digital world.

The stakes will increase in this struggle as evermore material is stored in the center/library only. This is inevitable because new technologies are voracious, simultaneously adding services and capacity as they mature. Thus we can expect evermore powerful and cost-effective computers linked to evermore efficient networks storing increasing amounts of data. What began as a text-driven library and message service has become a visual/auditory/hypertext resource. Whether the home computer also becomes a television controller capable of carrying 500 channels of movie and sitcom reruns is irrelevant. Whether one sees reruns on the computer or the television makes no difference. What is important is that digital documents will become richer, more data laden through hypertext, and the types of reports any user can call up will increase in number and kind. Powering this drive towards omnivorous dissemination will be the continuation of an economy of scale driving costs of data down, bite by bite.

For the foreseeable future the whole will remain a fertile field for hackers and rebels who seek greater access than they can afford, those who refuse the mix of low-cost public access and expensive private data realms which capitalism will impose on the whole. Certainly, evermore sophisticated search programs—software designed to roam the library at large, will be the medium by which those without seek to acquire the data of those with privileged accounts. People do not give up secrets easily, and companies are reluctant to give away what they can sell for a profit. The only way around this will be the age old qualities of stealth and deceit, attributes that we seem to have, in our species, in abundant supply.

Some things do not change. The logic of the system will remain hierarchical. Nobody has a better way of organizing vast data banks than through the one we now use combining a general system catalog (subject, title, author name) with key words—tags for specialized search programs—embedded. In the same vein, future systems will continue to be message—based, with queries sent by voice if not keyboard through a central hierarchical exchange. The whole will still carry questions and answers between users and resources. The center will be characterized by personal communication, either individual letter or group conversation. And, of course, users will continue to be frustrated and dissatisfied by the responses they receive. No matter how good the whole becomes, it will not offer omnipotence. Nothing can.

Even in maturity, the medium will not be the message. McLuhan's promise of a "global village" will remain a utopian dream. Why should we be surprised by this? Television carries images from around the world, telephones reach into every land, and the literatures of almost every people are available to us today, both in the original language and in translation. Yet struggle, injustice, prejudice, and strife remain the constants of our age. The "global village" resembles Karachi and Bogota, not heaven. Cultural history, economic class, linguistic preferences, religious differences, and political distance separate people despite geographic proximity and sometimes very similar goals. Members of various groups may find online both kindred spirits and fellow travelers in other parts of the world. They may share messages of hope and strategies of struggle. But the need for hope and the struggle for equality will not disappear because of this technology. Acceptance and rejection of the ideas carried by a mature center and library will remain, alas, a matter of class struggle and social battle, neither of which seems particularly susceptible to reason, information, or the obvious insanity of divisive social policies.

The developed system will not be perfection. Nothing ever is. It will not abolish poverty, prevent injustice, or assure a cure for aging, cancer, and the common cold. We create poverty through our studied misallocation of resources and our public policies. Similarly, injustice results from shortcomings in our social world, not the limits of our data–information system. All of today's vast array of knowledge is negligent in its understanding of the physical processes that we call aging (and the social discrimination that we assign to it). New systems may facilitate the exchange of data among researchers and assure more rapid dissemination of new findings when breakthroughs occur. They will not answer questions, however, any more than a telephone says "Honey, I love you" when you are traveling on the road. Your partner does that, and the phone carries that message forward. This, too, is nothing that will change. For users, the message is more important than the medium. And the message's creator is the most important element of all.

We have a talent for the comfortable, an affection for the pleasant but incomplete and half-truth. No matter how powerful the center may become, this is something it will not change. All great furies are subsumed in time, as James Agee said long ago. And so this resource will be bent, over time, to our limited perspectives and sometimes selfish needs. In user groups and conferences, people today complain about the inconvenience of the homeless, and about the cost of health care and its effect on the supposedly insupportable levels of public debt. In the center's library are documents, reports, studies, and articles that show conclusively that public debt is neither an unmitigated evil or the necessary result of public health-care systems. Similarly, we know that homelessness and poverty result from social inequities and our refusal to share wealth with our neighbors. Yet these are truths that we have chosen to ignore for hundreds of years. I see no reason to believe that a mature system, whatever form it takes, will guarantee the acceptance of these and other uncomfortable truths. No medium can insist that the appropriate message is accepted. They can only facilitate the search for the best available data.

At the best, what the conference center/library cum bazaar will present is greater access to alternate truths, a chance to bend the established view to one that fits fact to context and reality to hope. In the end, it may only permit a collective gasp across the network as environmental chaos and declining global living conditions slowly destroy the potential we might have achieved if only we had paid as much attention to the data made available to us all, the messages online, as we have to the medium itself.

NOTES

1. See, for example, Edward J. Taffe and Howard Gauthier, Jr. *Geography of Transporation*. Englewood Cliffs, NJ: Prentice Hall, 1973.
2. David Brin. *Earth*. New York: Bantam Books, 1990.
3. Trish Crawford. "Free Ride to the Future." *Toronto Star*. April 11, 1995, C4.

Selected Bibliography

Barlow, John Perry. Quoted in, "Currents section." *Utne Reader*. July–August, 1995, 35.

Basch, Reva. *Secrets of the Super Searchers*. Wilton, Ct.: Eight Bit Books, 1993.

Birkerts, Sven. *The Gutenberg Elegies: The Fate of Reading in an Electronic Age*. New York: Fawcett, 1994.

Brin, David. *Earth*. New York: Bantam Books, 1990.

Callahan, Daniel. *Setting Limits: Medical Goals in an Aging Society*. New York: Simon and Schuster, 1987.

Catalfo, Phil. "Welcome to America, Online." *New Age Journal* (1991) 39–47.

The Chronicle of Higher Education. July 13, 1994, A15. Quoted in Patrick Crispen, "Address Searches and Finger," Roadmap Lesson 25, University of Alabama at Tuscaloosa. December 6, 1994.

Conroy, Cathryn. "News You Can Choose: Nonstop Global Coverage Delivered Online." *Online Today* 8:1 (January, 1989), 16–21.

Conroy, Cathryn. "Making a Solid Case for Common Sense." *CompuServe Magazine*. December, 8, 1991.

Crawford, Trish. "Free Ride to the Future." *Toronto Star*. April 11, 1995, C4.

Crispen, Patrick. "Levels of Internet Connectivity," Roadmap Lesson 03, University of Alabama at Tuscaloosa. October 31, 1994, 2.

Eichorn, John, et. al. "Standards for Patient Monitoring During Anesthesia at Harvard Medical School." *Journal of the American Medical Asociation* 256, 1986, 1017–1020.

Endres, Fredreic F. "Daily Newspaper Utilization of Computer Data Bases. *Newspaper Research Journal* 7:1 (Fall, 1985), 34.

Fidler, Rogert. "Mediamorphosis, or The Transformation of Newspapers into a New Medium." *Media Studies Journal* (Fall, 1991), 115–25.

Gerver, Carol H. "Online Yesterday Today and Tomorrow." *Online Today* (July, 1991), 14.

Glossbrenner, Alfred. "CompuServe's Sigs: On the Frontier of Civilized Searching." *Database Magazine* (October, 1989), 50–57.

"Group Account Manager Undergoes Hearty Transplation And Experiences Adverse Reaction To Medication." *PaperChase Pulse* 3:1, 1990.

Hahn, Harley, and Stout, Rick. *The Internet Yellow Pages*. New York: McGraw-Hill, 1994.

Hutchins, Robert Maynard. *A Free and Responsible Press*. Robert D. Leigh, Ed. Chicago: University of Chicago, 1947: reprinted 1974.

Inlander, Charles B., Levin, Lowell S., and Weiner, Ed. *Medicine on Trial*. New York: Pantheon, 1988, 50–66.

Jorgensen, Bud. "The Buck Stops Here for Quebec." *Financial Post*. February 4–6, 1995, A3.

Kernen, Alvin. *Printing Technology, Letters, & Samuel Johnson*. Princeton: Princeton University Press, 1987.

Koch, Tom. *The News as Myth: Fact and Context in Journalism*. Westport, CT: Greenwood Press, 1990.

Koch, Tom. *Journalism for the 21st Century: Electronic Libraries, Databases, and the News*. New York: Praeger, 1991.

Koch, Tom. *A Place in Time: Care Givers for Their Elder*. New York: Praeger, 1994.

Koch, Tom. "The Gulf Between: Surrogate Choices, Physician Instructions, and Informal Network Choices." *Cambridge Quarterly of Healthcare Ethics* 4:2 (1995), 185–192.

Lewis, Thomas. *The Fragile Species*. New York: Collier Books, 1992, 18.

Lippmann, Walter. *Public Opinion*. New York: Free Press, 1965, 157.

Makulowich, John S. "Internet Resources on Alternate Medicine." 1994, via ftp://ftp.clark.net/pub.journalism/altmed.txt.

McLuhan, Marshall. *Understanding Media: The Extensions of Man*. New York: McGraw-Hill, 1964.

Moscow, Shirley. "Making Hospitals User Friendly." *American Medical News*. 34:3 (January 21, 1991), 7–9.

Moscow, Shirley. "Making Hospitals User Friendly: Computers Help Children Fight Isolation, Ease Recovery in Volunteer Program." *American Medical News* 34:3 (January 21, 1991).

Nachison, Andrew. "Reporting from Cyberspace." *CompuServe Magazine* (November, 1993), 46–48.

Postman, Neil. *Amusing Ourselves to Death: Public Discourse in the Age of Show Business*. New York: Penguin, 1986.

Postman, Neil. Quoted in "Currents Section." *Utne Reader*. July–August, 1995, 35.

Queenan, Joe. "Executive Search." *Barron's Weekly*. 1994.

Reuters. "U.S. On-line Subscribers Rise." *Toronto Star*. November 1, 1994.

Richards, Jim. "The Internet." *CompuServe Magazine* (September, 1995), 4.

Robinson, Martha. "No Guidelines in Boy's Death." [Vanocouver] *Sun*. May 30, 1980.

Sacks, Oliver. *Awakenings*. London: Pan Books, 1982.

Taffe, Edward J., and Gauthier, Howard. *Geography of Transporation*. Englewood Cliffs, NJ: Prentice Hall, 1973; revised ed. 1995.

"What Are We Doing On-Line?" *Harper's Magazine* (August, 1995), 36.

Weiss, Aaron. "Hop, Skip, and Jump." *Internet World* (April, 1995), 41–4.

Weizenbaum, Joseph. *Computer Power and Human Communication: Form Judgement to Calculation*. San Francisco: W. H. Freeman, 1976.

Whitcher, C., et al. "Anesthetic Mishaps and the Cost of Monitoring: A Proposed Standard for Monitoring Equipment." *Journal of Clinical Monitoring* 4 (January, 1988).

Index

About the Author

TOM KOCH is a geographer, journalist, and author of six previous books including *The News as Myth* (Greenwood Press, 1990) and *Journalism for the 21st Century: Electronic Libraries, Databases and the News* (Praeger, 1991).